The Daily Telegraph
BOOK OF OBITUARIES

'In this hilariously deadpan and highly selective selection of his favourite obits, Massingberd has chosen to ignore the great and the good and celebrate instead – one might almost say sanctify – the lives of a widely missed assortment of stage-door johnnies, dotty dowagers, showman peers, drunken journalists and other half-forgotten personalities whose existence has somehow added to the gaiety of the nation . . . The unstoppable and immensely lively book . . . deserves an honoured place beside the bed of everyone in this country who can still see the funny side of life.'

Andrew Barrow, *Evening Standard*

The Daily Telegraph
BOOK OF OBITUARIES

A celebration of eccentric lives

Edited by

HUGH MASSINGBERD

PAN BOOKS

For Teresa
with love and in the hope that
some of the contents will make her laugh

First published 1995 by Macmillan Reference Books

This edition published 1996 by Pan Books
an imprint of Macmillan Publishers Ltd
25 Eccleston Place, London SW1W 9NF
and Basingstoke

Associated companies throughout the world

ISBN 0 330 34979 1

1 3 5 7 9 8 6 4 2

A CIP catalogue record for this book is available from
the British Library

Typeset by CentraCet Limited, Cambridge
Printed and bound in Great Britain by
Mackays of Chatham plc, Chatham, Kent

INTRODUCTION

WHEN I TOOK on the job of obituaries editor of *The Daily Telegraph* in July 1986 many of my acquaintance appeared to regard me with a mixture of pity and contempt. Evidently I had taken leave of a never notably firm grip on my senses. Why was I masochistically immersing myself in the esoteric obscurity of such a dreary, stagnant backwater? Every newspaperman knew that the obits desk was the journalistic equivalent of Outer Siberia; had not Walter Burns, the fearsome editor in *The Front Page*, threatened some recalcitrant crippled hack with such a fate? Or was I turning into a vampire?

In fact, it was something I had long considered the best and most interesting job in Fleet Street (as it then still was), indeed one that I had dreamed of doing for years. For some reason the dear old *Telegraph* had never set great store by obituaries. In any event, severely limited efforts were made to compete with *The Times's* legendary superiority in this field, even when that newspaper was off the streets during the shutdown in the late 1970s. I first made an approach to see if there might be a role I could play in improving the "Cenotaph" obits at that time but I was given to understand that it was considered "rather bad form" to try to exploit the unfortunate absence of "Another Newspaper" in this way. I returned, chastened, to my task of seeking to enliven the narrative pedigrees produced by Burke's Peerage publications, of which I had become editor in 1971.

A few years earlier I had been inspired by a passage

in *Brief Lives*, Roy Dotrice's one-man show about the gossipy old 17th-century antiquarian John Aubrey. Picking up a work of reference, he read out an ineffably dull biographical entry about a barrister: Recorder of this, Bencher of that, and so on. He then snapped shut the volume with a "Tchah", or it may have been a "Pshaw", and pronounced: "He got more by his *prick* than his practice".

It was the blinding light for Massingberd. There and then in the Criterion Theatre I determined to dedicate myself to the chronicling of what people were *really* like through informal anecdote, description and character sketch rather than merely trot out the bald *curriculum vitae*. Aubrey's *Lives* were described by Anthony Powell, his best biographer and editor (and also to be a much-valued contributor to the obituaries columns under my editorship) as "that extraordinary jumble of biography from which later historians have plundered so much of their picturesque detail". This was to become my role model.

Eventually, nearly 20 years later, Max Hastings, the *Telegraph*'s new editor, generously gave me the opportunity to put my theories into practice. The paper had never had a separate obits "column" before; hitherto brief (often very brief indeed, in the form of notes, or "nuggets") biographies of notable people who had died had to take their chance with the rest of the day's news. Thus the obits editor came under the sway of the all-powerful News Editor. Now we were to form our own little enclave – a position somewhat analogous, I liked to think, to the tiny Grand Duchy portrayed in the Peter Sellers film *The Mouse That Roared*.

The beauty of obits is that the job is so straight-forward. You do not need to be told what to do, to attend conferences or "ideas meetings". The only requirement is to produce, albeit in short order, biographies of interesting figures who have died. Don't ask me to define "interesting"; suffice it to say that just as there is usually little doubt (with no disrespect to the Literary Editor) as to which of the 50,000–odd books published every year should be reviewed in the literary pages so do the handful of candidates for obits from the 200 or so people who "die in the *Telegraph*" every day largely choose themselves. The vital point is that the copy should be a good read, a lively, stimulating story.

For my part, I was only too happy not to be noticed by my peers as I proceeded about my arcane rituals amid the gold dust of ancient yellowing cuttings in "the Morgue" (as newspaper cuttings libraries are supposedly known). The trouble was that when buttonholed one was expected to answer such wearisome inquiries as "Isn't it all rather *morbid*?" (No, obits are about life not death); "But surely you've got everybody already on file?" (What? *Everybody*!); "Don't you find it embarrassing to approach the bereaved?" (Actually, it can be helpful therapy for them to deal with such matters). The embarrassment factor, in reality, is more prevalent in the tone of such questions: mention of obits for some reason (presumably the fear of death) always seems to provoke nervous titters.

Laughter of a more robust sort, though, certainly has its place in obits. As in a well-rounded address at a funeral or memorial service, an obit that makes you guffaw is serving a useful and healthy purpose. Often such laughter will be provoked by a feeling of exasperated affection about the deceased's shortcomings; a sympathetic acceptance, even celebration, of someone's foibles and faults is by no means out of place.

Apart from the pagan taboo about death, one's interrogators from among the harder-nosed fraternity of hacks sometimes barely disguised their contempt for "All that space being given to a load of *history* – which nobody reads anyway. Call yourselves *journalists?*" I can never understand why "history" is a dirty word in a newspaper office. If charged with producing historical material in the obits column I gratefully pleaded guilty, and priggishly pointed out that there were a fair number of readers that preferred straightforward biography to the usual diet of speculation, innuendo and fancy "angles".

The "big bang" of the new *Telegraph* column came in September 1986 – some little time, let historians note, before the *Independent* was launched with its lavishly illustrated and generously laid out personal tributes to "the loved one" that, according to mythology, are supposed to have made obits fashionable among the chattering classes. From the start I was determined that our obits must be anonymous, formal, detached, deadpan if you like, affording satisfaction, if necessary between the lines, to both friends and foes of the deceased. They should be distinguished from what is known in the trade as a "news obit" – a punchy report, possibly revolving around the dramatic circumstances of death – or some guff beginning with the dread cliché "Tributes poured in last night . . ."; or, for that matter, from an "appreciation" (*pace* the *Independent*) composed by a signed friend or admirer which usually tells one more about the writer than the ostensible subject. None the less, the *Telegraph* sometimes runs such pieces as an "add" underneath the main "anon" obit.

The tone I sought was sympathy, not sycophancy. Obits have their own peculiar, and enjoyable, form. Understatement is the golden rule and loaded messages can sometimes be conveyed in obit-speak. A notorious crook, for instance, might be judged "not to have upheld the highest ethical standards of the City". Our obit of Liberace ("He was unmarried") illustrated how even the most exotic material can benefit from being underplayed in a cool, distanced Olympian manner:

> Perhaps to lend himself an air of ruggedness with which nature had not chosen to endow him, he adopted the stage-name "Walter Busterkeys" when he embarked on his early career ... Liberace's private tastes were steeped in absence of sobriety. His master bedroom was painted with a re-creation of the Sistine Chapel ceiling, his lawn was centrally heated, his swimming-pool was piano-shaped and among his possessions – or "happy-happies" as he liked to call them – was a piano made out of 10,000 toothpicks.

Conversely, one can turn the tables the other way. John Allegro, the controversial Semitic philosopher was obituarised as "the Liberace of Biblical scholarship". Some readers who became used to a regular diet of robustly nicknamed brigadiers and air marshals ("the moustaches" as they were nicknamed on the desk), whose stirring yarns we felt honoured to publish, were horrified to find us giving space to such characters as "the obese female impersonator" Divine (once voted "the filthiest person alive"). Yet we were obliged, as recording angels, to cover the waterfront, from judges like the lamented Sir Melford Stevenson of Truncheons ("A lot of my colleagues are just constipated Methodists") to the medium Doris Stokes ("the Gracie Fields of the psychic world"); from Canon Edwyn Young (the first-ever chaplain of a striptease club) to the last Wali of Swat (with his fondness for Brown Windsor soup).

The joy of the job is capturing for posterity some little-known, or half-forgotten, figure who has made a hitherto undervalued contribution to some aspect of our times. Those who complain that they have never heard of half the people in the *Telegraph* obits column are rather missing the point. The scope embraces all sorts and types from the barman at the Ritz, Laurie Ross, and the intrepid botanist Margaret Mee to the *Oldham Chronicle*'s "Fellwalker" ("As he strode along, Chadwick would regale the young boys who were his most frequent companions – he was homosexually inclined – with interminable but inspired monologues, often in Esperanto") and the eccentric artist Adrian Daintrey (whose passing, Anthony Powell noted in his signed appreciation, "will bring a tear to the eye of more than one lady of quality and black bus conductress").

I confess to a particular soft spot for colourful aristocrats whose idiosyncrasies illustrate that P. G. Wodehouse was not quite such a fantasist as the more earnest literary critics like to believe. The Master would undoubtedly have felt at home with, say, the 6th Earl of Carnarvon ("relentless raconteur and most uncompromisingly direct ladies' man"), the 9th Earl of St Germans (whose recreations were "huntin' the slipper, shootin' a line, fishin' for compliments") and the "Cock o' the North", the 12th Marquess of Huntly ("I still have my own teeth. Why should I marry some dried-up old bag?"). Then there was the 3rd Lord Moynihan, who "provided, through his character and career, ample ammunition for critics of the hereditary principle". His chief occupations, we noted, were those of

> bongo-drummer, brothel-keeper, drug-smuggler and police informer, but "Tony" Moynihan also claimed other areas of expertise – as "professional negotiator", "international diplomatic courier", "currency manipu-lator" and "authority on rock and roll".

Descending from the peerage to the baronetage, we also celebrated the eccentric lives of such figures as the champion wrestler, Sir Atholl Oakeley, 7th Bt (author of *Blue Blood on the Mat* and pictured topless, flexing his biceps) and Sir Hugh Rankin, 3rd Bt (variously riveter's mate, cavalry trooper, sheep-shearer, Muslim, Buddhist, dwarf-fir forest subterranean crawler and self-styled "blood-red militant Communist in every possible way – *absolutely blood-red*").

My own conviction is that we are very fortunate to have been living through an optimum time for obits when some of the legendary figures of the 20th century – whose lives, indeed, throw the whole century into sharp relief – have been landing on the slab of contemporary history. It was a gratifying, and humbling, sensation to witness obit-fanciers emerging from the closet at last in the late 1980s and to hear the word spreading that the *Telegraph*'s "brief lives" could open the treasure-houses of good stories – even, dare one say it, the best read in the paper.

This book has come about as a result of the kind suggestions of numerous readers who wanted to read some of the obituaries again between hard covers. It does not pretend to be remotely comprehensive (how could it be, when there is room only for about a hundred obituaries in relation to the thousand published every year), or representative, or indeed anything like a weighty work of reference. It is merely a personal, subjective choice of some of the more remarkable and entertaining lives we celebrated during my eight years as obituaries editor of *The Daily Telegraph*, from 1986 to 1994 – when, with great reluctance, I had to retire from the chair because of ill health

In making this, inevitably, rough and ready selection, I have deliberately eschewed "the Great and the Good", the too obviously famous and notorious, and, on the whole, the worthy. I have also tended to turn a blind eye, for once, on the splendid set of military "moustaches" – the pride and joy of the *Telegraph* obits – which naturally deserve several volumes of their own (it is hoped that these will appear in due course). Americans and other nationals, which have provided some of the fruitiest material in the column (Liberace and Divine, of whose obits we had tastes earlier, being only two examples), have also been left on the tree for another bite at the cherry at some future date. This still leaves us with what I hope you will agree is a fairly juicy crop of illustrous, if obscure British eccentrics (a word used in its most affectionate sense, I hasten to say), whose lives seemed to call out for celebration in a more permanent form than newsprint. Their defining characteristic, I would suggest, is that they are larger than life, or death for that matter.

At the risk of breaching the obituarists' code of anonymity, I must acknowledge the guidance given to me at the outset of my stint on the obituaries desk of *The Daily Telegraph* by my wise predecessor, Augustus Tilley, and the help I received, especially in the early days of the column, from David Twiston Davies and Edward Bishop. I owe a special debt of gratitude to my deputy editor for seven years, David Jones, a master of the obituary form and author of many of our "greatest hits", who succeeded me. I should also like to offer my heartfelt thanks to all my other colleagues on the desk over the years — particularly Claudia FitzHerbert, Aurea Carpenter, Robert Gray, Will Cohu, Kate Summerscale (who, in turn, succeeded David Jones in the chair), Diana Heffer and, of course, our effervescent editorial assistant, Teresa Moore, to whom this book is dedicated. Teresa and Claudia, as well as my personal secretary Cynthia Lewis, all rendered invaluable assistance in preparing the material for publication; and I am grateful to Judith Hannam of Macmillan and Marilyn Warnick, the *Telegraph*'s publishing director, for enabling this long-held dream to be fulfilled.

Finally, I would also like to thank the brilliant team of specialist writers whose unfailing professional expertise and wit have been profoundly appreciated, but I know that several of them, quite properly, would prefer to remain *incognito* and it seems invidious to mention only some. Yet I feel that I must salute the great Philip Warner and such other stalwarts as John Winton, Eric

Introduction

Shorter, Hugo Vickers, John McEwen, Gavin Stamp, Ian Waller, Chaim Bermant and Dean Godson. They all contributed to making my job hugely enjoyable. I miss them, and it, very much.

HUGH MASSINGBERD
Louth, Lincolnshire
June 1995

GERALD WILDE

GERALD WILDE, who has died aged 81, was the eccentric artist on whom the novelist Joyce Cary based the character Gulley Jimson in *The Horse's Mouth*.

The part was played by Sir Alec Guinness in the film of the novel. Cary, like a number of others well qualified to judge, regarded Wilde as an unsung genius and acquired his paintings. But the seediness of Wilde's life far outdistanced that of Jimson.

His obituary appeared prematurely in this and other papers in 1970. This was because a man who had collapsed and died outside Wilde's home in Earlsfield had been promptly identified as Wilde by a neighbour.

Apart from art critics, Cary and Julian McLaren Ross were among the few writers to reminisce in print about Wilde. For many years his work was known only to a select few and he was 50 before a retrospective exhibition in 1965 won him wider recognition.

An inability to organise himself professionally made for difficulties with galleries, who were disconcerted by his practice of giving his latest painting away to friends or selling it for a few shillings. Most of his early work therefore went privately to friends and admirers such as Cary, Sir Kenneth Clark, Dylan Thomas and Iris Murdoch.

He was handicapped by losing the use of an eye in a childhood accident, the first of many afflictions he suffered throughout his life. For a period he was schizophrenic but recovered.

Gerald Wilde was born in 1905. He was already 21 when his parents' friends, Lord and Lady Alfred Douglas, persuaded them to let him enter Chelsea School of Art where he began his lifelong association with Henry Moore and Graham Sutherland. Sutherland and Percy Jowett were among his teachers.

Trained as a printmaker as well as a painter, his realistic 1929 lithograph, *The Dressing Table*, showed little hint of the extremes of expressionism which characterised much of his later work.

There had been periods of inactivity such as a wartime spell in the Pioneer Corps or when he felt he had painted himself out. But his premature obituary seems to have stimulated him, for after establishing his identity with the local police, he felt he was in some way resurrected and being given a second chance. His paintings took on a powerful vision. There followed a BBC2 feature of his life and work and a large retrospective show by the Arts Council. A few years later he was taken on as the star exhibitor of the American-run October Gallery, Queen's Square. Successive one-man shows finally established his reputation on a wider footing especially in America.

In 1972 the philosopher J. G. Bennett who like Wilde was a devotee of Gurdjieff, took him to his home in the Cotswolds. After Bennett's death in 1975, Wilde lived on in what he called his "graveyard", a stable with no mains water or drainage.

He lived on welfare and spent most of his money on drink. "Life is pure unadulterated hell", he reported.

October 7 1986

VICTOR DILL

VICTOR DILL, who has died aged 89, won the MC in the First World War, served in the Second as a lieutenant-colonel in the Pioneer Corps but was brought low by the Francasal affair of the 1950s.

This attempted betting coup resulted in the monocled Old Etonian being jailed in 1954.

In July 1953 a horse called Santa Amaro was secretly switched to run in the name of another, inferior, animal called Francasal in the Spa Selling Plate at Bath. About half an hour before the "off", the gang, of which the unfortunate Dill was a member, proceeded to place bets totalling £6,000 on "Francasal" with bookmakers throughout the country.

Soon afterwards, the bookmakers' "blower" telephone line was cut so that off-course bookmakers were unable to make contact with the course. Had they been able to do so the odds would have been radically shortened. As it turned out, "Francasal's" starting price was 10 to 1. He duly romped home. However, before bets placed off the course could be paid out, suspicions were aroused and payment was withheld on the advice of the National Sporting League, the bookmakers' association.

Before the abortive coup Dill was working for a bookmaker, doing odd jobs, including cleaning the office, for £5 a week.

Sentencing Dill to nine months in prison on each of the two charges of conspiring to defraud, the sentences to run concurrently, Mr Justice Byrne said: "I am distressed to see a man such as you convicted of this offence. You were down-and-out and were brought into this . . . to give an atmosphere of respectability to it."

A kinsman of Field-Marshal Sir John Dill, Victor Robert Colquhoun Dill was born in 1897 and educated at Eton and Sandhurst. He was commissioned in the Royal Artillery in 1915. He won the MC for gallantly putting out a fire, caused by a German shell, which threatened to blow up the howitzer battery he was commanding.

After the war he retired from the Army as an acting captain and joined Leslie Brabazon's racing stable in County Meath. This venture did not prove successful and he then went on the stage. Although he appeared in *Funny Face* at the Princes Theatre, his luck was mixed. Later he worked variously as a garage proprietor, salesman, sandwich-bar assistant and a washer-up at a club in Putney. When things were going well he owned the odd racehorse, and the great Gordon Richards once rode for him in a selling plate at Chepstow, finishing last.

In 1939 Dill was recalled to the Army, served in France with a Field Artillery unit and escaped from St Nazaire, after Dunkirk, in 1940. He became a staff officer in the Directorate of Military Training at the War Office and then a deputy assistant quartermaster-general for the Pioneer Corps, directing the work of clearing bombed sites in London.

He was promoted acting Lt-Col in 1941 and was invalided out in 1942. For three years he managed the old St James's Theatre and in 1949 settled at Maisons Lafitte, near Paris, where he set up as a bloodstock agent. There his tall figure, complete with monocle and pale corduroy cap as he rode an old-fashioned English bicycle, was a familiar sight in racing circles.

October 13 1986

LAURIE ROSS

LAURIE ROSS, who has died aged 78, was the revered barman at the Ritz in Piccadilly, celebrated for mixing legendary dry martinis and gin rickeys in the old Grill Bar downstairs in the hotel.

This intimate basement sanctuary, now replaced by the new Ritz Casino, was generally known as "Laurie's Bar" and was a favourite haunt of such varied luminaries as Nubar Gulbenkian, the Aly Khan, Graham Greene, Gregory Peck and Peregrine Worsthorne.

Ross began his career as a 13-year-old commis waiter at the Savoy and worked at the Café Royal, the old Delmonico Restaurant, and at hotels in Brighton and Newquay, before becoming chef de bar at the Carlton Hotel in the Haymarket in the 1930s. During the Second World War he served with the 51st Highland Division in North Africa and Italy. He joined the Ritz in 1946 and presided over the Grill Bar until the mid 1970s. He later worked as a wine steward at Buck's Club.

Away from mixing cocktails and counselling his many clients, Laurie Ross was a devoted student of paintings. He was particularly knowledgeable about 18th-century portraitists and the 17th-century Dutch School.

Peregrine Worsthorne writes: Laurie, who knew everybody, and was privy to many scandalous secrets, asked me once, just before his retirement, whether *The Sunday Telegraph* would like to serialise his memoirs. I was thrilled and awaited the manuscript eagerly. Imagine my disappointment when the first sentence of Chapter One read as follows: "Mr Thomas Driberg was a gentleman of the old school".

As is clear from that description, Laurie saw life through rose-coloured spectacles but that was what made him such a superb barman. All his old clients were treated in a manner appropriate to the status of "a gentleman of the old school". He flattered us outrageously and cosseted our egos − just as important a quality in a barman as being able to mix a good dry martini.

I suppose he was a bit of an actor. He cannot really always have been so pleased to see one as he seemed. But so convincing was his performance that while in his bar, and under his aegis, one felt oneself to be the most elegant, important, amusing person in town.

No wonder we all loved Laurie and returned to the Ritz bar, decade after decade, like homing pigeons.

December 5 1986

H. DE C. HASTINGS

HUBERT DE CRONIN HASTINGS, an influential figure in the world of architecture, who has died aged 84, was chairman of the Architectural Press and editor of both the monthly *Architectural Review* and of the weekly

Architects Journal which have played vital and differing roles in informing the professional and outside world of stylistic and technical developments in architecture.

In 1973 he became the first architectural publisher to receive the Royal Gold Medal for Architecture. The Royal Institute for British Architects' citation for the award stated that Hastings had been "a leading campaigner in drawing attention to many of the most crucial and controversial issues that have concerned the architectural profession in this century."

In the 1930s Hastings promoted the cause of Modernism, but he later led the "Archie Rev's" — as it was affectionately known — campaign for the rediscovery of "townscape," a phrase first coined in the magazine, and the preservation of historical towns and cities.

Although "H. de C." was certainly an inspiring and inspirational force, his undeniably awkward personality made him a difficult man with whom to work. He had a remarkable knack of bringing on young protégés with whom he would, almost invariably, later fall out.

Among the staff he recruited to the *Architectural Review* was John Betjeman who nicknamed his patron "Old Obscurity". They got on well, although Betjeman was openly impatient of the petty rules imposed by the management. On one occasion, infuriated by their insistence on seeing bus tickets stapled to expense sheets, he obtained a sackful of used bus tickets from the local station and tipped them over Hastings's desk. On another, during a particularly hot summer's day, the young poet donned the briefest of brief swimming trunks, in which he nonchalantly greeted Hastings senior and an eminent visitor.

The son of Percy Hastings, the proprietor of the Architectural Press who founded the *Architechtural Review* in 1896, Hubert de Cronin Hastings was born in 1902 and educated at Berkhamsted and University College, London. He also attended both the Bartlett School of Architecture and the Slade School of Art.

After assuming control of the *Architectural Review* as editor in 1927, he dramatically changed the layout of the magazine, deploying new concepts in graphic design and typography which were to develop into an identifiable style. There were regular sections on painting, sculpture, interior design and frequent excursions into architectural history, as well as occasional special numbers.

Apart from Betjeman, the new contributors included Osbert Lancaster, Robert Byron and Sacheverell Sitwell. Nikolaus Pevsner assisted Hastings in producing the magazine while the executive editor J. M. Richards was away serving in the Second World War.

The *Architects Journal*, which he edited from 1932 to 1973, pioneered the publication of systematic appraisals of buildings and cost analyses, as well as a library of technical information.

Hastings's outstanding quality was the ability to generate and disseminate original ideas which eventually became part of mainstream architectural thinking. Some of his notions were distinctly quixotic and the *Architectural Review* was often criticised for being absurdly romantic.

There are many stories of his eccentric behaviour and of stormy scenes at the offices of the Architectural Press, whose basement he stylishly adorned in the manner of a 19th-century public house, and which was known as The

Bride of Denmark. His attendance at editorial meetings was erratic, with prolonged absences when nothing was heard from him. Communication was restored, as often as not, with the arrival of a draft of a special issue or a pile of splendid photographs from some European capital.

Two of the most memorable special issues, which he wrote himself under the pseudonym Ivor de Wolfe, were *Italian Townscape* and *Civilia: The End of sub-Urban Man*, both later republished in book form. He was also the author of *The Alternative Society* (1980), and in the 1930s he had illustrated some of Betjeman's poems, as well as publishing a book of caricatures.

Hastings was always something of an enigma in the architectural world. When he received the Royal Gold Medal for Architecture, Sir Hugh Casson observed: "All those who have worked with him and those who have never set eyes on him – so often, in fact, they are the same – rejoice that so unusual, enterprising, perceptive, and elusive a talent has been at last publicly recognised and rewarded."

He married, in 1927, Hazel Rickman Garrard. They had a son and a daughter.

December 8 1986

SIR ATHOLL OAKELEY, BT

SIR ATHOLL OAKELEY, 7th Bt, who has died aged 86, was a champion wrestler, an impresario of giants, master of a former Bristol pilot cutter offering rugged holiday cruises and an authority on *Lorna Doone*.

A veteran of nearly 2,000 bouts, he described his career as a wrestler in an engaging autobiography, *Blue Blood on the Mat* (1971). He was heavyweight champion of Great Britain from 1930 to 1935, of Europe in 1932 and remained unbeaten on a 17-bout tour of America, helping to offset the traditional picture of horizontal British heavyweights.

Although only 5ft 9in tall, Oakeley was broad in the beam. He started wrestling seriously after being beaten up by a gang of louts and built up his body by drinking 11 pints of milk a day for three years. This regimen had been recommended by the giant wrestler Hackenschmidt, who later told Oakeley that the quantity of milk prescribed had been a misprint.

Giants always held a particular fascination for Oakeley. He liked to recall how he had bent a man of 9ft with a half-nelson which it took several other wrestlers sitting on his opponent to untangle.

He received his distinctive cauliflower ear in a bout in Chicago when, as he recalled, Bill Bartuch "got me in a scissors grip between his knees."

His active career came to an end in 1935 when he broke his shoulder. He then acted as manager to Jack Sherry, the world heavyweight champion, for four years, and later promoted championship wrestling at the Harringay Arena.

Among the wrestlers he staged was Gargantua, a 50-stone German with a 90in chest measurement, for whom special travelling arrangements had to be made with British Railways.

Edward Atholl Oakeley was born in 1900, the grandson of Sir Charles Oakeley, 4th Bt, a Bengal Cavalryman who was also an amateur heavyweight prize fighter. The baronetcy was created in 1790 for an ancestor who was Governor of Madras.

Oakeley was educated at Clifton and Sandhurst and commissioned in the Oxfordshire and Buckinghamshire Light Infantry. He was Army marathon and 10-mile track champion shortly after the First World War.

His interest in wrestling had first been aroused by reading *Lorna Doone* as a boy. The novel and its background remained a lifetime interest and in 1969 he published *The Facts on which R. D. Blackmore based Lorna Doone*. He mounted a lengthy and ultimately successful campaign to persuade the Ordnance Survey to change the map of Exmoor, showing that the Doone Valley was sited at Lank Combe rather than Hoccombe.

At the time he succeeded to the baronetcy on the death of his cousin Sir Charles Oakeley, 6th Bt, in 1959, Sir Atholl was making his living by taking people on cruises aboard his cutter *Seabreeze* from Hamble.

His first three marriages ended in divorce. He is survived by his fourth wife, the former Shirley Church; by a son of the second marriage; and by a daughter of the fourth. He also adopted a son.

The son of the second marriage, John Digby Atholl Oakeley, the well-known yachtsman, former America's Cup skipper and Olympic helmsman, now becomes the 8th Baronet.

January 8 1987

MARQUESS OF HUNTLY

THE 12TH MARQUESS OF HUNTLY, who has died aged 78, was premier Marquess of Scotland and did homage on behalf of the marquesses at the Coronation of George VI in 1937.

A few months earlier, Charles Gordon, a shy, unassuming character then working as a car salesman at Farnham, Surrey, had succeeded his great-uncle the 11th Marquess of Huntly in the marquessate, the five subsidiary peerages and a baronetcy. Apart from the titles, and the chiefship of the "Gey" House of Gordon, there was little for the new Lord Huntly to inherit, for his predecessor had sold the ancestral lands at Aboyne, Aberdeenshire, in 1922. But, with the help of his first wife, the former Pamela Berry, only daughter of the 1st Viscount Kemsley, the newspaper proprietor, Lord Huntly was able to buy back part of the old family estate. This was later made over to his son, the Earl of Aboyne, who has recently restored Aboyne Castle.

Lord Huntly lived in Surrey in a modest residence at Cranleigh. His first marriage, by which there is a son and daughter, was dissolved in 1965. In 1977, he married Elizabeth, daughter of Lt-Cdr F. H. Leigh.

His new bride, a nurse, was more than 40 years his junior. At the time his engagement was announced, he was quoted as saying: "I'm a very fit man. I walk my dog every day. I don't have to wear spectacles. I still have my own teeth. Why should I marry some dried-up old bag?"

These remarks appeared under the inevitable headline "I'm Cock o' the North" — an allusion to the designation borne by successive Lords Huntly since the military exploits of the 3rd Earl who commanded the left wing of the Scots Army at Flodden in 1513 but escaped the slaughter. The Marquessate was created in 1599.

Douglas Charles Lindsay Gordon was born on February 3 1908, eldest son of Lt-Col Douglas Gordon, equerry to the Duke of Connaught. He was commissioned in the Gordon Highlanders (the family regiment founded by the 5th Duke of Gordon in 1796) and served in the Second World War as a lieutenant.

Lord Huntly took his seat in the House of Lords as Lord Meldrum, a peerage of the United Kingdom created in 1815 for the 9th Marquess in the days when peers of Scotland could only be represented by certain of their number at Westminster.

Lord Huntly had great respect for the House of Lords. "Their intelligence is far and away above that of the House of Commons," he said. "That is why they are there." The Commons, he observed, "had hardly an 'h' between them." He was once also reported as saying that Harold Wilson "should be suspended from the end of a long pole."

Belying the popular image of a backwoodsman, however, Lord Huntly was a gentle, diffident, kindly man with a considerable talent for singing and painting. In 1961 he formed the House of Gordon Society to promote fellowship and kinship among members throughout the world. He was a familiar figure in his eagle-feathered bonnet at the Aboyne Highland Games.

His only son, the Earl of Aboyne now becomes the 13th Marquess of Huntly.

January 28 1987

Canon Edwyn Young

Canon Edwyn Young, who has died aged 74, was one of the Church of England's most colourful priests and claimed to be the first-ever chaplain to a strip-tease club, officiating at the Raymond Revuebar in Soho.

His claim was never challenged, and it is certain that he was the only Chaplain to the Queen and Chaplain of the Royal Victorian Order to hold such an office.

Young exercised a remarkably influential ministry among ordinary people in east London and central Liverpool, as well as those in the world of theatre and show business. He belonged to his Church's Anglo-Catholic wing, saw the Mass as the centre-point of parish life, and had an immense love of people which drove him in unusual directions in order to save their souls.

Cecil Edwyn Young was born in Colombo, Ceylon, in 1913 but his parents returned to England before his first birthday and he was brought up in Devon. After Radley, he entered Dorchester Missionary College in 1931 with a view to serving in the Church overseas, but this did not materialise and in 1936 he was ordained to a curacy at St Peter's, Wapping.

When the war came he was very much in the thick of it – ministering, under heavy bombing, to people in air raid shelters; to the dying and others who had lost their homes; and taking occasional breaks to visit parishioners who had been evacuated to the country. In 1941 he became priest-in-charge of St Francis, near Paddington station, and in addition to a tough pastoral ministry he was also an air raid warden. On his marriage in 1944 to Beatrice Mary Rees he was appointed rector of Broughton with Ripton Regis, Hunts, but he was in no sense a countryman and within three years was back in London as vicar of St Silas, Pentonville.

In this toughest of all London parishes he soon became the leading figure in the community. He mixed easily with the poor and the criminal, selling his lively parish newspaper in the public houses on Saturday evenings, and befriending stallholders and their customers in the local market.

It was during this time that he was invited to become chaplain to Collins Music Hall and, fascinated by the stage, quickly established a rapport with both performers and managers, the clothed and the unclothed. He also took another music hall, near King's Cross, under his wing and became greatly loved in the show business world.

In 1953 the Bishop of London persuaded him to leave Islington in order to become rector of Stepney, a parish of some 32,000 people and comprising five pre-war parishes. Here he built up a staff of six curates, three women church workers, two club leaders and a secretary, and through a combination of hard work and audacity the Church infiltrated virtually every aspect of Stepney's community life. At one time Young was a member of 44 committees.

The parish newspaper, reflecting the life of the whole

community and once again sold in public houses, was called *Stepahoy*; on one occasion, a member of the staff suggested that from time to time it might have a religious supplement. In fact, it contained many pictures of the rector in the company of actors and actresses, for he was also chaplain of the London Palladium and often invited "stars" to church services and parish events. Every summer he moved down to Kent for three weeks to minister to East Enders working in the hop fields.

In 1964 he went to Liverpool, spending the next nine years as rector of the parish church and also rural dean, becoming a canon diocesan of the cathedral soon after his arrival.

A city centre parish, with only a small resident population, cramped his style somewhat but he found plenty of scope for his pastoral energy in the public life of Liverpool and, besides theatre and night-club chaplaincies, inaugurated a new form of ministry in departmental stores. It was sad, but perhaps not surprising, that this vigorous and creative ministry was halted by a severe heart attack in 1973.

On his recovery the following year, Young returned to London as Chaplain of the Queen's Chapel of the Savoy. This was a strange appointment in many ways, but the duties were light and theatreland was on the doorstep. So also were a number of London's leading hotels and soon Young persuaded their managements that no hotel was complete without its visiting chaplain.

He is survived by his wife, two sons and a daughter.

March 2 1987

STEPHEN TENNANT

STEPHEN TENNANT, poet, painter and writer, who has died aged 80, made a singular contribution in bringing the exotic into English life.

He was a key figure in that group which included Cecil Beaton, Rex Whistler, the Mitfords and the three Sitwells.

Stephen James Napier Tennant was born in 1906, the youngest son of the 1st Lord Glenconner and his wife Pamela, who was latterly Viscountess Grey of Fallodon. Tennant's mother, born Pamela Wyndham, was famous for her beauty and is the central figure in Sargent's celebrated painting known as "The Three Graces". However, she was also distinguished for her artistic sensibilities and writing.

It was from her that the young "Steenie" inherited his ethereal looks and many of his talents. He would often refer to himself as "a mother's boy".

Educated at West Downs Preparatory School, Tennant was removed after two years as his mother considered him to be temperamentally unsuited to a conventional education. He was educated privately at home and in France, and he soon displayed a precocious talent for drawing.

He wrote poems and prose too, but he held his first London exhibition of paintings at the age of 16. Professor Tonks accepted him for the Slade School of Art, where he not only met and became a close friend of Rex Whistler, but began to develop the personality that was to make him a leader among the Bright Young Things of the 1920s.

Tennant's interest in his personal appearance was once again inherited from his mother. As he watched her applying make-up to her face, he saw no reason why he should not do the same. For the 1920s this was a move of considerable daring, but Tennant was never bothered by what others thought.

"I want to have bee-stung lips like Mae Murray," he would write with carefree abandon, and when Cecil Beaton first saw him riding *papier-mâché* horses at the circus, and blowing kisses to left and right, he realised that Tennant could be the inspiration he so badly needed. Tennant's uncurbed imagination, and his pioneer sense of "style" gave Beaton many of the ideas that he was to adopt both in his photography and stage design. When Beaton came to design the costumes for *My Fair Lady*, for instance, it was to Tennant that he went to learn about the fashions for Royal Ascot.

Fortunate to have been born with financial security, Stephen Tennant never commercialised himself. Apart from some anthologies and books of sayings which he illustrated for his mother — notably *The Vein in the Marble* — he published little.

Throughout his life he dreamt with a child's innocence of being famous, but preferred the dreams to the reality. The only complete book of his own that he brought out was *Leaves from a Missionary's Notebook*, which was first published in 1929 and reissued to celebrate his 80th birthday.

It concerns the adventures of Felix Littlejohn — a young and zealous priest — whose zeal gradually weakens under a hot, tropical sun and the merry cavortings of natives and sailors. Consisting of full page illustrations with captions, it gave Tennant the opportunity to explore his superb handling of comic draughtsmanship which was to surface again in his pen and ink watercolours of *louche* seaports and sailors' bars.

Outside his painting – which currently is enjoying a revival of interest – the work of art was Tennant himself and his home Wilsford Manor, in Wiltshire. This house of chequered flint and stone, built in the Arts and Crafts manner for Tennant's mother by the architect Detmar Blow became in time his fantasy land. He imported palm trees to rustle against mullioned windows, sand to create Mediterranean pathways between leaning cypresses and, within the house, riots of ice-cream colours.

Although such a thoroughly English house in its making, under Tennant's occupation Wilsford touched in the imagination all corners of the globe. It became the perfect resting place for his own restless mind.

For by the late 1950s Stephen Tennant decided that his travels to Europe and farther continents were over. He decided, also, that he would see few people and, on the whim that had directed so many of his passions in life, he retreated to Wilsford.

In the summers he lay by dripping fountains remembering his friendship with Willa Cather and the poems of Emily Dickinson; in the winters he took increasingly to his bed and played with his great novel of the Marseilles seaport that he must goad himself to finish.

Over the years Tennant became legendary as a recluse. His paintings – many of them vivid illustrations of Marseilles low life – were exhibited in London and New

York, but few saw Tennant himself. By the age of 60 he had retreated completely from the social scene.

Yet it was an irony that not more than half an hour away was another recluse, Tennant's former friend, Siegfried Sassoon. When Sassoon had met Tennant in the 1920s he had fallen instantly in love with him but, finally, Sasoon made emotional demands on Tennant which he felt unable to meet. Nonetheless, the affair was to drag itself out over eight years, changing what once had been happiness into frayed nerves on both sides.

So Tennant knew all the heights and depths of personal relationships and came to feel himself most at ease in the role of the solitary.

Recently Stephen Tennant had become something of a cult, in particular with a much younger generation. His excesses were always less frivolous than they appeared; what he feared most was that dullness in the English spirit that stifled life. One must live, he always said, "At the heartbreak of things".

Tennant was exceptionally shy about his achievements – or, as he once daubed on the back of one of his paintings: "The world famous, the very modest Stephen Tennant".

March 3 1987

LORD VENTRY

THE 7TH LORD VENTRY, the "lighter-than-air" Irish peer who has died aged 88, was a "certificated aeronaut", a balloonist, and an inveterate champion of the airship.

In 1949 he began work on the Bournemouth, the first airship to be built in Britain since the ill-fated *R 101* crashed in 1930. The sausage-shaped dirigible, with an envelope 108 ft long and a capacity of 45,000 cubic ft, was all set to make its maiden flight at Cardington, Beds, in July 1951.

Unfortunately the airship, designed to hold up to five people, failed to rise and the 17-stone Ventry was obliged to get out and allow a lighter man to take his place. The trials proceeded satisfactorily, but a month later, the airship, with Ventry aboard this time, "pancaked" on the roof of the gymnasium at RAF Cardington.

"We made a perfectly ordinary flight," said Ventry, "but as we were coming in to land one of the handling guy ropes caught on the catwalk of the gymnasium building and there we sat, just like a broody hen. It was a chance in a million."

Nothing daunted, Ventry made several more successful flights in the repaired Bournemouth until it was accidentally damaged in the hangar at Cardington in 1953. The vessel was eventually scrapped.

Arthur Frederick Daubeney Eveleigh de Moleyns (he later assumed the additional Christian name of Olav and was known as "Bunny") was born in 1898, the elder son of the 6th Lord Ventry, a substantial landowner. He succeeded his father in 1936.

He was educated at a private school at Langton Matravers, Dorset ("where unlike so many novelists I had the happiest of boyhoods") and at Wellington where he first became interested in balloons and airships.

From 1917 to 1918 he served in the Irish Guards and was wounded before transferring to the RAF as Cdre of

No. 902 County of London Balloon Squadron in the Auxiliary Air Force and served in the Second World War as a flight lieutenant in Balloon Command and Intelligence.

Both before and after the war Ventry campaigned ceaselessly for the revival of airships, pointing out that they were "in fact more reliable than present-day aircraft and of course vastly more comfortable."

He argued that airships could be used to locate submarines and mines in wartime and shoals of fish in peacetime. He also urged that an airship would be an ideal observation post for "monster hunting" over Loch Ness.

In old age Ventry lyrically recalled the pleasures of flying in the Graf Zeppelin from Lake Constance to Hanworth in about 12 hours. "For a good part of the time we flew at about 800 ft and so had a perfect bird's eye view. We had properly cooked meals and there was plenty of room to walk about between the control car, saloon and sleeping cabins: "I at least was never bored and the whole voyage was a sheer delight."

Ventry continued to travel in airships until he was almost 80 and kept abreast of the latest developments in the field. In 1981, for instance, he was recommending the value of a new British airship, Skyship 500, to the Royal Navy.

He was joint editor of *The Airship and Aero History* and chairman of the Airship Club. Besides articles on ballooning and airships, he also wrote about scouting, having served happily under Baden-Powell. "I can look back", he wrote, "on some of the happiest years of my long life with the Scouts, not only of this country but also of Norway . . . In my view, BP did more for the youth of the world than all the politicians put together."

A bachelor, Lord Ventry is succeeded in the peerage and the baronetcy by his nephew, Andrew Harold Wesley Daubeny de Moleyns.

March 10 1987

DENISA LADY NEWBOROUGH

DENISA LADY NEWBOROUGH, who has died aged 79, was many things: wire-walker, nightclub girl, nude dancer, airpilot. She only refused to be two things – a whore and a spy – "and there were attempts to make me both," she once wrote.

She was also a milliner, a perfumier and an antiques dealer; but her real metier, in early life at least, was what she called "profitable romance". Her opinions on the subject of presents from gentlemen would have done credit to the pen of Anita Loos: "I have never believed that jewels, any more than motors cars, can be called vulgar just because they are gigantic."

Her admirers included the Kings of Spain and Bulgaria, Adolf Hitler (whose virility she doubted), Benito Mussolini (whom she described as "a gigolo") and Sheikh ben Ghana (who gave her 500 sheep). When she lived in Paris, she had no fewer than five protectors – all "shareholders" as she termed them – and persuaded each, who was ignorant of his fellows, to part with a flat or a house.

23

She was earlier married to Jean Malpuech, the governor of Loas, who had died. But the climax of this stage of her career came in 1939 with her marriage to the 61-year-old 5th Lord Newborough as his second wife. They were divorced in 1947.

Denisa Josephine Braun was born on April Fool's Day, 1913, in Subotica, Serbia. In her early teens she ran away to Budapest, where for a time she slept under bridges with tramps. Then, styling herself "Baronne de Brans," she became a nude dancer and mistress of boyars, including a pair of twins. A decade of adventures followed, in Sofia, Bucharest, Paris, St Moritz and Berlin.

She spoke 14 languages. She served as a transport officer with the Red Cross at the beginning of the Second World War but was dismissed in 1941 because she was not of British birth.

In 1946, shortly before her divorce from "Tommy" Newborough, a receiving order was made against her for debts of £951, which she attributed to losses at bridge when her skill had been impaired by unhappiness. She recovered her finances by designing outrageous hats – "The Nicotine Hat", for example, which was covered with cigarettes, with half-smoked imitations hanging over the bridge.

In 1958, she published an autobiography, *The Fire in My Blood*, the flavour of which may be surmised from such chapter headings as "Gipsy Love," "Elegant Sin in Bucharest" and "On the Trail of the White Slavers".

She was convicted in 1964 of permitting her maisonette in Davies Street to be used for the purpose of habitual prostitution, though her conviction was quashed on appeal.

Lady Newborough was a great beauty and she was charming and funny. By conventional standards, her morality matched her flaming red hair but she remained as proud of the one as of the other.

She is survived by her daughter Juno, who is married to a dentist.

March 28 1987

THE VERY REV HUGH HEYWOOD

THE VERY REVEREND HUGH HEYWOOD, who has died aged 90, achieved wide publicity as provost of Southwell, first by encouraging miners to sing *Bring Out the Barrel* at a service and then by being arrested in Yugoslavia on suspicion of spying for the Russians.

On returning home from Yugoslavia, where secret police suspicions had been raised on finding him inspecting some ruins near the Greek border, Heywood had another brush with higher officialdom when he paid his overdue telephone bill, only to be cut off the next day. Recognising that no good could come of tangling with the colourful clergyman, the Post Office apologised profusely.

Heywood strongly believed that a church should be used as widely as possible. He criticised parishioners who hounded a couple out of a service because their baby was gurgling, put up a sign saying "dogs welcome", and organised a pageant in which whistling cyclists, courting couples and even a farmer with a shotgun went down the aisle.

He announced that he preferred to have his letters addressed to "Mr" rather than the "Very Reverend", and was not afraid to reveal the difficulties of living on his stipend of £23-a-week. That was in 1955. He pointed out that 10 years before, he had employed a man and a boy full-time all week in his three-acre garden, but now only had a single man for half-a-day a week.

There were few subjects on which he could not be relied upon for a sensible, genial opinion, whether it was the advisability of buying a wreath rather than picking wild flowers, or the best kinds of postcards. He even got Mr Tom Driberg, Labour MP, to raise in Parliament an incident in which he had been refused a glass of beer in Richmond Park because half a round of sandwiches did not legally constitute a whole round and therefore a meal.

But many of his friends felt that the beautiful Nottinghamshire minster over which he presided from 1945 to 1969 was not sufficiently demanding for a man of Heywood's considerable gifts. He had earlier been Dean of Gonville and Caius College, Cambridge, for 17 years.

Born in 1896, Hugh Christopher Lempriere Heywood joined the Manchest Regt. in 1914 and was quickly at the front, where he was wounded and mentioned in despatches.

In 1917, he was transferred to the Indian Army, serving in the 74th Punjabis, and remained in India, where he was a staff captain, until 1923.

He then returned to England to seek ordination and went up to Cambridge as a Exhibitioner of Trinity, where he soon became a Scholar. In addition to securing a First, with distinction, in both parts of the Theological Tripos, he carried off the coveted Carus Greek testament prize.

After being ordained at Ely in 1926, Heywood spent his final student year as curate of Greenford. But a year later he returned to Cambridge as Fellow and Dean of Gonville and Caius College.

His first book, *The Worshiping Community*, was published in 1938, but nothing more was to appear from his pen until 1960 and his later books were somewhat slight.

In 1945, the then Bishop of Southwell, Dr F. R. Barry, who admired men of academic distinction, invited Heywood to become provost of Southwell, but this quiet rural backwater offered no stimulus to a Cambridge scholar, and the pastoral responsibilities of the Cathedral parish diverted him from sustained reading and writing.

To the surprise of many, not least the Bishop and the Chapter, Heywood embarked on his programme of unusual activities designed to enliven the Cathedral community. Most of these were dismissed as gimmicks, and relations between the Provost and his colleagues, especially the Bishop, became strained. But Heywood continued in office until he was 73, and was much appreciated by lay people as a pastor and preacher. He then spent another seven years very happily as priest in charge of the country parish of Upton.

He married Margaret Marion Bizard in 1920 and they had a son and a daughter.

May 11 1987

DORIS STOKES

DORIS STOKES, who has passed over aged 68, was an internationally-celebrated medium, known as "The Gracie Fields of the psychic world".

She made much of her ordinariness, eschewing the mystery and glamour of Madame Arcati for a more cosy approach. In her highly-successful roadshow, *An Audience with Doris Stokes*, she appeared on stage in a chintz armchair with a simple flower display beside it, she wore studiedly dowdy frocks and a permanently waved hair-do, and invariably addressed her audiences (for the most part female and inclined to tears) as "lovey" and "dear."

Having warmed them up with a few jokes about sexual practices in the afterlife, she regaled them with a flood of "messages" – usually on domestic subjects (dining suites, garage doors) – from such dead relations as "Uncle Wilf" and "Auntie Dot". In recent years, when she had been raised by American television to the status of a "spiritualist superstar," she had much contact with dead celebrities (particularly John Lennon and Elvis Presley), and made extensive use of the medium of tabloid newspapers. Her followers included Ronnie Kray and Derek Jameson.

She claimed in her various books (*Voices in My Ear*, *More Voices in My Ear*, *Innocent Voices in My Ear*, *A Host of Voices*, etc) to have helped the police with a number of murder inquiries – though all the police forces she mentions have denied receiving any such assistance.

Doris Stokes was born in 1920 at Grantham, Lincs – a street away from the birthplace of Margaret Thatcher.

She described her childhood as "unhappy and confused," plagued as it was by inexplicable voices.

She first visited a medium at the age of 13, when her dead father announced himself to her. But she did not become a medium herself until she was 24 when she was invited to a spiritualist church after the death of her son.

She claimed to have visited "the Other Side," and said that its denizens "were not floating around in white sheets or sitting on clouds strumming a golden harp."

She said that the "voices . . . just spill out of my mouth and I don't know what I'm saying *half* the time. I suppose I'm a bit like a telephone exchange."

Some of her spillages gave rise to sceptical jokes about crossed lines. "He went very quickly," she told one member of her audience.

"He was ill for six months," came the reply. "Well, he went very quickly at the end, lovey."

Mrs Stokes lived in a bungalow in South London and a mobile home in Kent. She is survived by her husband John, a faith healer, and her adopted son Terry, a bus driver and part-time psychic.

May 12 1987

EARL OF WHARNCLIFFE

THE 4TH EARL OF WHARNCLIFFE, who has died aged 52, had a colourful career in which ultimately the comedy was overcast by a series of tragedies.

He was variously an able seaman, a stock-car driver, publican, garage mechanic, salesman and rock'n'roll drummer. But his life was blighted by a string of motoring accidents and convictions, culminating in a car crash near Barnsley in April 1979 in which a pub landlady was killed.

In the resulting court case of July, 1980, Lord Wharncliffe, who had himself been seriously injured in the crash, was found guilty of causing death by reckless driving and was jailed for six months. In 1981, a few months after his release from prison, Lord Wharncliffe's elder daughter, Lady Joanna Montagu-Stuart-Wortley-Mackenzie, was killed in a car crash near Caenby Corner, Lincs, aged 21.

Alan James Montagu-Stuart-Wortley-Mackenzie was born in 1935, the only son of the 3rd Earl of Wharncliffe by his wife, the redoubtable Lady Elfreda Wentworth-Fitzwilliam, who ran her own munitions works in the Second World War.

The barony of Wharncliffe was created in 1826 for James Stuart-Wortley-Mackenzie, Tory MP for Yorkshire. He edited the correspondence of his great-grandmother, the celebrated 18th-century woman of letters Lady Mary Wortley-Montagu, butt of Alexander Pope and pioneer of inoculation against smallpox. Fifty years later, in 1876, James's grandson was advanced to the viscountcy of Carlton and the earldom of Wharncliffe.

The Earl was educated at Eton and joined the Royal Naval Volunteer Reserve in 1952. He did his National Service in the Navy and was subsequently a member of the Supplementary Reserve. He succeeded his father in the earldom in 1953, and followed his mother as Master of the Ecclesfield Beagles.

As a student at the Royal Agricultural College,

Cirencester, he joined the Beards Society, making a vow never to shave, but after six months he applied the razor to his growth. The secretary of the society said he was "very annoyed to think that a peer of the realm could act in this way."

As drummer for the Johnny Lenniz rock'n'roll band Wharncliffe joined the Musicians' Union. The band, which included a fishmonger and a stone merchant, cut some discs, such as *Shake, Rattle and Roll* in 1957, and went on tours of Britain and the continent.

Later in the 1950s Wharncliffe became publican of the Wortley Arms on the family estate near Sheffield. "Now people come to enjoy a night out," he said in 1960. "Once they came to see if I had a head, two legs and two arms. I was something of a curiosity to them."

Apparently known as "Mad Ike" by the villagers, Wharncliffe caused a stir by shooting a black-and-white tom cat called Elvis which he had discovered in his kitchen. Behind the pub Wharncliffe ran Wharncliffe Engineering, a car repair workshop.

Although he was at one stage a member of the Institute of Advanced Motorists, Wharncliffe was banned from driving on several occasions in his motoring career. In 1976, when he was banned for three years for drink driving, the court was told that he had vowed never to drink again.

Fifteen days after this ban ended, Wharncliffe's estate car was involved in the fatal accident that led to his prison sentence. He suffered multiple fractures, and was unconscious for more than six weeks and on a life-support machine. At one stage he was pronounced clinically dead.

After the case had been adjourned to allow Wharncliffe time for rehabilitation, he fell from his crutches and broke another leg. He eventually appeared in court on sticks.

Wharncliffe was reported to have coped admirably with prison life, and one of his fellow inmates acted as his unofficial valet.

In 1974 he was elected the first president of the Yorkshire Sporting Club at Bradford. He enjoyed shooting, fishing and sailing.

In 1957 he married Aline Margaret Bruce, who survives him together with their younger daughter.

The heir to the earldom is his kinsman, Alan Ralph Montagu-Stuart-Wortley, who was born in 1927 and lives in Connecticut.

June 6 1987

LADY SIDNEY FARRAR

LADY SIDNEY FARRAR, who has died in Harare aged 87, was the first woman to be elected to the Old Kenyan Legislative Council and a vivid figure in settler society until forced to leave in 1969.

Bounding with energy and resourcefulness, she successfully built up a 2,000-acre dairy farm and never disguised her disgust with what she saw as Britain's betrayal of first the white Kenyans and later the white Rhodesians.

Lady Sidney Mary Catherine Anne Hobart-Hampden-Mercer-Henderson was born in 1900, the younger daughter of the 7th Earl of Buckinghamshire, and privately educated by a governess. She agreed to be a debutante, as a matter of family duty, on condition that she could go on to take a degree in history at London University.

When her parents objected to her choice of a husband she remained in her room, in the best Edwardian tradition, until they relented. After her marriage in 1924, she and her husband, Capt Thomas Farrar, the son of a bishop and great-nephew of Dean Farrar, author of *Eric, or Little by Little*, decided to farm in Kenya because of his damaged lungs.

On arriving at Mau Summit, one of the highest farms in the colony, which was 70 miles north of Nairobi, they had to hack land out of the bush. She found a snake curled up on her dressing table and contracted malaria and blackwater fever. For a time the couple also ran an hotel, not very successfully, in the gold rush district of Kakamanga.

But when Capt Farrar died in 1934, leaving his widow with an hotel, a farm and a son, nothing would induce her to return to England. Always an able public speaker, Lady Sidney was elected a member of the Legislative Council in 1938, earning a congratulatory telegram from Lady Astor, the first woman to take a seat at Westminster, and cheers in the chamber at Nairobi when she took the oath of allegiance.

War was already casting a shadow over most of the council's deliberations, but Lady Sidney had a notable clash with the libidinous 22nd Earl of Erroll. Never one of the colony's "fast set", she wholeheartedly supported a change in divorce law in line with A. P. Herbert's successful Private Member's Bill in the House of Commons, while the peer, who was later to be murdered in what was widely considered a *crime passionel*, piously declared that it favoured immorality.

Lady Sidney had founded the Kenyan FANY (First Aid Nursing Yeomanry) in 1931 and, once war was declared, found herself fully stretched.

Complete plans were drawn up for the evacuation of East Africa. Women sold their household goods and natives were told to destroy crops and drive cattle into the woods.

With only a few hundred men from the Kenyan Regiment, the King's African Rifles and a handful of women Territorials to face them, she could never understand why the Italians had not walked in, she told a recruiting meeting in Durban later.

In 1942 Lady Sidney reluctantly gave up command of the FANYs and her seat in Legco to go north to join Army headquarters in Cairo. On demobilisation, after being mentioned in despatches, she settled back into farming.

She carefully graded up a pedigree herd of shorthorn cattle and grew pyrethrum while also training Alsatians to be children's outdoor guard dogs and even making dog biscuits for sale. Rising shortly after dawn, she would join her native workers at milking, wearing her scruffiest clothing – though she could appear later immaculately dressed for lunch with neighbours.

Although she rarely visited England she displayed a surprising knowledge of a wide variety of subjects and had the latest books sent out for her large library. A kindly but firm employer who stood no nonsense, she was loyally waited on by members of one family always dressed in white clothes and red belts.

Lady Sidney never re-entered Legco, but she remained an indomitable champion of settler values, showing no fear at the height of the Mau Mau terror campaign when she was known to be on a list of intended victims. She was a caustic critic at public meetings of those who advocated compromise with the growing nationalistic forces.

After independence she was left alone for a time, prompting her to declare that she would only leave in her coffin. But when the farm was threatened with expropriation, she loaded her car with dogs and set off alone to drive the hundreds of miles to Rhodesia. She took no part in the politics of the increasingly embattled rebel colony, but built a house and devoted herself in her last years to looking after the animals of friends who were away from their homes.

A slim, striking-looking woman of middle height, Sidney Farrar had an outspokenness that could make bitter enemies. Yet her combination of breeding and indomitability spoke volumes about her British spirit that had departed elsewhere.

She leaves a son, Ewan, who lives in Zimbabwe.

June 25 1987

EARL OF CARNARVON

THE 6TH EARL OF CARNARVON, who has died aged 88, was one of the most colourful members of the 20th-century peerage, even if the brushwork in his Wodehousian character appeared somewhat crudely applied.

He was variously a soldier, sportsman, gentleman-rider, bloodstock breeder, landowner, clubman and *bon vivant*. He was also a pillar of the Ritz Hotel, an amateur actor, relentless raconteur and most uncompromisingly direct ladies' man. Always an outrageous exhibitionist, "Porchy" Carnarvon rejoiced in his manifestation, late in life, as a "television personality" following the publication of his racy memoirs *No Regrets* (1976).

Chat-show audiences were treated to frequent exposures of the carnationed Carnarvon baring his equine gums while he regaled Mr Michael Parkinson (or whomever) with renditions of how, as a young cavalry subaltern, he had been chased through the back gardens of Maidenhead by cuckolded husbands – or some similarly salacious anecdote. The irrepressible Porchy put on some remarkable performances, recalling nothing so much as the late A. E. Matthews overplaying the part of a rakish old "nob" in a Shafesbury Avenue farce.

Once aptly described as resembling a bookmaker in appearance, Porchy's physique was more that of a jockey's. Short of stature, he used to go down as a young man to Dick Dawson's stables at Whatcombe to "ride work". He became a legendary figure on the Turf, owning and breeding racehorses for over half a century. Under his beady eyes, the Highclere Stud (started by his father) bred Blenheim, which won the 1930 Derby for his crony, the "dear old fat boy" Aga Khan. Many years later Porchy's miler Queen's Hussar sired the great Brigadier Gerard.

Henry George Alfred Marius Victor Herbert (the sobriquet of "Porchy" derived from his courtesy title of Lord Porchester) was born in 1898, the only son of the

5th Earl of Carnarvon, a substantial landowner in Hampshire, Derbyshire and Nottinghamshire. The earldom was created in 1793 for a grandson of the 8th Earl of Pembroke.

He was educated at Eton and commissioned into the 7th Hussars, serving in the First World War.

In 1923 his career in the cavalry was cut short when his father, the Egyptologist, died of blood poisoning from an infected mosquito bite soon after he had helped discover the tomb of Tutankhamen. The 5th Earl's death gave rise to the legend of "Tutankhamen's Curse" – a rich seam of "copy" for the acutely publicity-conscious new Earl of Carnarvon.

In 1925 he was obliged to sell the Bingham estate in Nottinghamshire and from then on concentrated his resources upon the 6,000-acre property at Highclere on the Hampshire/Berkshire border with its "Jacobethan" Gothic castle designed by Sir Charles Barry. About a third of the Highclere land was made over to his son in the late 1950s.

A dedicated Gun, Porchy consolidated the pheasant shoot on the beautifully wooded estate at Highclere and he also shot regularly at Blenheim with his old chum and verbal sparring partner "Bert" Marlborough. The Duke and the Earl would swap the filthiest stories.

Soon after succeeding his father, Lord Carnarvon bred a couple of useful fillies at the Highclere Stud: Doushka, winner of the Yorkshire Oaks, and Nepeta, winner of the Newmarket Oaks. He inherited an outstanding brood mare from his father, Halva, who became the dam not only of Blenheim but of King Salmon and His Grace, both winners of the Coronation Cup at Epsom. King

Salmon was also runner-up to Hyperion in the 1933 Derby.

Racing parlance was Lord Carnarvon's preferred mode of speech, and his most celebrated *bon mot* was addressed to his old Army friend Sir "Jock" Delves Broughton after the baronet had been acquitted of murdering the 22nd Earl of Erroll in Kenya – the sensational case immortalised in James Fox's book *White Mischief*. Carnarvon sent the fortunate Broughton a cable (later framed at White's Club) which read: "Hearty congratulations on winning a neck cleverly."

When up in London, Carnarvon would hold court at White's and play bridge at the Portland Club but his metropolitan base was the Ritz in Piccadilly. At the hotel, the canny Carnarvon's chief concern was to find a suite not so much overlooking the Park as overlooking the rent. "In 1924," he recalled, "Billy Lurgan said that as I and my wife knew everybody, particularly in America, we could stay at the Ritz as guests of the hotel, and tell all and sundry of our pals to come and stay there." When the hotel celebrated its 75th anniversary in 1981, Lord Carnarvon, as the *doyen* of the Ritz, arrived in a horse-drawn landau, "mugging" for all he was worth in front of the television cameras.

His first wife, the former Catherine Wendell from New York, divorced him in 1936 and three years later he embarked on a disastrous marriage to the Viennese dancer and singer Tilly Losch (formerly married to the Surrealist patron Edward James), which was dissolved in 1947.

An inveterate stage-door johnny, the Earl had a lifetime's love of the theatre. "Gerald du Maurier told me that the secret of acting was to be yourself," he recalled.

He relished appearing in amateur theatricals and was once even invited to take up a career in Hollywood. In the 1950s he scored a memorable success in the West End charity production of *The Frog* which Princess Margaret helped to organise.

"Porchy' stole the show, much to the delight of the royal family, with whom he was apparently a particular favourite. In his second volume of memoirs, *Ermine Tales* (1980), he told how he satisfied King George V's fervent wish to hear a bookmaker on the rails at Newmarket shout that the favourite had been "f---d for fifty".

Lord Carnarvon rejoined his old regiment in the Second World War and ended up as a lieutenant-colonel, with the United States Bronze Star. He was hereditary High Steward of Newbury and entertained the Queen, Prince Philip and Princess Margaret at Highclere Castle, which, surprisingly for such a showman, he did not open to the public.

Carnarvon did himself well at the table and maintained a robustly Edwardian style of life at Highclere until retiring to a nursing home a few years ago.

He is survived by a son and a daughter by his first marriage. The son, Lord Porchester, who is the Queen's racing manager and married to Jean Wallop from Big Horn, Wyoming, now succeeds to the earldom.

September 23 1987

SHEILA VAN DAMM

SHEILA VAN DAMM, a pioneer woman rally driver who has died aged 65, spent three years at the wheel of the legendary Windmill Theatre until its quaint naughtiness was superseded by the onset of the Permissive Society.

Exuding a strapping, hail-fellow-well-met image she made no bones, on taking over the sole management on her father's death in 1961, about the contrast she made with the beautiful, shapely girls which were a byword for the theatre. At 39, she said, she had a constant problem with her weight and was all too aware of her own shortcomings to feel jealous

But despite having known the business for over 20 years she now faced unbeatable opposition which was emerging with the more daringly gyrating, if less sophisticated appeal of the neighbouring Soho strip shows. In 1964 she gave up, after three years, with good grace.

By then the well turned-out shows, which had encouraged the early careers of Jimmy Edwards, Michael Bentine and even Kenneth More, had been replaced in the popular imagination by antiseptic *poses plastiques* which contrasted curiously with the seediness of an audience consisting largely of macintoshed men of advanced age clutching their binoculars and sandwiches as they clambered over vacant seats for a better view.

Born in London in 1922, one of the three daughters of Vivian van Damm, she was educated at Queen's Gate and Frognal House before joining at 17 the publicity side of the Windmill, which her father had run since 1931.

On joining the WAAF after the outbreak of the Second World War, she became a driver for senior officers at RAF Stanmore. She showed that she was also a showbiz professional by using her leave to bring the Windmill lovelies – at the height of their fame for not letting Hitler keep them in their clothes for one night during the Blitz – on tours around the airfields.

Returning to assist her father after the war she joined the RAF Volunteer Reserve with whom she learnt to fly. It was only when her father persuaded her to enter a *Daily Express* rally in 1950 as a publicity stunt that her career as a driver took off.

She won first prize in the ladies section and so amazed Rootes's tough competition manager Norman Garrod that he invited her to join the company's works team.

During the next five years Sheila van Damm took part in 27 major rallies, winning the ladies sections of the Monte Carlo, Geneva and other rallies. Among her most outstanding achievements were her victory in the 1954 European Touring Car Championship ladies section and becoming the first British woman to win an Alpine Rally cup in 1953.

One of her few racing appearances was in the 1955 Mille Miglia in which she drove a Sunbeam Rapier with Peter Harper and they averaged 66.37 mph in appalling conditions to win their class. But she eventually had to give up when her father became ill.

Sheila van Damm was part of a closely-knit coterie which included the journalist Nancy Spain and the publisher Joan Wenner-Laurie. After the Windmill closed she settled in Sussex with her sister and became closely involved in several organisations, including the

International Spinal Research Trust. She was president of the Women's Motor Racing Associates Club, known as "the Doghouse Owners' Club", and wrote in 1967 an autobiography *We Never Closed*.

She was unmarried.

July 25 1987

DOROTHY LADY DE CLIFFORD

DOROTHY LADY DE CLIFFORD, who has died aged 85, was the second of the six daughters of "Ma" Meyrick, the notorious night-club queen of the 1920s, and the first of three to marry into the peerage.

Mrs Kate Meyrick, the wife of a Brighton doctor, came up to London in 1920 and took up running night-clubs in order to pay for her daughters' education. Her most successful establishment was the "43" (a basement in a house in Gerrard Street, Soho, once occupied by the poet Dryden) where luminaries such as the Prince of Wales, Noel Coward, Tallulah Bankhead and King Carol of Rumania would disport themselves, though one of Ma's previous establishments had been described by a magistrate as "a sink of iniquity".

Her daughters acted as dance instructresses, and in 1926 there was a sensation when it was disclosed that Miss Dorothy Evelyn Meyrick (known as "Dolly"), born in 1902, had secretly married 19-year-old Lord de Clifford, 26th holder of a barony created in 1299.

In fear of his mother (herself a former "Gibson Girl") withdrawing her consent to the marriage, Lord de Clifford falsely gave his age as 22 and came up in court before the Lord Mayor at the Mansion House. After explaining that he was not yet a man of means, the young peer was given two weeks to pay the fine. "Elsewhere," said the Lord Mayor, "the penalty would be seven years".

In 1935, Lord de Clifford, well known as a motor-racing driver, found himself the central figure in a far more spectacular trial when he became the last person to be tried "by God and my peers" in the House of Lords, having been accused of the manslaughter of a fellow motorist on the Kingston by-pass. Lady de Clifford sat among her fellow peeresses as the peers, resplendent in robes of scarlet and ermine, gave her husband a unanimous acquittal.

One of the few peers not to turn out in full rig was the 14th Earl of Kinnoull, who had married Dolly's elder sister, May. It was the only time this century that the House has been convened for such a trial.

Mrs Meyrick herself died in 1933, her health broken by a sentence of 15 months' hard labour in Holloway on conviction of bribery and corruption at the end of the 1920s. Her clubs, which included the Silver Slipper in Regent Street, had frequently been raided and she had twice previously been imprisoned for selling liquor without a licence, though she retained her indomitable spirit and good humour to the end.

Lord de Clifford, who became a colonel in the REME, later ran quarantine kennels in Somerset and was also a door-to-door dogfood salesman. He and his wife separated in the 1950s and the marriage, by which there were two sons, was dissolved in 1973.

September 25 1987

THE WALI OF SWAT

THE LAST WALI OF SWAT, MIANGUL ABDUL JAHAN-ZEB, who has died in his 70s, was a veritable Poo-bah, holding sway over that remote North-West Frontier principality for 20 years before handing over his ruling powers to Pakistan in 1969.

When the Queen dropped in on the Wali in 1961, many echoed the couplet of Edward Lear about his forbear: "*Who or what/Is the Akhund of Swat?*" It emerged that the Wali was a hard-working administrator of a state variously described as an "Islamic Ruritania" or a "Himalayan Switzerland".

He spent long hours at his desk in his modest rose-bowered bungalow palace overlooking the long green valley where orange trees contrast vividly with a breath-taking backdrop of the snow-capped Hindu Kush. A neatly turned-out figure very much in the English manner, the Wali favoured traditional English fare and had a fondness for Brown Windsor soup.

Sporting recreation was plentiful for this Frontier Highland laird and his guests, as Prince Philip found in his first visit of 1959, and then when accompanying the Queen in 1961. The palace had its own golf course and Swat is renowned for its hill partridges, wild duck and trout.

The Wali was a descendant of the mystery man in the Lear couplet who was in fact born Abdul Gaffur into a cowherding family of Upper Swat, in the early part of Queen Victoria's reign, and revealed mystic powers — eventually being recognised as a "Messenger of God", or Akhund.

The Akhund's ascendancy and accumulation of wealth owed much to the belief among the Swat Pukhtun that their success in 1863 in fighting the British to a standstill, was due to his *baraka*, or charismatic power. The Akhund's death in 1877 left a power vacuum which was eventually filled by the Akhund's only living descendant, Miangul Abdul Wadud. Styling himself the Badshah and assuming the powers of a total dictator, he created the state of Swat.

In 1926, the British, deciding to go along with the Badshah, sanctioned his rule, bestowing on him the title of Wali and granted him a subsidy. In 1949, two years after Swat joined the newly-created Pakistan, retaining local autonomy, the Wali abdicated and was succeeded by his son Miangul Abdul Jahanzeb.

The second Wali exchanged his father's despotic rule for a reign of firm benevolence, more in keeping with the 1950s, though continuing to control all aspects of life in Swat.

No argument was brooked; indeed lawyers were barred. The Wali *was* the law. The non-interference by Pakistan was assured by the marriage of two of the Wali's sons to daughters of President Ayub Khan.

Such was the Wali's prestige in Islamabad, that in 1966, President Ayub insisted he be addressed as "Highness" and received a 15-gun salute on all official occasions.

Unfortunately, Ayub's patronage eventually backfired with popular reaction against him in Pakistan. His fall combined with unrest in Swat which led to Pakistan's take-over and the conclusion of the dynasty in 1969.

In his later years, the Wali was pained by Swat's declining status as an increasingly lawless district in the Malakand division of the North-West Frontier province of Pakistan.

November 7 1987

NEREA DE CLIFFORD

NEREA DE CLIFFORD, who has died aged 82, was a doughty champion of British cats and a pillar of the Cats Protection league, which she joined shortly after its foundation in 1927 and served as president from the 1970s until the time of her death.

Among her many contributions to the welfare of cats – and to our knowledge of their ways – were the establishment of a sanctuary for them at New Malden, Surrey, and the publication of such reports as *What British Cats Think About Television*, in which she noted that "most cats show an interest of some kind, *though it is often of hostility*"; "a significant reaction . . . is the display of excitement when any picture, *especially of birds*, moves quickly across the screen".

Nerea Elizabeth de Clifford was born at Holland Park, West London, in 1905, and as a young woman was a distinguished breeder of cats. During the Second World War she devoted herself to the rescue of cats trapped in the rubble of the blitz, and thereafter to vigorous campaigns for free feline birth control and against catnapping.

She ran an adoption scheme, for which her "Homes Wanted" list contained some notably frank character sketches – "a little fiend in feline form"; "willing to do light mousework, and very good at it: non-union"; "a tough old stray", and so on – and made a point of feeding London's cats at Christmas, a favourite repast apparently being fish and chips. She also plumbed the mysteries of why cats purr – some because they have just murdered the Pekinese next door, others "for no damn reason at all".

De Clifford was also a much respected judge of cat shows around the country, and gave a series of lecture tours at schools on the care and training of cats.

December 16 1987

EARL RUSSELL

THE 4TH EARL RUSSELL, who has died aged 66, was the eccentric elder son of the philosopher Bertrand Russell and caused the occasional sensation in the House of Lords with his outrageous speeches.

In 1978, during a debate on aid for victims of crime, Lord Russell had to be called to order after a singularly rambling and incoherent discourse. As he was advocating total abolition of law and order, and saying that police should be prevented from raping youngsters in cells, he was interrupted by Lord Wells-Pestell, from the Labour Government's Front Bench, and reminded of the length of time he had been speaking. Without any further comment the Earl left the Chamber.

In his speech from the cross-benches Russell referred to modern society and the effects of automation in factories. Then he said: "There should be universal leisure for all, and a standing wage sufficient to provide life without working ought to be supplied . . . so that everybody becomes a leisured aristocrat – aristocrats are Marxists. . . . Police ought to be totally prevented from ever molesting young people at all, from ever putting them into jails and raping them and putting them into brothels or sending them out to serve other people sexually against their wills."

Peers seemed startled as he continued: "In a completely reorganised modern society, women's lib would be realised by girls being given a house of their own by the age of 12 and three-quarters of the wealth of the State being given to the girls so that marriage would be abolished and the girl could have as many husbands as she liked . . ." Finally Russell told the House of Lords: "Mr Brezhnev and Mr Carter are really the same person . . ."

The full text of this extraordinary outburst was published subsequently by Lord Russell's mother, Dora, and the old Etonian anarchist and playwright Heathcote Williams, who described Russell as "the first man since Guy Fawkes to enter the House of Parliament with an honest intention". The pamphlet, illustrated by Ralph Steadman, quickly became a collectors' item and essential reading for the "psychedelic Left".

In 1985 Russell received a less courteous hearing from Their Lordships when he read out a carefully prepared question on the leadership of the IRA and suggested that the organisation might have a legitimate role in resolving Ireland's problems.

John Conrad Russell was born in 1921 and received his early education at his parents' experimental co-education school in Hampshire where there were no compulsory lessons and the children were permitted to call their teachers rude names. At the age of 13 he proceeded to the progressive Dartington Hall in Devon and after his parents' divorce he joined his mother in Amercia, attending the University of California at Los Angeles, and Harvard.

From 1943 to 1946 he served with the RNVR and subsequently worked briefly for the Food and Agriculture Organisation of the United Nations in Washington and as an administrative assistant with the Treasury.

Following the dissolution of his own marriage to Susan Lindsay (daughter of the American poet Nicholas Vachel Lindsay) in the mid 1950s, Russell – or Viscount Amberley as he was styled by courtesy – became something of a recluse, spending his time writing and crocheting. His published works included a slim volume entitled *Abandon Spa, Hot Springs*.

To one visitor in the early 1960s he said: "I like to sit and think and write my thoughts. The few people who have seen my work find it too deep for them." He then pointed proudly to a pair of trousers hanging on the wall by a nail, "I crocheted these out of string," he said. "It took me a long while because I didn't have a pattern. I had to keep trying them on."

Although he succeeded to the earldom (created for the Victorian Prime Minister, Lord John Russell) in 1970, the new Earl received only an annuity of £300 from his father's £69,000 estate. The following year he issued a Chancery Division summons against Bertrand Russell's fourth wife and the executors.

He and his mother, who died in 1986, lived in a dilapidated Cornish cottage near Land's End. He died aboard a train to Penzance. A post-mortem was being held but police say there are no suspicious circumstances surrounding his death.

Lord Russell had two daughters, one whom survives. The heir to the title is his half-brother, Conrad Sebastian Robert Russell, Astor Professor of British History, University College, London, born in 1937, who now becomes the 5th Earl Russell.

December 18 1987

SIR MELFORD STEVENSON

SIR MELFORD STEVENSON, who has died aged 85, was celebrated as a no-nonsense judge – perhaps the sternest since Lord Chief Justice Goddard – whose handing down of stiff sentences led to occasional calls for his removal by the liberal establishment.

Regarded as one of the legal profession's most robust characters, the name of his house in Sussex, Truncheons, symbolised his singular blend of judicial toughness and humour. Upon his retirement after 22 years on the bench in 1979 at No 1 Court, Old Bailey, he was likened to a lion.

Stevenson's caustic court-room comments frequently stirred up controversy. Bookmakers were disgusted by his description of them as "a bunch of crooks" – as were Mancunians when he said of a husband in a divorce case: "He chose to live in Manchester, a wholly incomprehensible choice for any free man to make."

He once told a man acquitted of rape: "I see you come from Slough. It is a terrible place. You can go back there." Passing sentence after a bribes case, Stevenson said to another: "You have tried, and to some extent succeeded, in converting Birmingham into a municipal Gomorrah."

Sir Melford was both subject and source of numerous anecdotes, many of them emanating from his beloved Garrick Club. He was overheard to observe that the Kray twins had only told the truth twice in the course of their trial for murder, over which he presided: first when one brother referred to a barrister as "a fat slob," and secondly when the other brother claimed that the judge was biased.

Another story concerned Stevenson's unsuccessful attempt to enter Parliament as a Conservative at Maldon, Essex, in the 1945 General Election. He opened his campaign by announcing that he wanted a clean fight and would therefore not be alluding to "the alleged homosexuality" of his Labour opponent, Tom Driberg.

Stevenson's subsequent reference to the 1967 legislation reforming the homosexual laws as a "buggers' charter" led to a reprimand from the Lord Chancellor. One day in 1976, three of his decisions were changed by the Court of Appeal, driving him to criticism for which he later apologised. A Commons motion calling for his removal was then withdrawn.

Sentencing six Cambridge students in 1970 for a demonstration against the Greek regime which caused extensive damage at the Garden House Hotel, he caused a sensation by his remark that the sentences would have been more severe had the students not been "exposed to the evil influence of some senior members of the university."

Although staunchly in favour of the death penalty – soon after his retirement he called for its return for all murders – Stevenson's career at the Bar included a notable defence brief: that of Ruth Ellis who murdered her lover and became the last woman to be hanged in Britain. He also represented the Crown in Jomo Kenyatta's appeal against his conviction in the Mau Mau trial in Nairobi and was a member of the prosecution team in the famous murder trial of Dr Bokdin Adams, the Eastbourne physician.

When asked if he was hurt by criticisms during his career, Sir Melford commented: "A lot of my colleagues are just constipated Methodists."

The son of a minister at Beckenham Congregational Church, Aubrey Melford Steed Stevenson was born in 1902, educated at Dulwich and was called to the Bar by the Inner Temple in 1925, practising in common law. He took Silk in 1943 while serving in the Army, and as a major and deputy judge-advocate had plenty of experience of courts martial during the Second World War.

In 1945 he was judge-advocate at the Hamburg warcrime trial of German U-boat men who were sentenced to death for machine-gunning survivors of torpedoed ships.

Stevenson was Recorder of Rye from 1944 to 1951; chairman of West Kent Quarter Sessions from 1949 to 1955; and Recorder of Cambridge from 1952 to 1957 when he was made a High Court Judge and received a knighthood.

After four years in the Probate, Divorce and Admiralty Division, he was appointed to the Queen's Bench Division. He was presiding judge on the South-Eastern Circuit from 1970 to 1975. He became a Privy Councillor in 1973.

In retirement, Sir Melford enjoyed something of an Indian summer on television where his trenchant views, laced with dry wit, earned him a wide circle of admirers.

Twice married, Stevenson had a daughter by the first marriage and a son and a daughter by the second (to Rosalind Wagner, sister of Sir Anthony Wagner, the herald and genealogist).

December 29 1987

LEN CHADWICK

LEN CHADWICK, who has died aged 72, was perhaps the most gifted representative of that peculiarly northern institution, the outdoor columnist.

His weekly article for the *Oldham Evening Chronicle*, written throughout the 1950s and 1960s under the *nom de plume* of "Fellwalker", was a model of the columnist's craft and an inspiration to all ramblers and mountain walkers west of the Pennines.

Chadwick was an extraordinary character. Slight of frame, with streaming white hair, a lantern jaw and hooded eyes, he was dirty, unkempt and poor, dressed in disreputable cast-offs and always without a permanent home. He smoked incessantly, talked in a quick jabber through toothless gums and wrote – in prose or verse – with a boundless energy for the physical horizon.

His hardihood and appetite for miles defied belief: he would cover 30 or 40 each day of every weekend or holiday, at a spring-heeled step which most would term a run; and over any terrain, even among the peat-hags and mires of the Pennine moors which were his favourite haunt.

A classic autodidact, as he strode along Chadwick would regale the young boys who were his most frequent companions (he was homosexually inclined) with interminable but inspired monologues – often in Esperanto – on subjects ranging from the history of socialism or his prisoner-of-war experiences to the poetry of Ebenezer Elliott. The boys were often driven to the limits of their endurance, but if they lasted the course the experience was profoundly educative.

Aside from his writing Chadwick supported himself by a series of menial jobs – as a typist in a pool of 16-year-old girls, as an ice-cream salesman and as a clerk in a clothing factory. In the late 1970s his tenuous balance and careering pace of life were cruelly affected by a stroke; and when he recovered he was lamed by a broken ankle. Quite desitute, he spent his declining years in an old people's home at Oldham.

January 7 1988

JOHN ALLEGRO

JOHN ALLEGRO, the controversial Semitic philologist, who has died aged 65, was once aptly described as "the Liberace of Biblical scholarship".

Unlike most scholars in that field, Allegro was not himself a believer, having abandoned the faith after a brief period as a lay preacher and Methodist ordinand. He was, indeed, frankly hostile to the religious impulse – "to look on this life as part of a larger life is both unhealthy and unwise" – and particularly to what he called "these tales of this rabbi, Jesus, and his Mum and Dad".

In a series of increasingly fantastical books he claimed that Christianity was a cryptic version of ancient sex-cults inspired by the hallucinogenic mushroom *Amanita muscaria* or fly-agaric. By means of Sumerian etymologies he sought to establish that all the sacred rites in the Bible were mushroom rites; and that most of its leading characters, including Moses, David and Jesus, are in fact walking mushrooms. Thus Christ's final utterance on the Cross, *"Eloi eloi, lama sabachtani,"* is not a tragic appeal but "a paean of praise to the god of the mushroom".

The God of the Old Testament, on the other hand, is according to Allegro, "a mighty penis in the heavens" (*Yahweh* or "Jehovah" etymologically signifying "Spermatozoa"), who, "in the thunderous climax of the storm, ejaculated semen upon the furrows of Mother Earth."

Such theories did not find favour with the academic establishment. Dr Henry Chadwick, for example, wrote in *The Daily Telegraph* that there was "no particle of evidence for all this exciting conjecture", and that Allegro's work read "like a Semitic philologist's erotic nightmare after consuming a highly indigestible meal of hallucinogenic fungi". Allegro angrily denied that he ever consumed the mushrooms himself ("I wouldn't be so bloody stupid"); he was also a fervent teetotaller.

John Marco Allegro was born in London in 1923 and educated at Wallington County Grammar School. He served in the Royal Navy during the Second World War and then had a brilliant undergraduate career at Manchester University.

After a spell studying Hebrew dialects at Magdalen College, Oxford, he was invited in 1953 to join an international body of scholars working on the Dead Sea Scrolls in Jerusalem. He was personally involved in the opening and decipherment of the Copper Scroll, which was found five years after the Dead Sea Scrolls.

Allegro claimed to have found in the Scrolls references to a pre-Christian "teacher", whose disciples were to guard "the broken body of their Master" until Judgment Day – thus establishing "a well defined Essenic pattern into which Jesus of Nazareth fits". This claim caused great controversy. Others were quite unable to see Allegro's "findings", notably Fr Roland de Vaux, who was in charge of the scholars concerned. Allegro later wrote a play, with Roy Plomley, about this early brush with controversy – *The Lively Oracles* (1966), which was performed at Huddersfield.

In 1956 he published his theory in a book, *The Dead Sea Scrolls*, which is one of the best and almost certainly the most readable book on the subject. It was a bestseller, and having hit the jackpot he went on to write *The People of the Dead Sea Scrolls* (1958) and *The Treasure of the Copper Scroll* (1960), which, though still an original work of scholarship, carried more than passing echoes of *Treasure Island*.

He was, after all, a respected and popular lecturer in Comparative Semitics and Old Testament studies at Manchester University. But as the 1960s wore on his theories became increasingly *outré*, and the obsession with mushrooms took hold.

In 1967, at the height of the "counter culture", he traced the roots of Christianity to "a phallic, drug-taking mystery cult we none of us would want anything to do with". "They had visions. They went on a trip." He promised that "the Church is going to be scourged as never before".

In 1970 Allegro's theories reached their apogee with *The Sacred Mushroom and The Cross*, which did nothing for his academic reputation and which, in the words of one critic, "gave mushrooms a bad name". It excited more derision than outrage but nonetheless enjoyed a passing popularity, for those were the days of the drug culture gurus, and Allegro's ideas, if improbable, were at least in vogue, and he became something of a guru himself.

He followed it up with *The End of the Road*, which adhered to his mushroom theory and preached a new and more assertive humanism which was to replace the ancient faiths he had supposedly undermined by his discoveries. The title, however, was apt, for it marked the end of his academic career.

In 1971, unchastened and still flourishing his mush-rooms, he wrote *The Chosen People*, which suggested that

---

the Children of Israel were not so much chosen as stoned. Then followed *Lost Gods*, which as Anthony Quinton remarked in *The Sunday Telegraph*, has "all the freshness and coherence of the conversation of a very tired man in a crowded pub rather late at night". Allegro continued to publish until 1987, but his day had passed.

As a scholar Allego was no Pensoroso, being far too quick to draw conclusions: "Allegro," a senior colleague once admonished him, "*adagio, adagio!*" There was an almost nautical breeziness to even his most serious works, and it is that which gave them their popularity. He had a rare gift for illuminating obscure subjects, but was not averse to illuminating himself; and his tendencies as a showman finally overtook his devotion to learning. His intellectual abilities and literary skills were never in doubt, but his judgement was.

His marriage was dissolved in 1985; he is survived by a son and a daughter.

February 20 1988

EARL OF ST GERMANS

THE 9TH EARL OF ST GERMANS, popularly known as the "Bookie Peer", who has died aged 74, was an engaging eccentric whose recreations, according to his *Who's Who* entry, were "huntin' the slipper, shootin' a line, fishin' for compliments".

He used to describe his education in the same reference work as "at great expense to my parents", and it was at Eton that "Nicky" Eliot first acquired the taste for making a book. After the Second World War, in which he served as a major in the Duke of Cornwall's Light Infantry attached to the Royal Armoured Corps, he devoted himself to the Turf variously as an owner, trainer and bookmaker.

In 1950 he opened up a turf commission agency in Mayfair and three years later he was called as a witness in the celebrated Francasal betting coup case concerning the switch of two French racehorses at Bath. In his evidence Lord Eliot (as he then was) described how one of the accused conspirators had put to him several "quite childish ideas and suggestions".

The most concrete of these was that he should represent himself as an unofficial member of the Jockey Club and go and see the Chief Constable of Bath in order to have the matter of the cutting of the "blower" line to the racecourse dealt with quickly as a case of simple malicious damage. Another of the "childish suggestions" was that the Chief Constable's wife might like a fur coat.

Eliot declined to have anything to do with the matter and following the meeting telephoned Scotland Yard. A tall, rather cadaverous dandy with a Kaiser-style moustache, he cut a striking figure.

Nicholas Richard Michael Eliot was born in 1914, the elder son of the 8th Earl of St Germans who was a long-serving courtier, acting as Groom-in-Waiting to Edward VII, Groom of the Robes to George V and Extra Groom-in-Waiting to Edward VIII, George VI and the present Queen.

The Eliots, originally from Devon, acquired the Priory of St Germans in Cornwall in the 16th century and established their seat at Port Eliot which has an outstanding garden. Lord Eliot succeeded to the Earldom of St Germans in 1960 but made the 6,000-acre estate over to his son and heir and went into tax exile, settling in Tangier.

Calling himself the "Tangerine Earl" and with the telegraphic address of "Earls Court", St Germans was one of Tangier's most colourful characters. But on one occasion in 1963 – after an unfortunate incident in the Safari Bar when he apparently threatened customers with an unloaded and unauthorised gun – he found himself spending the night in a police cell.

St Germans, who enjoyed sailing in the Mediterranean, also lived in the South of France (changing the name of his villa from La Magnerie, "as I can't pronounce that", to Sea View) and latterly in Switzerland. But he always hankered for home and his beloved racing.

He particularly missed "the things about England that one never stops to think of when you live there", citing his club, steak and kidney pudding, treacle tart and "a decent game of backgammon". He recalled, however, that on one of his return visits, "when I got back to Dover in the pouring rain, I asked the dining car attendant on the train for anchovies and toast. 'The anchovies are off, sir', he said. 'So is the toast'. I must say I felt a little better about my exile then".

His first two marriages, to Helen Mary Villiers and Mrs Margaret Eleanor Eyston, were both dissolved; and he married thirdly, in 1965, Mrs Bridget Lotinga, daughter of Sir Shenton Thomas (Governor of the Straits Settlements when Singapore fell to the Japanese in 1942), who survives him together with a son and a daughter of the first marriage.

He son, Peregrine Nicholas Eliot, Lord Eliot, born in 1941, succeeds to the earldom.

March 16 1988

"FATHER JOE" WILLIAMSON

"FATHER JOE" WILLIAMSON, who has died aged 92, was a crusading East End clergyman celebrated for his campaigns to save prostitutes.

A deceptively frail figure with a bellowing voice, he regarded himself as *"called"* – having had "a vision" as he walked along Cable Street in Stepney where he was Vicar of St Paul's. "Suddenly," he recalled, "a woman called out to me: 'You walk past me because I'm a bloody prostitute, don't you?'

"I turned to her and saw she was young and very beautiful. Later I realised she was old and ugly with a razor-scarred face. But my vision was of the lovely girl she had been before prostitution destroyed her. Her name *had* to be Mary.

"It was a message from God," he explained. "I had to help women like her."

Williamson duly proceeded to turn Church House, Stepney, into a hostel for prostitutes; founded the Wellclose Square Fund on whose behalf he constantly toured the country and soon opened two more hostels in Essex and one in Birmingham. Troubled with failing eyesight he eventually had to retire from the parish in 1962 but continued as warden of the hostel.

Joseph Williamson was himself born into poverty in Poplar in 1895, as he described in his graphic autobiography, *Father Joe* (1963). His emancipation owed most to his remarkable mother – "one of Nature's greatest ladies".

At an early age he felt drawn to the priesthood and one day presented himself at the door of the local vicarage to announce this fact. The vicar, who was later to become Bishop of London, thanked him for the information and dismissed him with a curt good afternoon.

But he persevered and after attending St Augustine's College, Canterbury, was ordained in 1925 in St Paul's Cathedral as Curate of Fulwell. Following another curacy in Kensington he went to South Africa and served on the staff of Grahamstown Cathedral from 1928 to 1932.

He then returned to England and in the course of his career rebuilt four churches, partly with his own hands. At Fenny Drayton, Leics, he restored the church in the 15 months he was there by spending all his money on the work.

In 1934, when he went to Shimpling, Suffolk, he had to stand in water to conduct the services in the parish church. He continued the successful fund-raising while he was a chaplain to the forces during the Second World War.

Then Williamson moved to Little Dunham, Norfolk, where he became a spare-time carpenter and bricklayer for months in order to repair the church. He arrived at St Paul's Dock Street, Stepney in 1952 and undertook a major restoration of the church which had been bombed during the war.

From the platform of his provocative parish magazine, *The Pilot*, Williamson launched a series of outspoken conditions that prevailed in Stepney. In 1961 he described his parish to the London Diocesan Conference in a withering tirade: "We have developed into an area of low-level café-clubs for drugs, drink, gambling, and women. We have a hotbed of vice on gutter level. Humans are like rats, living in filth – two couples, four in a bed.

"We have actually been exhibited to sightseers in this setting. For one day a coach pulled into Ensign Street. They had an American guide; he led them to a Somali café-club – 'You'll find everything here!' he shouted – and indeed, they would!

"At the same spot, one evening before the Street Offences Act, I found a group of my schoolchildren with coloured adults watching a coloured man and a white girl having sexual intercourse. Girls screaming and fighting for their money, girls taking man after man in the open streets, girls being smashed to the ground by men, thrown down bodily and kicked ... There are people in this hall now who saw three men committing sodomy in the open in Wellclose Square.

"Right now I would move the unemployables, the impotent and the weakminded not back to Malta or Jamaica or Africa but to hutments around the Houses of Parliament and the Lords, Lambeth Palace Gardens and suchlike. Let Parliament enjoy a bit of 'Sophia Town' under its own nose".

He challenged the then Minister of Housing, Henry Brooke, to join him in a walk around Stepney – "he would be sickened and shocked".

Father Joe was one of the Church of England's great characters. He was rarely to be seen other than in his cassock and biretta and his notable work in the East End also included the chaplaincy of the Sailors Home and the Red Ensign Club.

Among the staunch supporters of Father Joe's campaign to rescue prositutes was Queen Elizabeth the Queen Mother. He was appointed MBE in 1975.

March 17 1988

CATHERINE GRIFFITHS

CATHERINE GRIFFITHS, who has died aged 102, was a Welsh nurse of fiery temperament; she was said to be the last surviving suffragette.

Mrs Griffiths played an active part in the militant "Votes for Women" campaign in the years immediately preceeding the First World War. Her finest moment was perhaps when she stole into the chamber of the House of Commons and strewed tin tacks upon the seat of Lloyd George ("To make him sit up" she later explained.) Subsequently she was jailed for breaking into the House of Lords.

After female suffrage was won, she went on to make a solid contribution to local government politics, eventually becoming Mayor of Finsbury. She joined the Labour Party as soon as membership became open to individuals (1918), was a founder-member of its Women's Section in North London, and gave distinguished service to the co-operative Women's Guild.

Mrs Griffiths cherished vivid memories of Keir Hardie, Clem Attlee, Aneurin Bevan and other stalwart socialists. In 1987 she received an award and a standing ovation at the Labour conference, responding with a happily-phrased speech. At 100 years old she still climbed three flights of stairs to her flat, but at 102 would consent to a short rest *en route*.

Born Catherine James in 1885 at Nanyffyllon, near Maesteg, she was the daughter of a miner and grand-daughter of the village blacksmith. Her father was literate and spoke both Welsh and English. Her mother was unlettered and knew only Welsh.

Catherine was proud of her Welsh ancestry and always retained the attractive lilt of her mother-tongue. She was one of five children brought up in the old respectable tradition of clean pinafore for school, Bible always on the parlour table, Sunday chapel and weekly Band of Hope meetings. She graduated from "board school" to higher school then trained for three years as a nurse at Merthyr Tydfil.

Since probationers were upaid, the family provided her with money for clothes – the mark of a modest social standing but still a struggle and when her pay rose from 10 shillings (50p) and then to 15, she was quick to "run home to Mam" with it.

Working as a Queen's Jubilee Nurse (district nurse) in Merthyr and Cardiff she often had to deal with mining and docklands injuries. What she saw in poor homes made her a radical and a suffragette. "A woman was just a slave – there to attend to the needs of men," she would recall.

Illiteracy was widespread and she was often asked to

write letters (sometimes in very stilted phrases) for the families she visited. But so great was the opposition to radicalism and the suffrage movement that some householders ordered her away rather than have their families attended by her.

She settled in London during the Second World War when her husband's work in education brought them to Finsbury. After his death in 1948 she concealed her age to get back into nursing work and even when forced to retire in 1965, undertook regular weekly voluntary work at the Great Ormond Street Children's Hospital until she reached 100. Even after this she remained a governor of Dulwich College, and Prior Weston School, and worked for the Amwell Society, a local conservation group.

Some of today's radical causes failed to win Mrs Griffiths's support, sometimes to the surprise of younger people. "You can't put words in her mouth, can you?" remarked one young BBC interviewer after Mrs Griffiths had declared of NHS abortion: "It's against nature." And she would often refer nostalgically to the firmer discipline of bygone days.

Mrs Griffiths is survived by a son and a daughter.

March 23 1988

SYLVIA GRANT-DALTON

SYLVIA GRANT-DALTON, who has died in her nineties, was the redoubtable châtelaine of Brodsworth Hall, Yorks, the least-altered Victorian country house in England, and had recently become a celebrity through her beguiling appearance in Lucinda Lambton's idiosyncratic televisison documentary, *The Great North Road*.

The warmth of her welcome, the liveliness of her mind and the gaiety of her spirit remained unaffected by old age, failing eyesight and the problems of maintaining the remarkable house in which she had lived for more than 70 years.

Born Sylvia Joan Cecil West, elder daughter of Reginald Cecil West, of Christchurch, Hants, she married two Grant-Daltons in succession: first, in 1916 Charles Grant-Dalton, the owner of Brodsworth and High Sheriff of Yorkshire, who died in 1952; and secondly, in 1959, his first cousin Major Eustace Grant-Dalton, of the Prince of Wales's Own (West Yorkshire Regiment), who died in 1970.

The Grant-Daltons were beneficiaries of the famous Thellusson Will, which is thought to have inspired the case of Jarndyce and Jarndyce in Charles Dickens's *Bleak House*. Peter Thellusson, a rich banker of Swiss origin, died in 1797, leaving nearly a million pounds to accumulate at compound interest and finally be inherited by the last survivor of his sons' sons. Ambiguity in the wording of the will led to such protracted litigation that when the estate was finally settled it amounted to far less than the huge sum envisaged by Peter Thellusson.

Nonetheless it paid for the rebuilding of Brodsworth Hall in the 1860s, to the designs of a mysterious Italian, the Chevalier Casentini. The result survives today with all its original decoration, fabrics and furnishings, including a large collection of Italian statues, which line the marbled walls of its halls and staircases.

The house is now inherited by Mrs Grant-Dalton's

only child, a daughter of the first marriage, although the contents remain the property of a family trust. Mrs Grant-Dalton was devoted to the house and loved showing it to visitors, but a complex of reasons have left it in need of substantial repair, and its future is likely to become a matter of major concern.

Lucinda Lambton writes: Sylvia Grant-Dalton was enchanting with a saintly nature and a turn of phrase with a quick-witted funniness that made one laugh out loud with delight.

She first came to Brodsworth when she was only 15 years old, courted by Charles Grant-Dalton who had decided to marry her when she was 12 and he was 30. After his death Sylvia married his cousin, Eustace: "He was so kind and so brave, he got into every war he could. He fought in the Boer War, the Kaiser's War and the last war. His first commission was signed by Queen Victoria . . . When he died he made me promise to look after the house and I have never left it for a single day."

Brodsworth is an electrifying and glorious time-warp of a prosperous 19th-century country house – a nationwide campaign must now be whipped up to save it – and Sylvia was its glorious occupant, whizzing about at top speed in her wheelchair through the mirrored maze of pillars and statuary. "Not quite my *gusto*, I'm afraid," she would say. "I'm a Georgian, I don't care for the hellish sentimentality of Victorian times, poor cold ladies."

She had a complete lack of vanity when being filmed for *The Great North Road* programme and she charmed the land with her unselfconscious complaining of "a scaggy nail . . . where's the gardener he's got a lovely thing of shears". Her reaction to being the shining star of the show was: "I've never known such a carry-on in all my bornly days".

She was loved by all who met her with her wondrous utterances – "all the plugs in the house are roundy-goes" (round pins) or "I'm freezy-frozy cold". Every split second spent in her company was a joy.

March 29 1988

SIR RANULPH "RASHER" BACON

SIR RANULPH BACON, otherwise "Rasher of the Yard", who has died aged 81, sparked a controversy in the mid-1960s when as Assistant Commissioner of "the Met" he advised the public to "have a go" against criminals.

Tall, convivial, popular with colleagues and earning respect, even affection, among opponents in the underworld, "Rasher" Bacon was always ready to speak his mind. Even now, almost a quarter of a century later, his urging of bystanders not to stand still or get out of the way but to "have a go" remains the subject of lively debate.

On another occasion he told a crime conference: "A shotgun is part of the adult Englishman's equipment."

After retiring from the Yard as Deputy Commissioner in 1966; he was appointed to the newly established Gaming Board and quickly asserted himself as the strong man of the club scene, policing London's gambling jungle. Bacon had already distinguished himself in that field in the Bahamas, where he investigated gambling scandals and sent Mafia operators scuttling back to New York.

Ranulph Robert Maunsell Bacon, who was born in 1906 and educated at Tonbridge and Queens' College, Cambridge, set his heart on becoming a policeman at the age when most boys decide to become engine drivers. On coming down from the University he joined the Metropolitan Police as a Bobby on the beat.

Brompton Oratory featured prominently in his early career. He made his first arrest there, dragging a brawling woman out of the church ("She was clinging to four seats and they came with her," he liked to recall); and he fell in love with a girl who often used the pedestrian crossing nearby when he was on point duty. PC Bacon married the girl – Alfreda Violet Annett – in 1932.

Two years later he was accepted for training on Course No 1 at the Hendon Police College, which the Metropolitan Police Commissioner, Lord Trenchard, fresh from "fathering" the RAF, had established with the aim of creating a Dartmouth, Sandhurst or Cranwell of the Police.

The Hendon equivalent of the Sword of Honour was a policeman's baton, the first of which was awarded to Rasher Bacon in 1935. Although Trenchard's attempt to create an officer class in the police failed to survive the outbreak of war in 1939, Bacon's course appeared to justify Trenchard's vision: it provided two Commissioners and seven Chief Constables.

A formidable rugby player, Bacon captained the Police XV, serving appropriately in the Twickenham sub-division of the Met. When Trenchard introduced a map room at Scotland Yard he summoned Bacon to help organise it.

Bacon was eager to transfer to the Armed Forces in 1939, but was unable to obtain permission until 1940, when he was seconded to the Provost Service in the Army. By 1942 he was a lieutenant-colonel and deputy provost marshal of the 9th Army in the Middle East, proceeding further in an easterly direction on his appointment in 1944 as Inspector General of Police in Ceylon.

But Bacon's heart remained at home and, eschewing a career in the Colonial Service, he returned in 1947 to serve Devon as Chief Constable. Fourteen years later he returned to the Met as Assistant Commmisoner responsible for the CID.

This post required him to head the British delegation at Internal conferences where he gained an international reputation for his professionalism and humorous, relaxed approach to the most complex and irritating problems.

In 1966 he was promoted to Deputy Commissioner at New Scotland Yard, serving immediately under the Commissioner, Sir Joseph Simpson – a reversal of their ranking at Hendon, where Rasher Bacon had headed "Joe" Simpson in the pass-out list. By now, though, Bacon was all but 60, and obligatory retirement later that year robbed him of the top post.

He was subsequently director and consultant of the American company, International Intelligence, and sat on the board of Securicor. His other appointments included the Presidency of the Gun Trade Association and of the Shooting Sports Trust.

Bacon was awarded the King's Police Medal in 1953

and knighted in 1966. Both his wife and their daughter predeceased him.

April 1 1988

SIR HUGH RANKIN, BT

SIR HUGH RANKIN, 3rd Bt, an eccentric remarkable even by the rarefied standards of the baronetage, who has died aged 88, was variously a riveter's mate in a Belfast shipyard; a trooper in the cavalry; a sheep shearer in Western Australia and runner-up in the All-Britain Sheep Judging Competition; president of the British Muslim Society and vice-president of the World's Buddhist Association; and a campaigner for "an independent Red Republic of all Scotland, excluding Orkneys and Shetland".

His death deprives *Who's Who* of possibly its most entertaining entry. He listed his recreations as "golf (holds an amateur record amongst golfers of Gt Britain in having played on 382 separate courses of UK and Eire), shooting, coarse fishing, hunting, motoring, cycling on mountain tracks to tops of British mountains (Pres. Rough Stuff Cycling Assoc. 1956), the study of ancient track ways; bowls, tennis, archaeology (wife and himself are only persons who have crawled under dwarf fir forest for last ½ mile of most northerly known section of any Roman road in Europe, terminating opposite end of Kirriemuir Golf Course) . . ."

Born in 1899 in the middle of the Tunisian desert, the elder son of the traveller and big game hunter Sir

Reginald Rankin (who survived being frozen to sleep in the Andes, shot the largest snow leopard on record in India and searched for the extinct giant sloth in Chile), he was christened Hubert Charles Rhys Rankin but later changed his first name to Hugh. At one stage he adopted the surname of Stewart-Rankin and during his Muslim period also briefly assumed the forename of Omar.

He was educated at Harrow but ran away to work in a Belfast shipyard before joining the 1st Royal Dragon Guards as a trooper. In 1921 he was broad-sword champion of the cavalry, but the following year, while serving in Ireland during the Troubles ("on the wrong side, I'm afraid"), he was shot by a sniper and invalided out of the Army.

Rankin, who wrote articles on agricultural stock, then devoted himself to the study of sheep, being elected president of the Clun Forest Sheep Breeders Association in 1928. Ten years later he represented British sheep breeders in petitioning the Government on the problems of the industry. At the time he succeeded to the baronetcy in 1931 he was a "piece-work" shearer in Western Australia, covering the area between Bunbury and Broome.

During travels in the Middle East, Rankin came under the influence of the Muslim peer, the 5th Lord Headley, whom he succeeded in 1935 as president of the British Muslim Society. But a few weeks later he resigned after a rowdy meeting: "They were very rude . . . and knew nothing of law and order or methods of procedure. I was disgusted with the whole lot of them."

He then formed a new society along orthodox and non-sectarian lines and in 1937 was the British representative to the first all European Muslim Congress in Geneva.

During the Second World War he served as a captain in the Royal Army Service Corps in India but on being demobilised, 'realised what an awful fool I had been to fight for Britain. If a revolution comes – and come it must after the next world war – I'll do my damnedest to see it succeeds."

He said that he had "always hated and loathed the Christian religion. The Muslim religion is a fighting one, so I dropped it and became a Buddhist." From 1944 he was a practising non-theistic Theravda Buddhist and claimed to be the second "Britisher" to perform the Holy Buddhist Pilgrimage.

In 1959 he declared it was "no news" that Abominable Snowmen existed: "It is part of our known belief that five Bodhisattvas ('Perfected Men') control the destiny of this world. They meet together once a year in a cave in the Himalayas to make their decisions. One of them lives permanently on the higher Himalayas. One of them lives in the Scottish Cairngorms." Sir Hugh said that he and his wife had clearly seen the latter Bodhisattva in the Larig Ghru Pass.

Rankin's political affiliations were equally varied: he joined the Labour party in 1939 and was subsequently a Dominion Home Ruler for Scotland, a Scottish Nationalist, a Scottish Communist and a Welsh Republican Nationalist. In *Who's Who* he stated that he held "extreme political views" and was "now left-side Labour".

In 1950 he was elected to Perth County Council and declared, "I am a blood-red militant Communist in every possible way. *Absolutely blood-red.*" He was a virulent critic of the Forestry Commission's alleged policies of depasturisation and turning out crofters and tenants.

In 1965 he claimed to be "the only baronet in the United Kingdom who is living on national assistance" and added that his title had always been a hindrance. Asked what job he might like, he replied: "Anything. Anything except being a butler. I hate snobbishness."

Among Sir Hugh's myriad distinctions were being Hereditary Piper of the Clan Maclaine and a "*News of the World* Knight of the Road (for courtesy in motor driving)".

His first wife Helen, widow of Capt Colin Campbell and eldest daughter of Sir Charles Stewart, the Public Trustee, died in 1945; he married secondly, in 1946, Robina Kelly, a nurse, who survives him.

There were no children of either marriage and the baronetcy passes to Sir Hugh's nephew, Ian Niall Rankin, born 1932, whose mother, Lady Jean Rankin, is a longstanding Woman of the Bedchamber to Queen Elizabeth the Queen Mother.

May 2 1988

DICK BRENNAN

DICK BRENNAN, who has died aged 78, founded the Wig and Pen Club, where his bubbling, beetle-browed welcome assured the success of that raffish establishment.

In the bars of his popular half-way house between Fleet Street and the Law Courts, Brennan was an enthusiastic participant in Warwick Charlton's plan to build and sail a replica of the Pilgrim Fathers' ship, the *Mayflower*, across the Atlantic.

In the event, Brennan sailed in *Mayflower II* from Plymouth in 1957 as its rumbustious Australian skipper Alan Villiers's second cook. Since then, administered by the Plimouth (*sic*) Plantation Trust, the ship has become a shrine in Massachussetts. During the 54-day voyage, as supplies ran low and thirst ran high, Brennan sorely missed his London watering-hole; as second cook he drew only one bottle of beer a day. The public relations value of the *Mayflower* crew's ordeal, however, worked wonders for the club – which, supported by the bookmaker Joe Coral, developed into a flourishing business.

Richard Brennan was born in 1909 and began his career as a night-club waiter. He founded the Wig and Pen Club after the Second World War.

Brennan's conviviality and readiness to sign up life members for £1 – or nothing, according to mood – produced an sometimes explosive cocktail of the less sober elements of Fleet Street and the Temple. At the start it was a popular haunt for the brigade of brightly button-holed columnists, led by that veteran of the *Evening News*, Eric Barker, who wrote under the Edwardian byline of "The Stroller" and sported the biggest button-hole of all.

Then there was Frank Owen, the celebrated editor, who sought refuge there after closing time at El Vino. Bill Connor ("Cassandra") headed a posse from the *Mirror* group, including Peter Wilson, "the Man They Could Not Gag".

Brennan's charm and skills broadened the clientele, so that one of the club's attractions was the opportunity for lesser lights to rub shoulders with cricketers such as

Denis Compton, Keith Miller and Ray Lindwall: he also served crime reporters, police chiefs and the occasional Soviet diplomat.

Some made the club a second home, among them Jimmy Guthrie, chairman of the Players' Union, who "freed the soccer slaves". Also regularly propping up the bar was the country writer Jimmy Wentworth Day (afflicted, it was said, with "Tally-hosis"), resplendent in striking houndstooth jacket and cavalry twills.

If many of the ghosts have since been laid to rest, the club decor, with its legal prints and framed front pages, remains as a monument to Brennan and to the friendliness of his wife, Babs.

May 17 1988

MICHAEL GABBERT

MICHAEL GABBERT, who has died aged 53, was the editor and joint founder of the *Sunday Sport*, the newspaper that fulfilled its promise to "out-*Sun* the *Sun*," and briefly the editor of the *Daily Star* which under his command became known as the "Daily Bonk" ("bonk" being a euphemism for sexual intercourse).

Gabbert was a man of simple tastes: "I personally," he once explained, "like outdoor pictures of topless girls. I think that's fantastic!" In the pages of the *Sunday Sport*, which he founded with the soft porn publisher David Sullivan, he indulged this predilection to the limit. The paper he created had a very small staff and low budget and eschewed such subjects as news and politics for colour photographs of naked women and "human interest" stories of a sexual flavour: a typical headline was "SEX BEAST BURNS WIFE'S MUM ALIVE!"

The *Sunday Sport* was barred from advertising on television by the IBA and was widely deplored by more sober newspapers; but within six months it had achieved a circulation of 500,000.

Gabbert brought the same spirit to the *Star*, of which he was appointed editor when Sullivan "linked up" with Lord Stevens of Ludgate, the proprietor of United Newspapers. Gabbert began his first editorial conference with an instruction that henceforth the paper would carry "the biggest boobs possible".

His editorial staff were not pleased by Gabbert's innovations. Commanded to produce articles illustrated by photographs of Zeta, Sullivan's girlfriend, posing provocatively in black leather, a number of journalists resigned, and the *Star*'s chapel passed a resolution expressing "dismay and disgust" at the paper's new policy.

One infamous story contained a quotation, of doubtful provenance, from a 15-year-old would-be topless model saying that she "quite enjoyed" the occasion when she was sexually assaulted.

Gabbert was unrepentant "Vulgar? Vulgarity is a very good thing. Smutty? No, I don't like that word. Soft porn? That's nonsense."

The *Star*'s readers were not impressed, however – nor were the advertisers. After two months Lord Stevens gave Gabbert a Havana cigar and said: "I thought I could live with a down-market paper and I find I can't. We must divorce."

Michael Gabbert was born in 1935 and began his

career as a journalist at the age of 15 on the *Portsmouth Evening News*. He rose through a series of local papers and Associated Press until he became the *People's* northern news editor in 1962.

In 1965 he was named Reporter of the Year for his investigation into a nationwide fraud to rig football matches. The next year he joined the *News of the World* as an assistant editor, where he remained until 1972. He then took a break from journalism and established the Silvermere Golf and Country Club in Surrey.

In 1982 he was appointed editor of the West Country's *Sunday Independent* before leaving in 1986 to found the *Sunday Sport*.

Gabbert lived in Norfolk, where he spent his time breeding golden retrievers, sailing, and doing *The Daily Telegraph* crossword in bed.

May 20 1988

RUSSELL HARTY

RUSSELL HARTY, the broadcaster and journalist who has died aged 53, reached the pinnacle of his career in the 1970s, when his television chat show, *Russell Harty Plus*, vied for massive audiences with one called *Parkinson*.

Harty made his name as a presenter in the relatively sober area of book and arts programmes before rising to become a ubiquitous figure in the media – a progress he likened to "climbing the north face of the Eiger in stiletto heels".

Like other presenters of arts and entertainment programmes at that time, Harty was an adenoidal Northerner. In his peers that vocal combination suggested sincerity and "grittiness"; but he revelled in his obvious lack of those qualities. As he once said: "I am not supposed to be an investigative journalist. I am a celebrant."

His own personality aroused mixed feelings. Many found him endearing. His style was cosy, effusive and relaxed, guaranteed to disturb neither the viewer nor – usually, at least – the "celebrity"; middle-aged ladies liked to send him pyjamas or little woolly things; and such catch-phrases as "You are, are you not . . ." were affectionately guyed by mimics.

Others, annoyed by his sweaty gaucheries, uniquely affected accent, baroque contortions of idiom and brazen sycophancy ("Since we got, *thank God*, to know you . . ."), agreed with the opinion of one acidulous *Daily Telegraph* columnist that Harty was "a networked Ozymandias, who has a lisp and a sneer which call us, not in vain, to look upon his works and despair."

Some of his guests seemed to endorse this verdict. In one celebrated incident Harty was belaboured by Grace Jones, an Amazonian disco singer, who felt she was being ignored.

He acknowledged that his personality could evoke "waves of mild antagonism" but said he did not lie awake worrying about it. Equally, his head was not turned by his successes: he cheerfully realised that he was of far less interest to his audience than the person he was interviewing.

In his series, *Russell Harty's Grand Tour*, he visited

numerous European cities to interview people and describe the sights; but the BBC's assignment seemed to have overstretched him. He was criticised for being trite and provincial, and his accompanying book showed a paucity of descriptive power and a flat approach to famous places.

Reviewing it in *The Daily Telegraph*, Dirk Bogarde wrote: "Mr Harty is no eagle, no hawk, swooping down on his delectable prey, tearing out the gut and the heart and making us see the cities and the places which he drifts through on his tour; rather he is a jackdaw, concerned with the glittering trivia." Earlier in the review, however, Bogarde paid him tribute: "He is a warm, sensitive, curious, funny, straight-down-the-line creature, and exceptionally good company, but, and this is the rub, I don't think that he writes nearly as well as he talks."

The actor also acknowledged the debt he owed to the broadcaster: when Bogarde appeared as a guest on Harty's show in the early 1970s a distinguished publisher, Norah Smallwood of Chatto & Windus, was so impressed by the quality of his talk that she offered to take him on.

In a subsequent television interview, filmed at Bogarde's house in Provence, Harty embarrassed his host with persistent questions about homosexuality. A few years later Harty was himself subjected to unwelcome publicity in the tabloid press over his alleged association with "rent boys".

Fredric Russell Harty was born in 1934 in Blackburn, Lancs, the son of Fred Harty, the fruit and vegetable stallholder who introduced the avocado pear to Blackburn market. From Queen Elizabeth's Grammar School, Blackburn, he gained a scholarship to Exeter College, Oxford, where he read English.

After Oxford he taught English and drama at Giggleswick School for six years, then spent two years as a lecturer at the City University of New York. On his return from America Harty answered a newspaper advertisement by the BBC and was given a job as a radio producer, working on such programmes as *World of Books*. In 1969 he moved to ITV television as a reporter on *Aquarius*, the London Weekend arts magazine, with which he won an Emmy award for a programme on the artist Salvador Dali.

Then came his apotheosis: a chat show of his own. His apparent social ineptitude, which might have been thought a handicap, was turned to surprising advantage, as guests ranging from the Prime Minister to a somewhat bemused Rita Hayworth did their best – whether out of embarrassment or pity – to compensate for the deficiencies of their host. As Harty once boasted: "If egg is dripping on my face, I can scramble it and serve it up to my own advantage."

In 1979 he replaced Desmond Wilcox on BBC Radio 4's chat show *Midweek*, on which he displayed greater assurance than when performing on television. At the same time he was on *Saturday Night People* with London Weekend, where he was said to earn £40,000 a year.

He joined the BBC full-time in 1980, with the idea that he might produce arts programmes; but his capacities as "pilot" of chat shows were again to take over and to direct his advancement.

On one such show in 1983 Harty decided to call,

unannounced and accompanied by a recording team, at randomly selected houses in Widnes, seeking "a cup of tea and a natter". Several of his victims turned him away. One woman said: "I'm busy," and shut him out. Another reported, "He didn't even introduce himself – just said 'Is the kettle on?' I said 'No.' He asked if I was going to put it on, but I was just going out and I told him 'No.'" The next day a newspaper reporter tried the same thing on Harty, calling at his Yorkshire home and asking if the kettle was on; he was not welcomed. Harty's personal assistant produced a cup of tea, but his master was disinclined to "natter".

Harty was frank about his ambition: "I want to be very, very rich," he said. "I want to be so rich it really hurts. I want a deep, vast reservoir of money which would buy me freedom. Then I think I would go back to being a schoolteacher, as I used to be in Giggleswick."

Recently Harty wrote a diary column in the *Sunday Times* and took over from Richard Baker on BBC Radio 4's Monday morning programme, *Start the Week*, in which he speculated on the coming week's events with assorted studio guests.

A bachelor, Harty lived in a converted barn near Giggleswick with a "daily" woman to look after his needs.

June 9 1988

REV MICHAEL BLAND

THE REVEREND MICHAEL BLAND, who has died aged 67, had an unhappy tenure as Rector of Buckland and Stanton with Snowshill, Glos, which combined the Church politics of a Trollope novel with the social comedy of one by Mrs Gaskell.

A former intelligence officer in the RAF, the bachelor Bland had the physical presence of a heavyweight boxer and what he himself described as "a latter Ciceronian haircut". He was appointed to the living in 1958 and remained there until shortly before his death: but his effective ministry ended in 1969 when he was charged in a Consistory Court at Gloucester for neglect of duties and conduct unbecoming a clergyman.

Wearing full convocation dress of cassock, gown, scarf and hood with white band, he made Anglican history as the first person to be tried under the Ecclesiastical Jurisdication Measure of 1963. He was tried on four charges of neglecting his duties: by leaving church before Divine Service ended; refusing to baptise a baby; preventing a parisioner from entering the church to declare publicly his dissent to the marriage of his son at the time the banns were published; and repelling another parishioner from Holy Communion without lawful cause.

Furthermore he was alleged to have written rude letters to six people; made offensive and hurtful remarks to parishioners; indulged four times in fits of temper in church, and to have have been generally short-tempered in the course of his dealings. Under the charge of making offensive remarks, Bland was alleged at a parochial church council meeting to have said in effect that he hated his parishioners.

He was also said to have called one parishioner a liar and to have told him he should be ashamed of himself for taking part in Holy Communion when his purpose in attending church was to hear his daughter's marriage banns read. Finally, Bland was alleged to have told the council that on the day he found no one in the church when he arrived to conduct a service, he would have achieved what he wanted to do: he could then run the church the way he wanted without the local squire's paid servants and tenants.

Bland, defended in court by Geoffrey Howe, was sentenced to be deprived of his living. But the verdict was overturned on appeal to the Court of Arches, which simply administered a formal rebuke and allowed him to return to his parish. The legal fees incurred by the diocese of Gloucester amounted to some £30,000.

Michael Bland was born in 1921 and read history and theology at St Peter's College, Oxford, before preparing for ordination at Wycliffe Hall.

Curacies at Southampton, Milford-on-Sea and Newbury from 1952 to 1958 were followed by his appointment to Buckland, and Stanton with Snowshill, where it was soon apparent that his ministry was not going to be a success.

Any hope that once the court case was ended there would be a recovery of pastoral relations between the Rector and his parishioners quickly was dashed, for Bland seemed incapable of carrying out his work in a way that was appropriate and acceptable. Asked about the angry emotions felt by some of his congregation, he said: "Quite right. Get the violence off the streets and into the Church where it belongs."

For many years Sunday services in Buckland were attended only by the Rector's housekeeper. All attempts by bishops, archdeacons and others failed and the sad situation came to an end only recently when Bland was persuaded to accept retirement.

July 2 1988

GERALD SPARROW

GERALD SPARROW, the former Bangkok judge and relentlessly prolific author who has died aged 83, was the eccentric central figure in the strange affair of the Club of Ten, the South African propaganda organisation, in the 1970s.

At first the irrepressible Sparrow – a large, bald, egg-like man – vigorously denied that the club, whose publicity campaigns he managed in this country, was a "front". He claimed in 1974 that its members were "all private individuals, deeply sincere and dedicated to the cause of answering Left-wing vilification of South Africa."

But then, in 1976, he had what he described as "a change of heart" over apartheid, which he found "no longer tolerable," and proceeded to reveal the names of the five South African millionaire "promotors" of the club which placed more than £100,000 worth of advertising in British publications.

A copy of Sparrow's manuscript revelations, *The Ad Astra Connection*, was among the papers mysteriously stolen from the Buckinghamshire home of Sir Harold Wilson in 1977. Although Sparrow had stood against Wilson in the 1970 General Election at Huyton for Desmond Donnelly's short-lived Democratic party, he had been impressed by the way the then Prime Minister took his defeat at the hands of Edward Heath.

In 1978 Sparrow went further in his recantation, alleging in a sensational series of articles in the *Rand Daily Mail* that the whole operation "to deceive the western press," and the Club of Ten, was financed and controlled by South Africa's department of information. He claimed that his go-between was the former director of information at South Africa House in London who "would ring me asking whether I needed more money. If so he would top up the account at Coutts".

Sparrow said that the advertisements were sent to him from South Africa and his task was to vet them for libel and place them in English, German and American newspapers. Sparrow's disclosures led to a spate of denials from South African officials.

His association with South Africa had begun in the early 1970s when he met a member of its tourist organisations in London who knew he had written a number of "sponsored books" for various countries. Six months later Sparrow was asked to submit a synopsis for a book; the "sponsorship" of his subsequent publication, *Not What I Expected*, excited much controversy.

Shortly before the Club of Ten was formed in 1973, Sparrow and his Thai wife, Chaluey, visited South Africa as guests of Dr Connie Mulder, the South African Information Minister, who arranged "honorary white status" for Mrs Sparrow.

John Walter Gerald Sparrow, the son of a barrister, was born at Buxton in 1905 and educated at Sherborne and Trinity Hall, Cambridge, where he was president of the Union. After being called to the Bar by Middle Temple he was appointed a Judge of the International Court in Bangkok – "the youngest judge in recorded appointments", he said – and later became legal adviser to the Thai Minister of Justice.

When the Japanese invaded Thailand in 1941 Sparrow was captured and suffered four years' imprisonment.

In 1950, after 20 years out East in which he had owned a string of racehorses and nightclubs (so exclusive, he claimed, that he "never greeted consuls or director-generals unless they were personal friends"), Sparrow settled in a seaside flat at Brighton. He retired "for three weeks but found idleness unbearable".

And so he set about producing an extraordinary ragbag of books: autobiography (*Land of the Moonflower*, *Opium Venture*, *Confessions of An Eccentric*); Eastern "faction"; travel (*Visiting Libya*, *Visiting Monte Carlo*); biography (*General Gordon*, *"Rab" Butler*, *King Hussein*); popular legal works (*Vintage Edwardian Murder*, *Satan's Children*); satire (*How To Become An MP*, *How To Become a Millionaire*); and a formidable series embracing *The Great Swindlers*, *The Great Impostors*, *The Great Forgers*, *The Great Abductors*, *The Great Traitors*, *The Great Assassins*, *The Great Intimidators*, *The Great Defamers*, *The Great Persecutors*, and so forth.

He concluded *The Great Judges* with this stirring verdict: "Never go to law. Pocket your pride and settle. Let the great judges entertain you, but avoid them like the plague. Avoid lawyers altogether. They will not champion your cause but try to compromise and this you can do better and more economically yourself. This is the best free advice ever given by a lawyer."

Sparrow was robustly critical of his fellow judges: "virtuous but dull . . . they should do a stint on a factory floor and see life as it really is." He fell foul of the Lord Chancellor, Lord Gardiner, when – billed as "Judge Sparrow" – he vigorously defended the Smith regime in Rhodesia and the Greek colonels' junta. Complaining of "an attempt to muzzle me", he proclaimed his resignation from the Bar in 1968.

Sparrow took an active interest in politics, first in the Conservative party, then the Labour party. He was adopted as prospective Labour candidate for Exeter in 1956, but resigned two years later, declaring that the local party had been "infiltrated by people who, though they deny that they are communists, advocate policies indistinguishable from communist doctrine".

Subsequently he joined forces with Desmond Donnelly's Democratic party, polling 1,232 votes in Huyton at 1970; but finally returned to the Tory fold, joining the Monday Club.

In 1972 he announced that he would be contesting his home constituency of Brighton Kemptown as an Independent Conservative at the next election, describing his platform as "large-scale voluntary repatriation, the rule of law, the restoration of discipline in schools and universities, implacable opposition to imperialist aggression (such as by India against East Pakistan), and all-out support for Loyal Ulster".

In the event he did not stand but continued to include politics among his recreations together with beagling and trout fishing; and to maintain that he was still fascinated by "this wonderful business we call life".

August 28 1988

DUKE OF ST ALBANS

THE 13TH DUKE OF ST ALBANS, who has died aged 73, belonged to that element of the peerage so beloved of the popular press: the distant kinsman in a workaday job who inherits an illustrious title.

But apart from the dukedom, an earldom, a brace of baronies and the hereditary sinecures of Grand Falconer of England and Registrar of the Court of Chancery, Charles Beauclerk's inheritance did not amount to much in material terms when he succeeded his second cousin in 1964.

There was no family seat or large estate, merely the right to receive the occasional haunch of venison from Windsor; even the ducal privilege of driving down Birdcage Walk appeared to have lapsed. It was almost as if King Charles II's dying injunction, "Let not poor Nelly starve", had been ignored as far as the Cockney whore's descendants were concerned: the dukedom had been created for Nell Gwyn's "little bastard" by the Merry

Monarch and its successive holders had tended to lack both cash and distinction.

Charles Beauclerk's predecessor "Obby", the delightfully dotty 12th Duke, once arrived to stay at an Irish country house with a brown paper bag containing pyjamas and a toothbrush and used to tell the hall porter at Brooks's Club to "wind up my watch for me, there's a good fellow".

In 1953 the 12th Duke caused a flutter in the Royal Household when he announced his intention of turning up at the Coronation with a live falcon in his capacity as Hereditary Grand Falconer of England. On being told he could bring only a stuffed bird, he declined to attend the ceremony at all.

At the time he succeeded to the Dukedom of St Albans Charles Beauclerk was working for the film division of the Central Office of Information and so became allegedly the first Duke in history to work at a regular salaried job.

It was revealed that he had once been employed as a salesman living in furnished rooms (and had actually lived in St Albans itself), as well as a journalist on the old *Star*, the London evening newspaper, writing feature articles on such topics as Peak Frean biscuits.

The 13th Duke decided to put his title to profitable use in boardrooms, but as he ruefully admitted in 1977, after chequered commercial ventures in property, travel, advertising and finance, "My involvement in the business world has brought me nothing but problems".

Indeed he found himself involved in a series of financial scandals, earning censure in a Department of

Trade report, and at the end of the 1970s decided to settle on the Continent.

While there was sympathy for the genial Charles St Albans in his determination to replenish the ancestral coffers and to recover historic heirlooms, it was generally held that he had shown scant judgment in the company he had kept in the City.

Charles Frederic Aubrey de Vere Beauclerk was born 1915, only child of Aubrey Beauclerk, of Aldeburgh, Suffolk, a junior descendant of the 8th Duke of St Albans. He was educated at Eton and Magdalene College, Cambridge, where he read Law and Modern Languages.

His fluency in French and German was valuable during the 1939–45 War when he worked in military intelligence and psychological warfare, becoming a colonel in the Intelligence Corps. He was appointed OBE in 1945.

Afterwards he was Controller of Information Services in the Allied Control Commission for Austria. He was chief books editor at the Central Office of Information for seven years from 1951, then chief films production officer for two years.

In 1960 he was appointed director of the films division, carrying on in the post for six months after inheriting the dukedom in 1964. He was also president of the Federation of Industrial Development Associations.

After a few years as chairman of Grendon Trust, a property company, the Duke was criticised in 1973 for selling his holding to a young entrepreneur called Christopher Selmes – a one-time Slater Walker executive who set out to make a fortune on his own – when the board was trying to secure a higher counter-bid. The deal brought the Duke £793,000, and sharp criticism from his fellow directors. The Take-Over Panel found no evidence of conspiracy, but called the sale "a severe error of judgment".

Inspectors appointed to inquire into the Selmes companies twice interviewed the Duke about his dealings. In 1974 the Duke took an interest in another property company, Isle of Man Overseas Properties. Angry shareholders unsuccessfully petitioned for an inquiry when this showed a loss of £138,000 in 1975.

After the Inland Revenue sued him for £182,000 in back taxes and interest in 1978, the Duke sold two houses in Chelsea, paintings and furniture. He protested against the eventual Department of Trade report in 1979 which accused him, when chairman of Grendon Trust, of conspiring to lie to the City Panel on Takeovers and Mergers.

The report told the "almost incredible story" of how Mr Selmes obtained a £17 million loan from the Keyser Ullman merchant bank with "worthless guarantees". Directors of the bank were accused of incompetence.

The loans were made to Mr Selmes to help finance his takeover of the Grendon Trust. The Duke and another director were criticised in the report for the way they sold their shares to Mr Selmes, giving him control of the company, while a better price was being negotiated with the Metropolitan Estates and Property Corporation.

Mr Selmes left Britain for America with more than £20 million owing after the collapse of his companies. The Duke went to live in the south of France, where his second wife's family had property, but returned regularly to London to have his hair cut at the Ritz.

The bespectacled Duke, who had a certain look of his royal ancestor, Charles II, took a passionate interest in his family history. But he never sat in the House of Lords, nor possessed a ducal coronet or robes. "I don't enjoy dressing up," he said.

He was a staunch champion of the claims of his ancestor, Edward de Vere, 17th Earl of Oxford, to have written Shakespeare's works – or at least to have been part of "the team" behind him. The Duke was patron of the Shakespearean Authorship Trust and his other appointments included the presidency of the International Families Fund.

His first marriage to Nathalie Chatham Walker was dissolved in 1947; he married secondly later that year, Suzanne Fesq, an author and artist, who survives him together with a son by the first marriage and three sons and a daughter by the second.

The Duke's eldest son, Murray de Vere Beauclerk Earl of Burford, a chartered accountant born in 1939, succeeds to the title.

October 11 1988

ADRIAN DAINTREY

ADRIAN DAINTREY, who has died aged 87, was an underrated English artist and engagingly eccentric Bohemian figure who produced delightful cityscapes in the Post-Impressionist manner.

Much to his surprise and satisfaction, late in life he

became what he called a "film star" thanks to a bizarre television documentary about a police stake-out at the country home of his friend Laura Duchess of Marlborough. The police, tipped off about a likely burglarly at the Duchess's house in Buckinghamshire, arrived with a television crew in tow which did not prove to the liking of another house guest, Sir Arthur Bryant.

Feeling that the constabulary were not treating "the two old gents" (as they referred to Bryant and Daintrey) with quite the proper degree of respect, the artist took an officer aside and confided, in front of the camera, that Sir Arthur happened to be an extremely distinguished historian and that he himself was "a semi-well-known painter".

The film included such hilarious moments as the Duchess warning Daintrey that unless he did up his fly-buttons he would be arrested for indecent exposure. "Surely that is one of the more minor offences?" Daintrey asked the attendant policeman.

But as an artist he was worthy of more serious consideration than such farcical incidents suggested, possessing a delicate sense of place, an affection for buildings and a deep love of nature.

Daintrey was an enthusiastic traveller; Paris, Bangkok, Istanbul, Singapore, Delhi and most of Italy featured in his work. But London seemed his real subject.

Daintrey used the metropolis, as he liked to put it, as a tourist, setting up his equipment in the middle of Trafalgar Square or South Kensington and painting the view (sometimes, as he recalled, he would be thrown a few coins). He was also adept at giving an atmospheric insider's view in such interiors as the Travellers' Club, the Crush Bar at Covent Garden and the Winter Garden at the Ritz.

His friend John Betjeman placed Daintrey in "the great tradition of London from Thackeray and Sir John Leech to Max Beerbohm and Osbert Lancaster." Betjeman (with his teddy bear Archibald) and Lancaster were among the subjects of Daintrey's sympathetic portraits, together with other friends such as Anthony Powell, Peter Quennell and Paddy Leigh Fermor in Cretan costume.

Adrian Maurice Daintrey, the son of a solicitor, was born in 1901 and brought up in Tooting and Wimbledon. He disliked his time at Charterhouse ("mass bullying, persecution or sending to Coventry"), but won the drawing prize and a place at the Slade School of Art, then ruled by the formidable Henry Tonks, with whom he soon crossed swords.

His preferred teacher was Wilson Steer who told him "Well, you can't do better than the Old Masters: we all know that". Daintrey took to copying paintings in the National Gallery (where he became friendly with Vanessa Bell and Duncan Grant) and continued this practice in the Louvre when he went to Paris in 1924.

His modern heroes were Utrillo, Manet, Derain and Matisse, though the latter, he was always careful to stress, he never attempted to imitate. As a student he became a drinking partner of Augustus John, having boldly approached him in the street and asked if he could visit his studio. John invited him round and presently said: "I have to go now, but stay as long as you like." John often steered him to a pub where they would meet "some charming girl behind the bar who well merited a visit."

Daintrey's first one-man show, shared with Paul Nash at the fashionable Warren Gallery in 1928, brought him many aristocratic patrons most of whom he retained throughout his working life. Despite this, he experienced continual financial problems and never acquired the steady support of a gallery until recently: his last show at the Sally Hunter Gallery in 1988 was a great success.

On the outbreak of the 1939–45 War he joined the ARP; then, in 1940, he switched to the RASC as a driver before transferring to the Camouflage Corps and taking the opportunity to paint in such exotic locations as Iran, Iraq, Egypt and Italy.

At one stage he was surprised to find himself appointed Garrison Engineer of Sardinia. The legendarily ineffectual Daintrey explained to the authorities that although he was indeed attached to the Royal Engineers, this was rather out of his line.

After the war he held regular exhibitons of his own work at his Chelsea flat and also contributed art criticism to *Punch* where his friend Anthony Powell was literary editor.

Daintrey's reminiscences, *I Must Say* (1963), moved with much charm from pre-war Bohemia to the world of the socially smart in a way faintly reminiscent of Powell's great novel sequence, *A Dance to the Music of Time*.

Daintrey was an endearing, very untidy and in many ways rather innocent man: in the 1930s he shared a house and played golf with Donald Maclean, later observing that he found his political views rather strange but nothing more sinister.

In recent years he became a familiar figure in the so-called "Paddington Set", the coterie that gathered round

Lady Diana Cooper in Little Venice. Although often looking faintly bemused and bewildered, his interest in the fairer sex, wine and cigars remained undiminished to the end.

Daintrey described himself as "an incurable sentimentalist who liked savouring memories of the past" and used to say "I am always in love with somebody". He appeared to take the vicissitudes of his life cheerfully, mainly because he was fundamentally very serious about his art.

Daintrey was fond of quoting Derain's remark "Sit down in front of nature and show whether you are an imbecile or not". His rhythmic drawings, full of life and acute observations, and with broad patches of carefully observed colour describing so precisely atmosphere, light and texture, show just how studiously he took this dictum.

Anthony Powell writes: Adrian Daintrey a was a friend of mine for over 60 years. He was one of the few artists I have known who could specify the precise moment when the visible world took shape for him in painters' terms. He was coming back from school, standing on Earl's Court Station platform and a cigarette kiosk suddenly came to life as a pictorial composition.

Daintrey had a peculiar wit of his own. I remember him commending George Orwell's *Down and Out in Paris and London* to me with the words, "You *must* read it. You'll never enjoy *sauté* potatoes again."

Early in our acquaintance we spent Easter at Le Havre, a holiday which opened in some commotion as Daintrey mislaid the tickets for the night boat. They turned up later in his suitcase. I believe some rebate was recovered but fresh tickets put some strain on our limited resources.

Daintrey was keen to cross the bay to Honfleur, painter's country, where Bonington, Corot, Courbet, Boudin, the Impressionists, had all worked. He wanted specially to visit a pub called La Ferme Saint-Simeon, between Trouville and the sea, where some of these painters used to find cheap accommodation. We found La Ferme Saint-Simeon without too much difficulty, and decided to lunch there. I see now with the sophistication of age that the bright yellow shutters ought to have been a warning. We were each handed a menu bound in leather.

We studied it aghast: "You never ought to have allowed me to come here," said Daintrey. We lunched as modestly as we could, spending the last couple of days in Le Havre with extreme economy. In the glossy papers one occasionally sees pictures today of provincial French restaurants with many stars, among which La Ferme Saint-Simeon is likely to figure.

Daintrey's friendship with Augustus John had given him some of John's gruff manner which did not indicate an enemy of conviviality. Daintrey also shared John's wholehearted admiration for the opposite sex, many of whom showed their appreciation in the most practical manner.

Like his fellow Carthusian, Thackeray's Colonel Newcome, Daintrey ended his days in the Charterhouse where to the end he was visited by many charming young women. I have lost an old friend, and I do not doubt that

Daintrey's passing will bring a tear to the eye of more than one lady of quality and black bus conductress.

October 13 1988

FLORENCE NAGLE

FLORENCE NAGLE, the racehorse trainer and dog breeder who has died aged 94, achieved a remarkable double, against long odds, in breaching the all-male preserves of both the Jockey Club and the Kennel Club.

In 1966 she took on the Jockey Club single-handed in the courts and won a famous victory, forcing racing's ruling body to give licences to women trainers. Eleven years later the Jockey Club admitted, for the first time in its long history, three women as members.

At an industrial tribunal the next year Mrs Nagle turned her sights on the controlling organisation of dogdom, the Kennel Club, accusing it of sex discrimination by its insistence on exclusively male membership. Although she lost this case on a technicality, Mrs Nagle was generally given the credit when shortly afterwards the Kennel Club decided to allow women members.

The redoubtable grey-haired great-grandmother became a national celebrity for her doughty campaigns. "Women always have to fight for things, and someone has to stick her neck out," she said. "I don't believe in equality for its own sake. People are the same as animals, and you can get idiots in any litter. What I want is the best, whether it is a man or a woman."

Florence Watson was born in Manchester in 1894,

the only daughter of a dairy tycoon, William George Watson, who was created a baronet in 1912. During the First World War the Watson family seat of Sulhamstead Abbotts, Berks, was used as a hospital and there she met a gassed soldier, James Nagle, an Irishman who had emigrated to Canada and had come back to fight with the Canadian Highlanders and the 60th Rifles.

The Nagles were both keen on racing and in 1929 they had a useful sprinter called Fernley; but James Nagle was a gambler, and they could not afford to go on owning horses. "He was a gay spender," Mrs Nagle recalled. "We had a wonderful time. Then he ran off with one of our kennel maids and that was that." The marriage was dissolved in 1928, and Nagle died in 1933.

"We had our ups and downs," Mrs Nagle said. "At one time I ran a tearoom at Stonehenge, and used to have to clean out the lavatories myself." She added with characteristic good humour: "In fact, I suppose that is the only thing I am qualified in, lavatory cleaning."

She had been allowed her first big dog, an Irish wolfhound, on leaving school and went on to make her name in the dog world, breeding Irish wolfhounds and Irish setters. She won 18 field trial championships with her dogs.

In the 1930s she tried her luck on the Turf again and in 1937 was unfortunate not to win the Derby with Sandsprite, who was narrowly beaten by Midday Sun. Sandsprite was "nobbled" in his next race at Ascot and was not much good afterwards.

Three decades later she was to make racing history. Until Mrs Nagle's intervention the Jockey Club had consistently refused to give licences to women trainers, though at the time women trainers such as Helen Johnson-Houghton (widow of the trainer Gordon Johnson-Houghton) were training with much success with a male friend or stable-lad holding the licence.

Twice the Jockey Club was able to block Mrs Nagle's efforts to have the case heard in the Court of Appeal. At the third attempt she succeeded, and the judges did not mince their words.

"If Mrs Nagle is to carry on her trade without stooping to subterfuge she has to have a training licence," said Lord Denning. "In my opinion," said Lord Justice Danckwerts, "the courts have the right to protect the right of a person to work when it is being prevented by the dictatorial exercise of powers by a body which holds a monopoly."

After such a damning indictment the Jockey Club quickly capitulated, and Mrs Nagle at last received her licence to train. In 1969 she duly became the first woman trainer in Britain to saddle a winner under the rules of racing.

During the Second World War Mrs Nagle had moved her stud from Sulhamstead to Westerlands near Petworth, Sussex, where she was joined by Miss F. Newton-Deakin, who also had mares there.

After the war Mrs Nagle trained – with her head lad, W. Stickley, holding the licence – several notable winners, including Elf Arrow, winner of the Liverpool St Leger and the Royal Hunt Cup runner-up, Gelert.

Mrs Nagle retired from training in 1976 and decided to emigrate to America to set up a stud farm; but she did not care for the way the Americans treated their animals and returned home, settling at Hunters Moon in Sussex.

She is survived by her son.

November 1 1988

MABEL STRICKLAND

MABEL STRICKLAND, who has died on Malta aged 89, was for many years a dominant figure in the public affairs of that island, as proprietor and editor of the *Times of Malta* and as a fiercely pro-Commonwealth politician.

Large and imposing and with her hair parted in the middle, she had the appearance of a Victorian governess and was always known to the Maltese as Miss Mabel. She wielded considerable influence, both through her journalism and her formidable personality, but her political career cannot be accounted a success. She attributed this to her sex rather than her policies, and would often clutch at her ample breasts and moan: "If it wasn't for *these* I would be Prime Minister of Malta!"

Miss Strickland's finest hour was during the siege of Malta in 1940, when she continued to publish her two newspapers throughout the enemy bombardment. The onslaught began on June 11, and Malta's air defences rested on three Gladiator bi-plane fighters, known as Faith, Hope and Charity.

The *Times of Malta* and *Il Berqua*, her other daily, were bombed out of their editorial and publishing building. But the redoubtable Miss Strickland had installed their presses in a rock cavern deep below Valletta, the capital, and though some copies were charred by fire not a single edition was lost.

This was not her only contribution to the islanders' morale: a keen gardener and a member of the Royal Horticultural Society, Miss Strickland produced large crops of oranges, tangerines and grapefruit to help to feed the island's children.

In 1944 she was appointed OBE, and such was her influence by the end of the war that it was said that the island was ruled by three people: the Governor, the Archbishop and Miss Strickland.

Her post-war attempts to translate this influence into actual power proved disastrous, however. The party she created received little support; and she herself — its only member in the Maltese Legislative Assembly — was soon unseated on a technicality.

In the election of 1955 she was comprehensively defeated by Dom Mintoff. Twenty years later the *Times of Malta* was banned from using its presses under a police order, which it defied; and in October 1979 its offices were burnt out by a mob of Mintoff supporters, which had broken in while the police watched. But, as in the 1939–45 War, the *Times* was on the streets again the next day.

Mabel Edeline Strickland was born on Malta in 1899. She was the third daughter of the 1st and last Baron Strickland of Sizergh and 6th Count della Catena and the former Lady Edeline Sackville, daughter of the 7th Earl De La Warr.

Strickland had served Malta as chief secretary to the

Governor at the turn of the century, and later held
appointments in Tasmania, New South Wales and Western Australia, where Mabel was educated privately.

The family returned to Malta in the 1920s, and
Strickland took as his second wife Margaret Hulton, sister
of the newspaper proprietor Sir Edward Hulton. Strickland was Prime Minister of Malta from 1927 to 1932;
and in 1931 Mabel became assistant secretary of his
Constitutional party, a post she retained until 1945.

Miss Strickland first demonstrated her political mettle
in the 1930s, when she proved such an implacable
opponent of the Italian fascists who were seeking to
dominate the island's trade that they nicknamed her
"Malta's She-Devil". During that decade she also had the
foresight to urge industrial developments aimed at
making the economy less dependent on its role as a major
British defence base.

After Malta had settled down from the upheaval of
the war, Miss Strickland gave up her editorship of the
Times of Malta to seek election to the Legislative Assembly
in 1950. Three years later, emboldened by early success,
she founded the Progressive Constitutional party, "to
fight for constitutional and social progress for Malta as
part of the British Commonwealth". But in the 1955
election her party failed to win a single seat and when
she campaigned against the Nationalists and Socialists
she was stoned.

Mintoff, who had defeated Borg Olivier in the 1955
election, called for the integration of Malta with the
United Kingdom, and a referendum approved this suggestion by a three-to-one majority. Miss Strickland

opposed integration, fearing sectarian violence, and demanded as an alternative the appointment of a Minister of State for Maltese Affairs in London.

Neither plan came to anything; and after Olivier's National party defeated Mintoff's Socialists in 1962, Duncan Sandys, the Commonwealth and Colonial Secretary, decided in favour of independence, which was duly declared in September 1964. Thereafter Miss Strickland maintained a fundamentally pro-Western attitude; and after Mintoff returned to power in 1971 she continued in her outspoken opposition. Though her newspaper quickly bounced back after the arson attack of 1979, Miss Strickland herself never recovered from the shock.

As well as editing the *Times of Malta* and the *Sunday Times of Malta*, she was managing director of Allied Malta Newspapers and chairman and director of the Progress Press Company. Her publications included collections of essays on Malta, and *Maltese Constitutional and Economic Issues, 1955–1959*. The new owner of the *Times of Malta* is Miss Strickland's great-nephew, who lives in England.

November 30 1988

MARGARET MEE

MARGARET MEE, the intrepid and brilliant botanical artist who has died aged 79, devoted her life to recording the threatened flora of the Amazonian rainforests.

Besides being one of the foremost experts of the art of flower portraiture Margaret Mee was a redoubtable traveller in the great female tradition of Mary Kingsley and Freya Stark. Wearing a straw hat and packing a pistol along with her sketch pad, brushes and watercolours, this deceptively frail and intensely feminine woman braved snakes, poisonous spiders, cannibals and blood-sucking buffalo gnats to penetrate the deepest Brazilian jungle in pursuit of rare species.

She would make her way in a small boat, with a local boatman as her only companion, and suffered several bouts of malaria and hepatitis. One night a band of drunken gold prospectors burst into her hut in an Indian village, but she sent them on their way, reminding the ruffians that it was not proper to enter a lady's hut when she was alone.

When the leader of the gang unwisely made another incursion into the hut some hours – and bottles – later, he found himself looking down the barrel of Mrs Mee's .32 Rossi revolver. "I haven't had a lot of shooting practice," she recalled, "but really I think I'm quite good. After all, a steady hand and a good eye are absolutely essential qualities for a painter, wouldn't you say?"

Her last Amazon expedition took place this May when she fulfilled her long-held ambition to record the *Selenicereus wittii* (the Amazon Moonflower). On previous journeys in the Igapo flooded forest she had seen the celebrated cactus (which flowers just once, on one night a year) but never succeeded in capturing it with her brush. Once, in the late 1970s, she caught a glimpse of it in bud, but its surrounding creek proved impenetrable in the dark and when she returned in the light of day the flower had closed.

But on her final journey Mrs Mee succeeded in painting the opening flower and, for the first time in the wild, noted many points of its unusual natural history. In her diary she recorded how she waited for the buds to open: "As I stood there with the dim outline of the forest all around, I was spellbound. Then the first petal began to move and then another as the flower burst into life". She then had merely a few hours of darkness left to commit the flower to paper for posterity.

Margaret Hendersen Brown, of Swedish seafaring descent, was born at Chesham, Bucks, in 1909 and, although she studied art as a girl, made her initial mark in the political sphere. In 1937 she was delegate of the Union of Sign, Glass and Ticket Writers to the TUC in Norwich, where she made a stirring speech.

During the Second World War she served as a draughtsman in an aircraft factory and afterwards resumed her art studies at the Camberwell School of Art under Victor Pasmore and then at St Martin's, where she met her husband, Greville Mee, a commercial artist.

In 1952 the Mees moved to Brazil, where her sister lived, and Margaret began her travels to capture the beauty of flowers. In the course of her early journeys, she concentrated her efforts in the coastal rainforests around Sao Paulo, finding a host of subjects which she illustrated with unerring accuracy and a sensitive technical style.

These early paintings are all the more important because this coastal rainforest has since virtually disappeared. They were exhibited in Brazil in 1958 and in London in 1960 when she was awarded the Grenfell Medal of the Royal Horticultural Society. In the early 1960s she travelled into the arid north-east of Brazil where she sketched and painted for Dr Lyman B Smith, the authority on the family *Bromeliaceae*.

Margaret Mee's great Amazonian odyssey began in 1956 with a visit to the Gurupi river which forms a border between the states of Pará and Maranhão. In 1967 she became the first woman traveller to climb on the south side of the Pico de Nebline, Brazil's highest mountain. From this journey her interest in and concern for the future of the forest Indians began and then grew in intensity over the years.

A high point in Mrs Mee's career came in 1967 when she exhibited at London's Tryon Gallery, a show timed to coincide with the publication of a folio edition of *Flowers of the Brazilian Forests*, containing 32 plates. The edition was created under the patronage of Prince Philip and the paintings were widely acclaimed.

More Amazon journeys followed, with two in 1971–2 funded by a Guggenheim Fellowship. These were immensely successful as Mrs Mee discovered an area south of the main Amazon stream which was rich in new species – notably *Aechmea polyantha* and *Aechmea Meeana* brome-liads which have never been found since and which are known only from Margaret Mee's Amazon Collection of 60 paintings.

The next 18 years of her life were devoted to further Amazon journeys from which the major part of the Collection was derived.

She was appointed MBE in 1975 and elected a Fellow of the Linnean Society in 1986.

At the time of her death, in a motor accident in the English Midlands, she was campaigning passionately for the conservation and future of the Brazilian jungle and promoting her remarkable new book, *In Search of Flowers of the Amazon Forests*. A major exhibition of her work, Amazon Collection, is currently on show at Kew.

Mrs Mee, who saw the beginning of the destruction of the Amazon forests in the late 1960s, realised the scientific value of her work and determined never to sell an original first painting of any species. Thus she created a unique record of Amazon plants in permanent gouache, a medium which, if well conserved, should last forever.

She is survived by her husband.

December 3 1988

BARONESS PANNONICA DE KOENIGSWARTER

PANNONICA DE KOENIGSWARTER, who has died in New York aged 74, was the daughter of a British Rothschild and the wife of a French diplomat, but rejected her native milieu to become a notable patron of jazz.

She was known as the "Bebop Baroness", as her friends and beneficiaries were leading exponents of the Bebop school which revolutionised the American jazz scene in the 1940s and 1950s. They included Dizzy Gillespie, Charlie Mingus, Thelonious Monk, Miles Davis and Charlie "Bird" Parker – who spent his last hours in "Nica" Koenigswarter's Manhattan apartment.

The medical report on Parker indicated that his death was due to an excess of drugs and alcohol; that he was a jazzman and she a baroness proved a heady mixture for the press. The headlines included: "BOP KING DIES IN HEIRESS'S FLAT and "THE BIRD IN THE BARONESS'S BOUDOIR."

She featured in all the books on Parker and is portrayed by Diana Salinger in the Clint Eastwood film *Bird*. She is also to be seen in *Straight, No Chaser*, a documentary film about Theolonious Monk – in which she comes across a lively and beautiful woman, her cutglass accent, without a trace of Transatlantic overtones, contrasting starkly with Monk's unintelligible mumblings.

The Baroness was witty, sardonic and outspoken. She painted abstruse canvases, using a mixture of acrylic, milk, Scotch whisky and scent; she was fascinated by African sculpture, Afro-American music and negritude generally.

She dressed casually in highly expensive clothes. Her Rolls-Royce (which she described as her "Silver Sparrow"), her furs and gold pocket-flask were familiar to the habitués and staff of the jazz clubs in Greenwich Village and Harlem.

The eccentric Monk was her closest associate, and he recorded *Pannonica* as a dedication to his benefactress; other dedications were *Nica Steps Out* by pianist Freddy Redd, and *Nica's Dream* by alto-saxophonist Gigi Gryce.

It was Monk who introduced her to Parker, who was much impressed by this unexpected vision of *haute* Bohemia, by the Baroness's politeness in dealing with servants and her casual handling of complaints by her outraged landlords. He was amused, too, to find in the Fifth Avenue *salon* of this eccentric aristocrat a haven from the pressures of poverty, the hostility of the critics and the attentions of the Narcotics Squad.

Kathleen Annie Pannonica Rothschild was born in 1913, the youngest daughter of the banker Nathaniel Charles Rothschild – and a sister of the late Lord Rothschild, another notable jazz enthusiast, and of the naturalist Miriam Rothschild.

Pannonica had a conventional upper-class childhood, attended a finishing school in Paris and a coming-out ball in London but she showed early signs of atypical behaviour by becoming an aviatrix.

She met her husband-to-be, Col Baron Jules de Koenigswarter, Minister Plenipotentiary at the French Embassy in New York, at Le Touquet Airport. They were married in 1935 and had five children; the marriage was dissolved in 1956.

During the Second World War the Baroness was variously a decoder with Gen. de Gaulle's intelligence service, a private in the Free French Army, a broadcaster from a propaganda station in Brazzaville, Equatorial French Africa, and later a driver for the War Graves Commission.

In 1951, bored with life as a diplomat's wife at the French Embassy in Mexico City, she left her husband and took up residence in a luxuriously-furnished suite at the Hotel Stanhope on New York's Fifth Avenue, which soon became a "crash pad" for a number of black jazz musicians.

Thelonious Monk was often to be seen in the hotel lobby wearing a red shirt, deer-stalker hat, dark glasses and carrying a white cane, much to the disgust of the other excessively respectable residents who complained to the management, adding to the many complaints about jam sessions going on until the early hours of the morning. An annoyed but respectful management doubled her rent – a matter of little import to a Rothschild.

It was Monk who persuaded her to abandon hotel life, with its tiresome constraints on the playing of Behop jazz throughout the night, and together they moved to an apartment overlooking the Hudson River.

Since Monk's death in 1982 she had been virtually a recluse, living with an assortment of cats.

December 10 1988

"COCKIE" HOOGTERP

"COCKIE" HOOGTERP, who has died aged 96, was one of the last links with life between the wars in East Africa, which encompassed such figures as Baron Blixen, her second husband, Elspeth Huxley and the denizens of "Happy Valley" portrayed in the film *White Mischief*.

While married to Blixen (whose previous wife Karen – the author of Isak Dinesen – wrote *Out of Africa*), Cockie entertained the Prince of Wales and Lady Furness on safari in Tanganyika, and he was much diverted by her company.

Cockie Hoogterp certainly added to the gaiety of nations and enriched the public stock of harmless pleasure. She was invariably witty in conversation, some-times wickedly so, and given to impromptu practical jokes. It was no great surprise to her friends – though it gave some of them cause for concern – when she returned to London after her divorce from Blixen and found work on the gossip column of the *Daily Express*.

One joke which was not of Cockie's making was the report in 1938 in *The Daily Telegraph* of the death of Baroness Eva von Blixen-Finecke, who was confused with Cockie Hoogterp. In March 1988, when we reproduced this report in our "50 Years Ago" column, Cockie was hugely amused, recalling that in 1938 she had marked all her bills "Deceased" and sent them back.

Many of the Happy Valley crowd were Cockie Hoogterp's friends, though she was not one of the "set". She did not take drugs, as many of them did, but enjoyed describing one, Kiki Preston, as being "clever with her needles".

She saw Sir "Jock" Delves Broughton, Bt (later tried and acquitted of the murder of his wife's lover, the 22nd Earl of Erroll) a few times in Johannesburg in 1940, shortly before he married Diana Caldwell and they made their fateful way to Nairobi.

"Cockie" Hoogterp was born Jacqueline Harriet Alexander in London in 1892, the daughter of James Alexander, a banker of Irish Ascendancy stock, and his wife Lady Emily Boyle, eldest daughter of the 9th Earl of Cork and Orrery.

"Cockie" was thrice married: first, in 1914, to Major Benedict Birkbeck, a fellow officer of her brother Ulick (later Keeper of the Privy Purse to King George VI); then to Blixen; and lastly to Jan ("Hookie") Hoogterp, a South African. There were no children.

Elspeth Huxley writes: Cockie's father had assured his family that when he died there would be nothing left. As they lived in such an opulent style, they assumed that he was joking. He was not. After his death in 1915 Lady Emily was left with £350 a year, and Cockie without a *dot*.

When the 1914–18 War ended, she and Ben Birkbeck emigrated to Kenya, where ex-servicemen could obtain title to undeveloped land on easy terms. Capital, however, was needed to develop it.

When Ben returned to England to try to raise some, Cockie fell in love with Baron Bror von Blixen, the husband of the future writer Karen (or Tanne). The von Blixens' marriage had already foundered, and Karen had embarked on her much publicised love affair with Denys Finch Hatton. Cockie and Blixen were married in 1928 in Sweden. Providentially, a friend offered them £800 a year to establish a coffee plantation in a then remote part of Tanganyika Territory (later Tanzania), 100 miles from the nearest township.

This was real pioneering, and at Babati Cockie spent what she described as the happiest time of her life. Blixen doubled the roles of coffee planter and white hunter, with the emphasis on the latter. In 1928 and again in 1930 he, with Finch Hatton, took out the Prince of Wales, with Cockie as a lively member of the party.

"Membership" (as if it had been a club) of the so-called Happy Valley set has sometimes been, quite wrongly, attributed to Cockie. The Happy Valley was a small glen in the Aberdare Mountains. Cockie was either some 350 miles away in Tanganyika (sometimes even further in the Belgian Congo, or South-West Africa) or 6,000 miles away in England visiting her two brothers, to whom she was devoted, and her numerous friends. She was neither promiscuous nor an alcoholic, although a gin-and-tonic seldom came amiss.

She used her social contacts to recruit safari clients such as the immensely rich American hostess Laura Corrigan, who engaged an aeroplane to fly her wig to Nariobi twice a week for a shampoo and set, and to return with fresh milk, cream and other necessities such as champagne.

Cockie's frequent visits to England, combined with Blixen's roving eye, undid the marriage. On her return from London in the mid-1930s Cockie was greeted at the airport by Blixen and Eva, a glamorous racing motorist and fellow Swede, with the suggestion that they should stay with a friend *à trois*. Cockie declined.

The following year, perhaps partly out of pique, she married Jan Hoogterp, a handsome, ebullient and temperamental architect and former pupil of Sir Herbert Baker, who had carried out an ambitious programme of public building in Kenya.

They moved to Johannesburg, and it was here that Cockie read her own obituary in a newspaper which had confused her with Eva, who styled herself the Baroness Blixen and had been killed in a motor accident near Baghdad. The apologetic editor agreed to Cockie's stipulation that the correction should be published in her own words. These were: "Mrs Hoogterp wishes it to be known that she has not yet been screwed in her coffin."

"For God's sake, Cockie," a friend admonished her on her third marriage, "don't make a third mistake." It soon became apparent that she had. After the outbreak of the 1939–45 War the Third Mistake as Cockie sometimes called him, joined the South African Air Force and Cockie withdrew to the Cape, where she made a somewhat chequered living in a variety of jobs and became an ornament of Cape Town society.

When she finally returned to England she settled in a cottage near Newbury, Berks, where her wit, sparkle and genius for hospitality, exercised on an apparently elastic shoe-string, endeared her to a wide circle of friends of all ages.

Cockie was a lily of the field now submerged beneath the manners of a harsher age. Few women, other than the very rich, can have survived into the late 1980s without ever having boiled an egg or made her own bed.

Laughter and the love of friends were her lodestars. She could elevate a visit to the hairdresser's into an uproarious drama that had her audience in stitches. Parties were the breath of life, along with making plans and re-arranging them, and shopping in flea markets, and going to the races, and enlivening the lives of those who lived in stately homes.

Her species has become extinct.

December 13 1988

ARTHUR MARSHALL

ARTHUR MARSHALL, who has died aged 78, was in turn schoolmaster, actor, broadcaster, essayist and critic, and often more than one of these things at once.

It was comparatively late in life that he also became – as a leader of a team in *Call My Bluff* – a "television personality", a role which, though he would have mocked the phrase, he greatly enjoyed. On hearing of Marshall's death his co-panellist, Frank Muir, said: "Arthur was the bubbles in the champagne, and now things will all go a bit flat." Marshall's principal pleasure was the exchange of laughter between friends, of whom he had an enormous number. "I have made laughter," he said, "my prime consideration in life".

He gave joy for many years to readers of *The Sunday Telegraph* through his book reviews and, from 1977, his fortnightly column. His short essays (800 words were his best length) are masterpieces of apparent inconsequentiality constructed with great care. Many thought he was at his best when sympathetically mocking the social amenities of the upper-middle classes, from which he came. Some fans were less certain about his *tendre* for scatological puns.

Behind it all was an intolerance of pomposity, officiousness and self-regard, and he could be sharp with busybodies who tried to interfere with the harmless pleasure of others. He once wrote: "My view of God is a simple one, namely that if He exists at all He must be an outstandingly disagreeable old gentleman." It was said of him that he never intentionally gave pain, but in print he could cut down a public figure with the lightest of reproofs, probably in brackets (of which he was a master).

Charles Arthur Bertram Marshall was born on May 10 1910, the son of an engineer in charge of a firm called the Pimlico Wheel Works. His obsession with everything theatrical had developed by the age of five. He acquired through the years a fine stock of theatrical anecdotes and was particularly strong on amateur mishaps – such as the production in which Lady Macbeth, "evidently keen on following the text while in the wings, made her entrance for the sleepwalking scene wearing a large pair of horn-rimmed spectacles".

From school at Oundle he went up to Christ's, Cambridge, where, according to Peter Wright, author of *Spycatcher*, he was called "Artie" and knew "who was sleeping with whom in the Burgess and Blunt circles". At Cambridge Marshall became, almost inevitably, president of the Amateur Dramatic Club, where, in those days of all-male casts, he specialised in women's roles.

In 1931, his parents having dissuaded him from drama school, he returned to his beloved Oundle to teach modern languages. He stayed, with an intermission for the Second World War, for 23 years and became a bachelor housemaster.

He served in Intelligence throughout the war, was taken off the beaches of Dunkirk, worked at Combined Operations at HQ in London, then transferred to Eisenhower's staff at Supreme Headquarters. His habit of giving girls' names to various brasshats – "Brenda Montgomery" was a super prefect – can hardly have harmed morale. The Armistice found him, by then a lieutenant-colonel, at Flensburg, one of his tasks being to interrogate members of the German High Command, another to seek the suicidal Himmler.

At Oundle he perfected his monologues impersonating eccentric schoolmistresses. ("There's ever such a dainty hellebore by your left plimsoll, Cynthia"). Part of his secret was an intimate knowledge of that queen of girls' school fiction, Angela Brazil; he became an expert in the genre, and in 1935 the *New Statesman* asked him to review for it. The association lasted until 1981, when his incurable levity (one of his japes was to arrive at Great Turnstile saying "*Cooee*, isn't Mrs Thatcher doing well?") became too much for the then editor, Bruce Page, and he was summarily sacked.

At a party in Cambridge in 1934 he was doing one of his impressions of a hockey mistress when a BBC producer spotted him and he joined a distinguished company in the monthly radio show *Charlot's Half Hour*; the next year he cut five records of his sketches and became famous. In 1943, when he was with Combined Ops, he was invited to fill in with a sketch of a bossy hospital nurse for a BBC comedy series which soon became known as *A Date with Nurse Dugdale*.

Marshall left Oundle in 1954 to be secretary to Lord Rothschild, an old friend, then at the Department of Zoology at Cambridge. People who knew only his public performances might think him never anything but frivolous. They would be mistaken.

Four years later he joined H. M. Tennent as a script-reader and stayed there until 1964, since when he had worked as a full-time freelance, achieving his apotheosis on television in *Call My Bluff*.

His publications include several collections of his *New Statesman* and *Sunday Telegraph* pieces and an engaging autobiography (*Life's Rich Pageant*, 1984).

Since 1970 he had lived in the Devon cottage known to his readers as "Myrtlebank". One of his pleasures was to read in bed every night a few pages of P. G. Wodehouse, so that, as he said, if he died in his sleep it would be with a smile on his face.

January 28 1989

PETER LANGAN

PETER LANGAN, the erratic Irish-born *restaurateur* who has died aged 47, was celebrated more for the eccentricity and extravagance of his behaviour than for the real merits of the restaurants with which he was associated.

His greatest success was the brasserie in Mayfair's Stratton Street, which bore his name and became a popular haunt of the famous and notorious alike. It opened in 1976, on the premises of the old Coq d'Or, an ailing dinosaur of the Maxwell Joseph period, where it achieved a remarkable transformation. His immediate success set the standard for a host of imitators, none of which could match the original in terms of style, consistent quality of cuisine and modish appeal.

Langan's partners in the venture were the actor Michael Caine, whose association with the restaurant gave it a show-business presence of British and American actors and their camp followers – and Richard Shepherd, formerly chef at the Capital Hotel.

"I'm a great *restaurateur*," Langan claimed, "but businesswise . . ." The restaurant worked because Shepherd organised its every aspect, turning out 400 or 500 covers a day and providing interesting and constantly changing dishes to a high standard. But the idea was Langan's and it was his vivid personality and astute awareness of the uses of publicity – even publicity that others might think self-defeating – that stamped the Brasserie on the public consciousness.

Langan's personal notoriety, his reputation for behaviour variously disconcerting, outrageous or disgraceful, was sometimes justified – especially when liberally fuelled by his favourite Krug. He could seem a demonic figure; but the excesses attributed to him often owed something to the embroidery of certain journalists.

Of the many anecdotes in the Langan canon, few are printable. He was celebrated for his insults and had a highly public quarrel with his partner Caine.

It is said that tabloid newspaper editors, when short of copy, would dispatch youngish female reporters to interview Langan with the express purpose of being shocked. Langan invariably obliged, though he strenuously denied the allegation that he had vomited into his napkin before one woman journalist. He insisted that a small piece of food had unfortunately caught in his throat: "I'd never vomit. I'm particular about my manners."

Among the tales he did not deny was that of the cockroach which a distraught customer had found in the ladies' room. "Madam," he exclaimed after studying it closely, "that cockroach is *dead*. All ours are alive." He then apparently swallowed it, washing it down decorously with a glass of vintage Krug.

Langan would regularly launch himself at customers he found, usually for some unfathomable reason, offensive. Often he would pass out amid the cutlery before doing any damage, but occasionally he would cruise menacingly beneath the tables, biting unwary customers' ankles.

Not known for his delicacy towards the fairer sex, Langan rejoiced in daring attractive young women to strip naked in the bar in return for limitless champagne. Patrons of Langans' haunts were only safe when he lay like a white whale in his crumpled suit, snoring sonorously by the Colony Room Club's piano, underneath a table, or on the floor in the gentlemen's lavatory at his Brasserie.

Peter Daniel Langan, son of Dan Langan, the Irish rugby full-back and a prominent figure in the Irish petrol industry, was born in Co Clare in 1941 and educated in Ireland. After a spell working in petrol in Britain, Langan made his first foray into the restaurant world as the chef, and soon the moving spirit, at Odin's in Devonshire Street, Marylebone, in 1966. There he evolved the idiosyncratic style which distinguished his later enterprises.

The virtues of Langan's largely self-taught cooking were soon apparent and the happy chance that his real passion for pictures was complemented by the presence upstairs of the artist Patrick Procktor. The tables of Odin's came to be frequented by what are now the great names of contemporary British painting while their early works hung on the walls.

Odin's became the works canteen of such artists as Francis Bacon, R.B. Kitaj, Lucian Freud and David Hockney, as well as Procktor. In the manner of a Rive Gauche café proprietor, Langan would exchange meals for the painters' work.

Procktor's mural of Venice still hangs in the unfashionable upstairs room at Langan's Brasserie; and he also designed its distinctive menu, on which a blue-faced Langan looks bemused while Shepherd appears concerned to separate him from an admonitory Caine.

Odin's prospered and removed next door; the original site became Langan's Bistro — still, 20 years on, a pleasing setting for simple dishes of unusual merit. The Dublin Bay Prawns, for example, were appropriately and exceptionally good – even if Langan himself would occasionally nod gently off with his head in a bowl of the crustaceans.

Those who condemned his excesses almost always overlooked Langan's intelligence and wit. For all his flaws he could be a charming and kindly companion and a princely host.

That he was often misunderstood is perhaps understandable but for all his occasional grossness he was a man whose delights, in Shakespeare's phrase, "were dolphin-like, they showed their backs above the element they lived in." Langan had a great delight in life and his exuberant vitality, sometimes tinged with melancholy, was an unfailing diversion to his friends.

Latterly, his thoughts had turned towards the franchising of his name in this country and especially in America where, after long years of abortive negotiation, the first transatlantic Langan's Brasserie has opened its doors in Century City, Los Angeles – though Langan himself was barred from the premises.

His wife, Susan, injured in the fire that cost Langan his life, survives him.

December 9 1988

BRIAN DE BREFFNY

BRIAN DE BREFFNY, author, genealogist, architectural historian and *soi-disant* Baron, who has died aged 58, was something of a mystery man in Ireland, where he lived grandly in a Palladian pile staffed by Indian servants on the Kilkenny/Tipperary border at Carrick-on-Suir.

His foxhunting neighbours were vaguely aware that he was a "writer chappie"; and foreign ambassadors to Eire, bidden for the weekend, attempted without success to find their kind host in any reference book. His marbled seat, known as Castletown Cox and one of the most important houses in Ireland, which he restored splendidly, belonged – de Breffny liked to explain – to a Panamanian company owned in turn by a family trust, and he lived there under a caretaker agreement.

"The Baron" was, in fact, born Brian Michael Leese at Isleworth, Middlesex, in 1931, the son of a Jewish father (a turf accountant turned taxi-cab driver) and an Irish Catholic mother.

Young Brian's schoolboy passion for genealogy became an obsession. The discovery that his great-great-grandmother's maiden name was Breffni stimulated his interest in the Irish O'Rorkes, Princes of Breffny, and he identified with the exiled French and Russian branches of this ancient Gaelic family. Later he took the name "de Breffny", and variously styled himself as a "7th Baron of the Holy Roman Empire", "Baron O'Rorke de Breffny" and "Count O'Rourke". Among his most treasured possessions were flags and swords said to have been carried at the Battle of Aughrim and a miniature of Mary of Modena which he claimed to be a family heirloom.

As a romantic young man, Leese/de Breffny lived in Rome, sometimes working as a professional genealogist. His American clients, believing themselves to be of "Famine Irish" ancestry, were astonished and greatly pleased when he produced pedigrees showing that they too were descended from the 17th-century exiled Irish landowners known as the Wild Geese.

His first book, inspired by a visit to the late Percy Paley of Castle Hacket, Co Galway, owner of the largest genealogical library in Ireland, was a *Bibliography of Irish Family History*, a slim volume which remains the most valuable reference book of its kind. In collaboration with the Irish genealogist Rosemary ffolliott, de Breffny edited a journal, *The Irish Ancestor*, and together they produced a delightful book, *The Houses of Ireland*, with photographs by George Mott.

While working on this project "the Baron" presented himself, unannounced, on numerous Irish doorsteps. Mr Charles Haughey was among the several country house owners to be taken with de Breffny's considerable charm and amusing conversation.

Only in deepest Munster did de Breffny meet with a stern rebuff, upon walking into the hall of a big house and praising the plasterwork. The owner's wife, unaccustomed to having her home commented upon by architecturally-aware strangers, showed him the door. Retreating down the avenue, he met the owner on his horse and informed him that his servant had been rude. With words based on the great tradition of the music-hall, he roared back: "That was no servant, that was my wife" before chasing "the Baron" off his demesne.

During the 1970s de Breffny published books on Irish castles, churches and abbeys, and edited three large coffee-table volumes, culminating in *Ireland: a Cultural Encyclopaedia*. He was a dedicated fund-raiser for the Wexford Opera Festival and for the pioneering Irish Architectural Archive.

He also wrote a novel, *My First Naked Lady*, telling of an Irish boy who discovers his relations are grandees moving in fashionable society in the South of France.

De Breffny married first, Princess Jyotsna, daughter of the Maharajadhiraja Bahadur of Burdwan; and secondly, Ulli, widow of Sir Stafford Sands, Minister of Tourism and Finance in the Bahamas, and daughter of Lauri Castren of Helsinki.

He is survived by his wife and by a daughter of the first marriage, Sita-Maria, who married in 1987 the 7th Viscount de Vesci, nephew of the Earl of Snowdon.

February 14 1989

MARIGA GUINNESS

MARIGA GUINNESS, who has died aged 56, was an inspired champion of architectural conservation and did much to awaken interest in the endangered Irish heritage. Tall, striking and dramatic – and a German princess by birth – she was also a legendary character.

Mrs Guinness and her former husband, Desmond, revived the defunct Irish Georgian Society in 1958, and she became a driving force against the property developers then bent on destroying Dublin. She fought hard to save Georgian houses in Lower Fitzwilliam Street and Mountjoy Square in the 1960s, as well as many other buildings. On one memorable occasion, in order to save Tailor's Hall in Dublin, she paraded the streets attired in a sandwich board.

Normally, she preferred to dress in flamboyant 18th-century costume, cutting an unforgettable figure. The remarkable Mrs Guinness was the subject of many anecdotes celebrating her idiosyncrasies.

One visitor to the Guinness household was startled to hear Mariga say: "I've spent my last two shillings on Whiskas for Lord Longford." In fact, the cats were named after the Pakenhams – of whom Mariga commented: "They have left Ireland for reasons of *literature*, I believe".

She spoke in an inimitable manner and always addressed people, however well she knew them, formally as "Mr" or "Mrs". The singer Mick Jagger for example, who was a regular house guest, curiously became "Mr McJaeger". Mrs Guinness would also use amusingly archaic terms – speaking, for instance, of "television machines".

Her enthusiasm for architecture knew no bounds: "From the age of three," she claimed, "I have always been more impressed by buildings than people." Stories were told of how she climbed into houses generally regarded as impenetrable. One country house owner in the West of Ireland was surprised when lying in bed to overhear an expert guided tour being delivered by Mrs Guinness to her companions.

Her influence extended well beyond Ireland. In America she promoted the Georgian cause and in Britain pioneered the renovation of early 18th-century Huguenot weavers' houses in Spitalfields in London's East End.

Princess Hermione Marie-Gabrielle Petronella Sophia Devota Florestine of Urach was born on Sept 21 1932 – the diminutive "Mariga" derived from her second and third Christian names. Her father was Prince Albrecht of Urach, sometime diplomatist and a director of the Daimler-Benz motor company. He was the third son of the 2nd Duke of Urach (a title created in 1867 for a scion of the Royal House of Württemberg who had contracted a morganatic marriage). Mariga's mother was the former, Rosemary Blackadder, whose ancestry was part Scottish, part Scandinavian.

Of her childhood, Mrs Guinness recalled: "I was born in London and immediately taken to Japan where my father was the German press attaché. An eccentric great-aunt brought me up, by mistake I think . . . and I had a lot of governesses . . . 12 perhaps, no, more."

In the early 1950s she arrived as an undergraduate at Oxford where she caused a sensation. In 1964 she was married to Desmond Guinness, second son of the 2nd Lord Moyne (Bryan Guinness, the poet and novelist) by his first wife Diana Mitford (later Lady Mosley). They had a son and a daughter.

Although forbidden to do so by her great-aunt – who believed Ireland was "full of Fenians and consumptives" – she settled in that country with her husband.

At first they rented Carton, ancestral seat of the Dukes of Leinster. It was there – at a tea party in 1958 – that the Irish Georgian Society was launched.

In the mid-1970s Mrs Guinness and her husband

became estranged and, after an interlude in Co Antrim, she finally departed from their subsequent home, Leixlip Castle, in 1983 following a divorce settlement.

Latterly, she had been based at a house in Offaly on the Birr demesne of the Earl of Rosse.

She was buried underneath the spectacular Conolly's Folly at Celbridge on the Castletown demesne, which she had been inspirational in restoring.

Christopher Gibbs writes: Mariga Guinness had a poet's vision and a patrician disdain for all forms of vulgarity.

Leixlip Castle, which Desmond and Mariga restored in the 1960s, stands on a steep, wooded bluff with the long, painted street of the town at its feet and the salmon leap of the Liffey, now harnessed to light Dublin, beside it. In the 18th century, white gothic windows pierced the thick walls, and spacious rooms were shaped behind them.

Desmond and Mariga furnished it with bold grace, filled it with friends and then bought and revived the great palace of Castletown next door. The boldness and vigour of Irish decoration, combining rustic strength and 18th-century elegance, brought fresh life to empty rooms.

Huge canvases in carved frames of shabby gilding; fireplaces where fossils sprawled across mouldings; great consoles where eagles beaks held garlands of black mahogany – all were garnished with Chinese pots, marble busts and sparkling Irish silver. Sixty soup plates of worn Staffordshire Imari brimmed with honest Irish broth, wine flowed freely, peat fires smoked and scented the tapestry rooms, fountains of fresh beech leaves or peacock feathers waved from gilded dairy pails in the draughty halls.

Busy, friendly folk from the kitchen and pantry mingled, danced and sang with the couple's children, Patrick and Marina Guinness, with dons from Trinity College, friends and neighbours. Bemused Americans met musicians from London, art historians, subalterns; wild and beautiful girls and boys met endless cousins, poets and painters, antique dealers, artisans, grandees, genealogists and horse-copers.

Thus were two generations infected with this generous understanding of Irish art and history. They were whirled in carriages and hearses – and occasionally motorcars – up rutted rhodedendron-choked drives to surprise dozing gentry and startle nuns in the search for tumbling Palladio, obelisks, dairies and grottoes, Chinese bridges and flinty bone houses.

Great forays of Irish Georgians were led abroad to Russia, Scandinavia, to Italy and India, introduced to international architecture and admonished to bring their own vodka or a marble egg to wrap in their flannel (no bath plugs in Russia). More intimate friends were taken to Mariga's Norwegian retreat to talk away the nightless days among the midges and the pinewoods.

Latterly, Mariga spent more time in England, exploring, encouraging, nourishing and inspiring old friends and new.

She will be remembered for her wit and zest, her energetic pursuit of beauty and her deep yet lightly-worn sense of history.

May 10 1989

PAMELA LADY GLENCONNER

PAMELA LADY GLENCONNER, who has died aged 85, was the first wife of the 2nd Lord Glenconner and a legendary character in a variety of circles.

She was born Pamela Winifred Paget on Aug 7 1903. Her father was the eccentric amateur scientist Sir Richard Paget, 2nd Bt, who had married Lady Muriel Finch-Hatton, only daughter of the 12th Earl of Winchilsea and Nottingham. Lady Muriel spent much of her life rescuing English governesses stranded in Soviet Russia. Sir Richard was often embarrassed by her exploits, and was once heard to answer the question "Are you related?" with the evasive if truthful reply, "Only by marriage."

Pamela Paget grew up in a large Victorian house in Somerset, where she had often to play the part of hapless collaborator in – or victim of – her father's experiments. She threw herself, for example, backwards off an omnibus proceeding at 30mph down Park Lane, in order to demonstrate Sir Richard's theory that the force of the air behind her would see to it that she landed safely on her feet, which she did. Sir Richard filled his three daughters' ears with treacle and invented a sign language.

In 1962 the Paget Gorman Society was formed for the promotion and development of the Paget Gorman Signed Speech. Lady Glenconner was a member of the society's committee until her death.

Pamela was an obedient daughter to both her parents.

Her mother, as well as her work with English governesses, established field hospitals on the Russian front and helped Thomas Mazaryck to found Czechoslovakia. When a telegram arrived for Pamela saying "COME TO RIGA FOR NIGHT", it never occurred to her not to do so.

Lady Glenconner inherited her mother's concern for British subjects repatriated from Russia, and in 1961 she was elected to the Russia Company, which provided financial aid to many of those repatriated in the 1930s.

Pamela Paget read English at Newnham College, Cambridge, and in 1925 she married the 2nd Lord Glenconner in Wells Cathedral. The wedding was lavish, being designed by the bridegroom's exotic brother, Stephen Tennant (*qv*), who had the bridesmaids dressed in the colours of stained glass and turned up with both a snake and tortoise concealed in his pockets.

But Lady Glenconner found herself unable to play the conventional wife to the respectable head of the somewhat wayward Tennant family into which she had married, and in 1935 she divorced the man she adored.

As well as the charitable responsibilities she inherited from her parents, which included many years' work with the Invalid Kitchens of London (which have since developed into Meals on Wheels), Lady Glenconner was a remarkable governor of the North London Polytechnic. In the 1960s she joined the sit-ins of rioting students, developing brochitis and pneumonia as a result.

Lady Glenconner lived in the Admiral's Lodge in Hampstead before moving to Campden Hill in 1949. Here she was to be found with her grumpy bearded maid, who once opened the door to a pair of royal personages, muttering, "Two *more*!"

Pamela Glenconner was a well-known and much-loved figure in the neighbourhood, running down and scrambling up the precipitous Hillsleigh Road several times a day on her straightish legs. She was wont to whistle slightly, and always wore curiously old-fashioned bonnets.

She is survived by her two sons.

May 23 1989

LAWRENCE ISHERWOOD

LAWRENCE ISHERWOOD, the artist who has died aged 72, was driven by his muse to abandon a career as a cobbler. To begin with he painted the women of his native Wigan but he later found a more lucrative market with imaginary nude studies of such public figures as Barbara Castle, Field-Marshal Viscount Montgomery of Alamein and Mary Whitehouse.

"I would rather paint the women of Wigan than any film star," he said early in his career, "particularly the old women in their shawls. Old faces have more character and colour." His work of that time showed the characters, mills and narrow streets of the town, fitfully illuminated by the eerie light of sulphur fumes.

There were hints of Isherwood's future direction in 1962, when he exhibited a portrait of Princess Margaret with the infant Viscount Linley in her arms, done entirely in blue. The other pictures in the show were painted over a series "of Lady Chatterley in the altogether," abandoned, he explained, because "no one seemed to appreciate them. They were pretty near the bone, you see."

Isherwood's first major celebrity nude was of the singer Dusty Springfield (1966), which infuriated her but was sold to a Hampshire pig farmer for 75 guineas. Inspired by his frequent difficulties with traffic wardens, he went on to paint a nude of Mrs Castle, who was then Minister of Transport, with her body decorated by such signs as "NO ENTRY," "NO WAITING" and "NO THROUGH ROAD".

A later portrait of Mrs Whitehouse showed her with five breasts; it was bought by Sir Hugh Carleton Greene, a former Director-General of the BBC, which elicited the response from its subject: "I am rather surprised that Sir Hugh wished to have a full-frontal nude of me on his wall: I think it is unreasonable." Subsequent subjects for this imaginative approach included Field-Marshal Montgomery naked save for his medals, and George Best, the footballer.

Isherwood himself was plump and bespectacled, with a blond beard and moustache.

The son of a cobbler, James Lawrence Isherwood was born at Wigan on April 7 1917 and studied art at Wigan Technical College from 1934 to 1953. To make ends meet he followed his father's trade.

In 1956 he exhibited at Wigan, to a mixed reception from the locals. Several exhibits were damaged; the titles under portraits of a Nigerian nurse and a coalminer were switched; and a miniature sculpture in wire and plaster, entitled *Wigan's Wire Women*, was entirely crushed. "Must have been somebody who didn't like modern art," Isherwood said.

His output was prolific and eventually he was able to give up cobbling, though his finances remained precarious. He often paid hotel and garage bills with his work and once offered a watercolour of Wigan jetty in payment of a court fine for speeding, though the magistrate declined the barter. In the early 1960s he was asking an average price of eight guineas for his works, though he admitted: "If anyone offers me four I snatch their hand off — it's a couple of beers and bed and breakfast, isn't ·it?"

Isherwood would paint until he had enough pictures to fill a van and would then set off on a sales tour with his mother, Lily, who frequently sat for him. He had innumerable one-man exhibitions, often at unusual sites — beneath Boadicea's statue at Westminster, for example, or in a lay-by on the East Lancashire Road. He regularly exhibited at Oxford and Cambridge, and when the Prince of Wales was an undergraduate at Trinity he bought a seascape by Isherwood.

The standard critical response to his work was epitomised by the opinion of Lt-Col A. D. Wintle (celebrated for debagging his solicitor), who championed the artist at an exhibition in a Trafalgar Square coffee house in 1959. "What I like about Isherwood's paintings," announced the monocled colonel, "is that there is no doubt about which way they hang."

In the late 1970s Isherwood travelled extensively through Europe and established a permanent exhibition of his work at Torremolinos; he also showed in Malta, where in 1976 he painted both the Prime Minister and Miss Malta.

In 1979 he opened the Isherwood Suite at a hotel in

Southport and the next year established the Isherwood Gallery in Wigan, which burned down in 1983.

June 14 1989

THE DOWAGER COUNTESS OF ELGIN AND KINCARDINE

THE DOWAGER COUNTESS OF ELGIN AND KINCARDINE, who has died aged 99, was a spirited and versatile character whose adventures evoke forgotten eras of social and political life.

As a young woman the red-haired Kitty Cochrane cut a considerable dash in the Foreign Office. Recruited as a temporary clerical assistant during the First World War, she fast rose to become head of a sub-unit which both extracted and concealed messages in letters to and from prisoners of war. She was then secretly recruited to a special division and given the responsibility for preparing the expected peace negotiations and a catalogue of all declared war aims and relevant international commercial treaties.

Miss Cochrane's *War Aims Index* proved invaluable. When she left London for Versailles in 1919 she and her colleagues were pursued by the press, whose story ran: "FOREIGN OFFICE LOVELIES LEAVE LONDON FOR PEACE CONFERENCE".

But the women were not treated as mere lovelies in

Versailles: badly housed and poorly fed, they worked round the clock to keep their masters supplied with information. Miss Cochrane was a staunch defender of her files, which were never allowed to leave the office. She had once to expel from her lair Harold Nicolson, whom she found sprawled on the floor with her precious papers scattered around him. His feeble excuse, "they are needed for the PM," cut little ice.

She did, however, once bend the rules for Lloyd George – who appointed her MBE. Later she was advanced to DBE for her sterling work on the Empire Exhibition held in Glasgow in 1938.

Katherine Elizabeth Cochrane was born on March 16 1890, the third daughter of Thomas Cochrane, MP, later 1st Lord Cochrane of Cults, by his wife, Lady Gertrude Boyle, eldest daughter of the 6th Earl of Glasgow.

Young Kitty had a boyish girlhood, divided between politics, cars, horses and golf. She was brought up with her father's political battle song in her ears:

> *Vote, vote, vote for Tommy Cochrane*
> *We'll go and fetch a gun*
> *Shoot the Liberals up the bum*
> *And vote for Tommy Cochrane in the morning.*

And she remained a steadfast Tory all her life.

Her father was the proud owner of two early motor-cars, one of which Kitty and her brothers spent hours dismantling and assembling. All three suffered from a desire to make everything connected with the new internal combustion engine go better.

Riding was also a passion from an early age. Her

138

myopia made hunting a hazardous exercise, but she was taught how to fall properly by learning to pole-vault.

When war broke out in 1914 she helped an elder sister, who was suffering from tuberculosis, to create a market garden. The sister died as the first crop of strawberries ripened, and Kitty struggled on alone – she marketed all the produce and kept a faithful financial account.

Then she did a brief stint as a nursing auxiliary, but her ways were not theirs and she left the Red Cross for the Foreign Office. Her time in Whitehall had its lighter moments: a women's team was assembled to challenge their counterparts at the War Office at cricket. "Plum" Warner acted as the coach, and they scored a glorious victory by 66 runs.

In 1921 Kitty Cochrane married Edward James Bruce, 10th Earl of Elgin and 14th Earl of Kincardine; they had six children. The banns were nearly called off on account of her grandmother's illness; but Lord Elgin, emboldened by love, acted swiftly. He had cream and porridge fed to the old lady in her Edinburgh nursing home: she made a spectacular recovery, returned home to Fife and lived for another 12 years.

As mistress of the family seat of Broomhall near Dunfermline the new Lady Elgin had occasionally to battle with obsolete practices among the domestic staff. "Why," she demanded of the housekeeper, "did mutton cutlets come up every day for breakfast?" The servant replied: "His late Lordship used often to take one."

To teach history to her children Lady Elgin engaged a local lass, Miss Marion Crawford, whom her pupils nicknamed "Cuppa". She later became famous under another sobriquet – bestowed on her by two subsequent charges, Princess Elizabeth and Princess Margaret Rose – "Crawfie".

During the 1930s Lady Elgin spent much time and energy on the voluntary agencies for the unemployed, forging a number of life-long friendships all over central Scotland. She chaired the women's section of the Empire Exhibition in 1938, had a Women's Pavilion designed by a woman architect and almost covered her costs.

? 2nd

During the First World War she remained in Fife, where her husband was Lord-Lieutenant, and became deeply involved in looking after the Polish Army, who were based there from 1941. Once again she established a market garden, and visitors – from admirals downward – were expected to spend an hour or two weeding onions and lettuce.

After the war Lady Elgin became an active force in rural politics, building cottages, sitting on hospital boards and campaigning for the wider use of solid fuel. In the 1950s she masterminded the restoration of the derelict Culross Abbey, a 17th-century ancestral house with a 16th-century garden.

Her husband died in 1968, and Lady Elgin, increasingly crippled by rheumatism, remained at Culross until 1985. She sped round her beloved garden in an electric wheelchair, pulling behind her a trailer full of garden tools. She was impossible to keep up with, and spry young companions were fast reduced to panting wrecks.

Kitty Elgin returned to Broomhall for the last years of her life, when she drew great pleasure from television.

She was apt to live a little too vicariously: one day last year, as the wind was blowing a gale in Fife, the Dowager Countess sat watching Wimbledon, and was heard calling out to her nurse: "It is over 100 degrees at Wimbledon, you had better open the window."

Lady Elgin retained her zest for life until the end — last December she remarked to the minister of the parish: "This is going to be an interesting year . . . in March I have my 99th birthday, and that will be interesting. In April my granddaughter's wedding, and then I shall look forward to my 100th birthday, but I may die before that, and that will be very interesting too.'

July 3 1989

LARRY PARNES

LARRY PARNES, who has died aged 59, emerged in the late-1950s as the pre-eminent manager and impresario of British rock and roll.

A reluctant rag-trade retailer, beguiled by Soho nightlife, Parnes stumbled into his gold-mine in 1956, when the publicist John Kennedy approached him to finance the promotion of an unknown coffee-bar skiffler called Thomas Hicks. Renamed Tommy Steele, Hicks was soon hailed as England's answer to Elvis Presley; he became an overnight "teenbeat" sensation and the role model for a string of successors, celebrated as "Larry Parnes's Stable of Stars".

Though Steele devised his own stage name, Parnes insisted on renaming such subsequent discoveries as

Marty Wilde (Reg Smith), Billy Fury (Ron Wycherly), Johnny Gentle (John Askew), Dicky Pride (Richard Knellar), Vince Eager (Roy Taylor) and Georgie Fame (Clive Powell). The Cockney guitarist Joe Brown, however, refused to become Almer Twitch.

An all-powerful figure in the burgeoning teenage music industry, Parnes's great strength was his ability to exploit star potential. A Parnes management contract practically guaranteed a recording deal, TV and radio exposure and a place in his touring shows, in which half a dozen acts would share the billing.

He had no ear for music and relied on record company arrangers to guide his artists. They often did so ineptly. But pop music was then seen merely as a stepping stone to pantomime, theatre and film: the common goal was to emulate Tommy Steele, and become an all-round entertainer.

There was an element of *Minder*'s Arthur Daley in Parnes's business approach, and his financial acuity earned him the nickname "Parnes, Shillings and Pence". In 1959, for example, he arranged a press conference for Vince Eager's 19th birthday, for which he gave him a new Triumph Herald.

"It's yours, Vince, because you've been a good boy and always been punctual for rehearsals." Eager later complained: "After everyone left, the man who had delivered the car drove it back to his showroom. Then Larry told me the whole thing was a stunt." Parnes later said of his protégé: "The boy's ingratitude appals me."

In the mid-1960s tastes in pop music underwent a dramatic shift. Parnes's supremacy was ended by the

Beatles, whose potential he had badly underestimated some years earlier when he grudgingly hired them to make their first foray beyond Liverpool, backing Johnny Gentle on a lacklustre tour of the Scottish hinterlands.

Laurence Maurice Parnes was born at Willesden, London, in 1930. One of his uncles was a pre-war music hall star called Len Young the Singing Fool.

Parnes left school at 16 and began working in shops, "picking up pins with a magnet". By the age of 18 he was running his own dress shop in Romford, with a half share of a club in Romilly Street and a stake in a touring play called *The House of Shame*.

After a decade as the Svengali of pop, Parnes was eclipsed by the new Merseyside groups and broke up with Steele, who had been his principal earner. In 1967 he announced that he had "outgrown" pop and would be devoting himself to the theatre.

The next year he put on *Fortune and Men's Eyes*, a play about homosexuality in a Canadian prison. After losing £5,000 on the venture he said: "I'm going back to staging family entertainment."

In 1972 he bought a 12-year lease of the Cambridge Theatre, where he concentrated on musicals. Alongside the management of John Currie, the ice skater, this occupied him until 1981, when he retired from show business after a brain haemorrhage.

Parnes is said to have renamed some of his stars for their sexual potential, but though he undoubtedly adored the company of young men he was circumspect about mixing business with pleasure. The greatest loves of his life were two Alsatian dogs, Prince and Duke, whose cremated remains were prominently displayed in his South Kensington penthouse.

August 7 1989

JULIAN "MO" ANTHOINE

JULIAN ANTHOINE, who has died aged 50, was one of the best loved characters in modern British mountaineering; his Rabelaisian approach to life sometimes disconcerted even hardened fellow climbers.

He began climbing in the 1950s with a select group of friends known as the Wallasey Mountaineering Club whose bacchanals soon became legendary. "Mo" Anthoine was himself the inaugurator of their regular concluding ritual, the so-called "dance of the flaming arsehole" – an exhibition which impressed itself forcibly on anyone who witnessed it.

In August, 1966, after climbing the Old Brenva route on Mont Blanc, Anthoine survived the great storm which swept the mountain and claimed many lives, including those of two of his companions. The other mountaineers were reduced to awed silence by the mischievous manner in which Anthoine, at the height of the gale, pranced around outside the snowhole near the mountain summit and invited the Almighty to "either crank up the wind machine another notch or two or *fuck off*".

He was in some demand as a stunt man and more than once stood in for merely mortal actors – his short powerful physique passed for that of Jeremy Irons in *The Mission* and Sylvester Stallone in *Rambo III*.

Julian Anthoine was born in 1939 and educated at King Charles I School in Kidderminster where his father was a carpet designer. He started rock climbing in Snowdonia and soon became one of the leading pioneers of the 1950s.

His first ascents – most notably that of the Groove of Llech Ddu – include some of the great climbs of the area. When it came to describing the tactics used on the climbs Anthoine eschewed the self-inflating duplicity which was then the norm in such accounts.

From 1961 to 1964 Anthoine and his travelling companion Foxey – a former boxer – went on a world tour which left a trail of devastation and potential diplomatic incidents across five continents. He returned, slightly chastened, to Britain and enrolled at a teacher training course at Coventry College of Education. It was here that he met Jackie Philippe, whom he later married.

Anthoine coped admirably with savage weather conditions more than once in his mountaineering career. In 1964 he took the Comici route on the Cima Grande di Lavaredo with the writer Al Alvarez, and was caught out in a storm high on the face. Ill-equipped, soaked and frozen, they survived a fearful bivouac and climbed to the summit in dreadful conditions the following day.

Alvarez's account of this experience, thinly veiled as fiction, was later published in the *New Yorker*. Last year Alvarez published a deeply felt tribute to Anthoine entitled *Feeding the Rat: Profile of a Climber*.

His self-reliance and strong vein of anarchical irreverence were sufficient to distance Anthoine from the new professional conformity which marked out Himalayan mountaineering in the 1970s. The smooth men who ran their slick, big money operations in the mountains had no desire to prejudice them by inviting along a rebel who, however reliable he might be in the survival stakes, might not prove so at the press conference or the official function. Anthoine was quite without the gift of glibness.

But successful expeditions to Roraima in the Guyanan jungle in 1973, and to the Trango Tower in the Karakoram in 1976 – on both of which Anthoine distinguished himself and the latter of which he led – made his presence increasingly difficult to ignore.

In 1977 he was invited, along with his old friend Clive Rowlands, on an expedition to the difficult, unclimbed 24,000ft peak of the Ogre in the Karakoram. His role was as a cameraman, to record the activities of Chris Bonington and Doug Scott.

His presence was fortuitous, for shortly after reaching the summit Scott fell, breaking both ankles; a little later Bonington fell, breaking two ribs; a prolonged storm blew up. Only through Anthoine's great reserves of skill, experience and strength were the two famous mountaineers brought safely down from the mountain.

When the expedition returned to England the media contrived to write Anthoine out of the "celebrities' feat of endurance" saga, a process he accepted with his customary sharp humour, but without rancour.

Anthoine accompanied two expeditions to the northeast ridge of Mount Everest in the 1980s, the second of them taking place shortly after a major operation to remove a brain tumour. This condition was almost certainly caused by his employment, 25 years previously, in an asbestos mine in Australia.

In true amateur tradition he financed his travels from

the proceeds of the mountaineering equipment company, Snowdon Mouldings, which he had founded with his wife, who survives him with their son and daughter.

Anthoine was the staunchest upholder of the great traditions of British climbing, and the most merciless critic of those who traduced them; he was also a master of earthy and waspish badinage, and the kindest and best of friends. With his death, a dimension of sanity and sheer fun has gone which British climbing could ill afford to lose.

August 17 1989

ANN GEORGE

ANN GEORGE, the actress who has died aged 86, earned a huge following for her distinctly idiosyncratic performance as Amy Turtle, the obnoxious factotum in the long-running ITV series, *Crossroads*.

First seen as a shop assistant in the emporium run by the Midlands motel owner Meg Richardson's sister, Kitty Jarvis, in the mid-1960s, Amy Turtle was subsequently moved to the motel itself as a charlady. The bustling, bespectacled beldam of diminutive stature with an impenetrable "Brummie" accent soon developed into the busybody that viewers loved to hate.

For connoisseurs of *Crossroads*, Miss George's somewhat erratic grasp of the script lent the programme a peculiar charm. It was thought that Julie Walters's wickedly funny characterisation of Mrs Overall in *Acorn Antiques*, the spoof "soap" on Victoria Wood's television programme, may have owed something to the Turtle *persona*.

In any event, Amy Turtle became one of *Crossroads'* legendary characters, indeed virtually its "Second Lady" after Meg Richardson (played by Noele Gordon). The part was suitably built up and Amy found herself in some singular situations.

She was, for example, accused of shoplifting, and imprisoned. And in one episode she was even accused of being the notorious Russian spy "Amelia Turtlovski".

But in February 1975, Miss George was abruptly dropped from the show ("I heard the awful news from the wardrobe mistress," she recalled. "She just told me to clear out my things as I wouldn't be coming back"). The storyline intimated that Amy Turtle had gone to visit her nephew in Texas. Nothing more was heard of her, however, and some viewers organised a "Bring Back Amy" campaign.

Then, in 1987, Miss George was unexpectedly invited to rejoin the cast of *Crossroads* and Amy Turtle made the occasional appearance before the programme was finally taken off the air in 1988.

Miss George was born Ann Snape at Erdington, Birmingham, in 1903 and trained as an actress and singer. She appeared in operettas and musicals and at one stage was a member of the D'Oyly Carte Company.

On Amy Turtle's return to the *Crossroads* set after an absence of nearly a dozen years the cast and crew burst into applause, reducing the much-loved actress to tears. In retirement Miss George carried on entertaining fellow pensioners at a club near her Birmingham home.

Her first husband died in 1962. She is survived by

her second husband, Gordon Buckingham, and by a son of the first marriage.

September 12 1989

LT-COL SIR WALTER BROMLEY-DAVENPORT

LT-COL SIR WALTER BROMLEY-DAVENPORT, the former Conservative MP for Knutsford who has died aged 86, epitomised the qualities of continuity and public service which have been the squirearchy's special contribution to Britain's social fabric over the centuries.

By the time he completed his 25 years' service in the Commons in 1970, however, Sir Walter was one of a diminishing number of "Knights of the Shire" at Westminster.

During the years he adorned the back benches with his Brigade of Guards tie, he was reputed to have had the loudest voice in Parliament, even if its stentorian tones from a sedentary position – more closely akin to barks and growls than accepted human speech – tended to be employed in interjections or in questions rather than speeches.

Bromley-Davenport – who had, perhaps, a somewhat *simpliste* view of politics – laid no claims to intellectual prowess or political ambition. His vocal contributions in the chamber generally reflected either shock at what he perceived to be the latest socialist outrage, or unqualified loyalty to his own party.

Behind such sentiments, though, was a robust common sense and good nature. His overriding preoccupations were his constituents, his beloved county of Cheshire and the management of the Capesthorne estate, with its vast Victorian pile by Blore and Salvin and its own theatre. The felon with a rope round his neck in the family crest is depicted on the staircase at Capesthorne with the features of the arch-enemy Gladstone.

Bromley-Davenport resigned the one office he held — as a junior whip from 1948 to 1951 — in order to devote himself more fully to those interests.

Walter Henry Bromley-Davenport was born on Sept 15 1903, and educated at Malvern. He served in the Grenadier Guards from 1922 to 1937, and in 1926 became welterweight boxing champion of the British Army; he later fought as a middle and light heavyweight.

At the outbreak of the Second World War in 1939 he raised and commanded the 5th Battalion of the Cheshire Regiment.

He held the Territorial Decoration, was appointed a Deputy Lieutenant of Cheshire in 1949 and became a member of the British Boxing Board of Control in 1953. He was knighted in 1961 and a year later survived a stabbing attack on him by a madman.

An enthusiastic cricketer, he was a stalwart of the Lords and Commons XI and was credited with "a deadly bowling style".

In 1933 he married Lenette, daughter of Joseph Jeanes of Philadelphia, who predeceased him by a few days. They had a son and daughter.

Julian Critchley writes: Walter Bromley-Davenport was a great Parliamentary character. Noisy, opinionated and robust of opinion, he was a low comedian every bit as much at home on the boards of his great house, where amateur theatricals were the order of the day, as he was in the Commons.

He would tell Labour MPs to take their hands out of their pockets (the results varied); and at meetings where there was too much noise he would bellow in military style: "Quiet! You young officers."

A story is told of his time in the whips' office when he was supposed to have caught sight of a colleague sneaking off home before the 10 o'clock vote. Having failed to attract his attention by shouting, Walter pursued him down the corridor and booted him up the backside: it turned out to be the Belgian ambassador.

Walter Bromley-Davenport was much loved by both his constituents and his colleagues. He was one of the class and generation that saw service in Parliament as an extension of its sense of social obligation.

He was as loyal as he was obstreperous, as cheerful as he was hard-working.

December 28 1989

LADY BONHAM CARTER

LADY BONHAM CARTER, who has died aged 96, was a remarkable patron of the arts, a tireless supporter of good causes and a perennial presence at cultural gatherings.

Charlotte Bonham Carter's ubiquity became part of

folklore: people across the British Isles would swear they had all seen her bent, benevolent figure – clad in her customarily eccentric clothes – contemporaneously at multifarious events.

The only daughter of a colonel in the King's Royal Rifle Corps and a scion of the Ogilvy Baronets of Inverquharity, Charlotte Helen Ogilvy was born in London on Aug 22 1893. She was educated at Miss Wolff's School, Eastbourne, and then "finished" in Dresden.

She came out as débutante in 1912 and enjoyed the social round of *la belle époque*, retaining vivid memories of dancing at the newly-built Ritz Hotel to Casani's orchestra.

During the First World War she served in the Foreign Office. At one stage she was seconded to the infant MI5, where she was involved in the tracking down of Lenin before the Russian Revolution as he crossed Germany.

In 1919 she was assigned to the British Delegation at the Paris Peace Conference. Afterwards she occasionally attended lectures at the London School of Economics. In 1926 she became a founding director of the Ballet Rambert.

In 1927 she married Sir Edgar Bonham Carter, one of three knights among 11 brothers, and a brother-in-law of Lady Violet Bonham Carter. Sir Edgar, a legal public servant and chairman of the First Garden City (Letchworth), died in 1956.

In the 1930s Lady Bonham Carter gained a pilot's licence and on the outbreak of the Second World War she joined the WAAF, being commissioned in 1941 and working in the photographic interpretation department.

She also served in the Ministry of Economic Warfare and afterwards presided over the Women's Advisory Housing council.

In 1947 she inherited the estate of Binsted Wyck in Hampshire, where she became a dedicated gardener and dairy farmer. She was a county councillor and chairman of the Hampshire planning committee, as well as sitting on the Paddington Borough Council.

Passionately fond of music, Lady Bonham Carter was a champion of the Aldeburgh, Windsor and other festivals and gave many treasures to museums. Her other special interests included archaeology and travel.

In 1978 her devoted circle of friends commissioned a portrait of her by Peter Greenham which now hangs in the Tate Gallery.

Nathalie Brooke writes: Charlotte Bonham Carter, for anyone who had the joy and privilege of knowing her, was one of the Immortals.

For who else remained who had actually been present at performances of Diaghilev's *Ballet Russe* before the First World War? Who else had visited Fortuny's establishment in Venice and bought dresses there from the *couturier* himself? Who else had attended every artistic, musical and learned event for the past 75 years?

Charlotte was possessed of the greatest curiosity and interest in all aspects of *La Vie Humaine* – but she did not remain buried in the past. For her, the new, the forward-looking and, above all, young people, were overriding interests.

It was for this reason that she will be remembered as one of the last great hostesses, both in London and in

Hampshire, at her celebrated "aconite" lunches in February – for her love of bringing together of people of all ages, all professions, all ways of life.

All learned, musical and amenity societies and charities will feel her loss most keenly. There was never an appeal unanswered, never a charity auction without a gift from her, never an event for which tickets were not taken.

The most vivid memories of this indomitable, unique personality remain. Standing in the crush bar of the Royal Opera House at some glittering first night, saluting all her countless friends; apparently fast asleep in a drawing room filled with people, yet suddenly waking to make the most penetrating and apposite comment on the conversation.

And, finally, a fragile, tiny body being carried off the Royal Yacht in teeming rain by a burly sailor.

December 28 1989

LORD PAGET OF NORTHAMPTON

LORD PAGET OF NORTHAMPTON, who has died aged 81, was firmly in the mould of the great English eccentrics: a rich foxhunting squire, lawyer, artist, sailor and, as Reginald Paget, Labour MP for Northampton from 1945 to 1974, when he was created a Life Peer. "Reggie" Paget looked and sounded every inch the country gentleman and represented much that his fellow socialists abhorred: his politics, on the other hand, were anathema to his peers in the Shires. Yet the Pytchley made him their MFH, and few Labour MPs raised an eyebrow when on occasion he arrived in the Division Lobby fresh from the hunting field, still attired in scarlet and breeches.

For what no one could question was his passionate determination to fight injustice; he was instinctively on the side of the underdog and unshakeable once his feelings were aroused. A striking and highly controversial example of this was when he undertook, without fee, the defence of Field Marshal Von Manstein before a War Crimes Tribunal in 1949. The public mood had little sympathy for Manstein's fate. But Paget believed that a serving officer in the field should be distinguished from Nazi war criminals; and his sense of justice was offended by the absence of proper defence facilities for him.

Paget was tall, dignified and spoke in grave ponderous tones – he had the record of being the Commons' slowest speaker – as if each judgment was engraved on stone. His pronouncements were often quite incalculable – he once advocated executing an IRA internee for each person killed by an IRA bomb – and his tongue could have a vitriolic edge.

During the debate on the Obscene Publications Bill in 1964, he said that there was no greater source of brutality, sadism and murder than the Bible, and that he thought it better to leave alone the job of deciding which books were suitable for reading.

Paget staunchly defended Profumo as a gallant officer, whatever his other misdemeanours; and when Lord Hailsham launched a moralistic attack on Profumo, Paget attacked him as "an unctuous beast [giving] a virtuoso performance in the art of kicking a fallen friend in the guts".

Harold Wilson, whom Paget originally much admired, also felt the lash of his tongue: "A conman . . . all the troubles of the Government can be summed up in one word – Wilson."

Paget had only a brief spell as a front bench spokesman on defence and, inexplicably, was not given office by Wilson in 1964, an omission which undoubtedly wounded him. He subsequently resigned the Whip over Rhodesian sanctions, although he remained loyal to Labour on most issues.

Paget had owlish eyebrows and a puckish sense of humour, speaking with a slight catch in his voice. Harold Macmillan once remarked: "I always enjoy Paget's interventions but never know whether they are epigrams or paradoxes."

He spoke often and vigorously in the House of Lords, notably on the advisability of restoring National Service; and in 1987, when a butterfly collector employed a swordstick to fight off a drunken attacker on the London Underground, Paget appealed for donations to pay off the £3,000 legal fees.

Reginald Thomas Paget was born on Sept 2 1908 at Sulby Hall, Northants, the son of a foxhunting Conservative MP who in 1952 was killed out hunting with the Fernie – "a death my father would have chosen".

He was educated at Eton and Trinity College, Cambridge, and when a seat fell vacant at Market Harborough in his final year, his father suggested that he follow the last five generations of Pagets and become a Tory MP.

Instead Paget decided to spend an extra year at Cambridge learning more about politics.

It was the time of mass unemployment at home and the rise of fascism in Europe. Paget sat at the feet of Maynard Keynes – whom he described as the greatest man he ever met – and was converted to socialism.

He dallied for a time with Communism, but unlike some of his Trinity contemporaries, he never succumbed to it: he was always a patriot and a democrat. His father did not demur when the young Paget announced his conversion, beyond suggesting that he had better start earning a living; he was called to the Bar in 1934 and practised with some success until the beginning of the Second World War.

Although as a young man he had broken his neck and other bones in a bad fall, Paget joined the RNVR and served as a lieutenant in command of a landing flotilla until he was invalided out in 1943 with severe gout.

He had stood for Northampton in 1935, and in 1945 he won the seat and began a distinctly idiosyncratic Commons career.

His great love was hunting and he wrote lyrically of "The cry of hounds, the smell of the woods, the flicker of white that ripples along a pack as it turns to the line, all these things delight with a hereditary joy."

Another enthusiasm was painting, which he took up during the war when his ship was detained in Freetown harbour for six months; he improvised the necessary equipment by borrowing an iodine brush from the ship's doctor and a few pots of paint from the maintenance crew.

In 1988 he celebrated his eighth decade with an exhibition of unpretentious landscapes at the Fine Arts

Gallery. Richard Dorment described the exhibition in The Daily Telegraph as "on the whole, a very impressive debut". Paget was modest about his achievement: "If you get spots of the right colour on the right places, you have a picture."

He also wrote three books: *Manstein – Campaigns and Trial* (1951); *Hanged – and Innocent?* (about the Craig and Bentley Case, with S.S. Silverman, 1958); and *The Human Journey* (1979), an extraordinary history of the human race, written with a lordly disdain for correct dates but full of diverting aperçus.

Paget married, in 1931, Sybil Gibbons; they adopted two sons and two daughters.

January 4 1990

LADY EVE BALFOUR

LADY EVE BALFOUR, who has died aged 91, was the founder of the Soil Association and the instigator of the organic movement in British farming.

Although she did not expect to see any results from her work during her own lifetime, the indefatigable Lady Eve lived to see the principle of holistic agriculture pass from ridicule to wide acceptance.

Evelyn Barbara Balfour was born in London on July 16, 1898, and spent the first two years of her life in Dublin, where her father, Gerald Balfour, MP, was the Chief Secretary for Ireland. Her mother, Lady Betty, was the eldest daughter of the 1st Earl of Lytton, the poet and Viceroy of India.

In 1930 Gerald Balfour succeeded his brother, the former Prime Minister A. J. Balfour in the Earldom of Balfour, and his fourth daughter duly became styled Lady Eve.

She was educated privately and divided her childhood between Fisher's Hill, near Woking, the house her uncle Edwin Lutyens had designed for her parents, and Whittingehame in East Lothian, the Scottish seat of A. J. Balfour.

The bachelor "A.J." made Whittingehame home to his two married brothers, their wives and 11 nieces and nephews, who knew the politician as "Nunkie". Lady Eve later recalled that her older cousins, Nunkie, and the fascinating conversation of the guests at his house parties, were the most significant elements of her education.

At the age of 12 she decided to become a farmer and in 1915, since she was too young for war work, went to Reading University to read for a diploma in agriculture. In the last year of the First World War – with an "official age" of 25 – she took over a farm, training Land Army girls on behalf of the Women's War Agricultural Committee.

In 1919 she bought New Bells Farm at Haughley, a village between Stowmarket and Bury St Edmunds in Suffolk. It was there in the 1930s that she became a champion of the local farmers, who were fighting for justice in the Tithe Wars.

Originally one-tenth of the value of certain crops, tithes were levied on values established in 1836, when the sale price of the produce was three times greater than in the years of the Depression a century later. Lady Eve's pamphlet and her evidence to the Royal Commission on

Tithe were influential in changing the law to end this punishing tax.

In 1938 Lord Lymington (later the 9th Earl Portsmouth) published *Famine in England* and introduced Lady Eve to the relationship between different agricultural practices, healthy soil and the "wholeness" and health-giving properties of food. Her subsequent research led her to write a now classic work, *The Living Soil* (1943), which has run to nine editions.

She discovered that by eating compost-grown vegetables in a mainly lacto-vegetarian diet she could cure her own recurring colds, rheumatism and tooth decay. Although throughout her life Lady Eve held tenaciously to her own objectives, she had a flexibility of mind and understanding that made her always receptive to other points of view.

In 1939 she initiated the Haughley Experiment at New Bells Farm to compare organic and inorganic methods of farming. Lady Eve published the findings in 1975 as an addendum to the reprint of *The Living Soil*.

They provide a unique research document, particularly important today when, as the Environment Editor of *The Daily Telegraph*, Charles Clover, has put it, "organic and low-intensity farming are seen as the provinces of the prescient and not the cranky".

Lady Eve never liked to stick to just one track. In her early days in Suffolk in the 1920s she founded a dance band and herself played a moody saxophone. The evenings at her dance club at the Great White Horse in Ipswich were so successful that the band was booked for a week's appearance at Sherry's, the well-known Brighton dance hall.

In the 1930s, when flying lessons cost half-a-crown (12½p), she passed her pilot's licence. Only the arrival of the Second World War, and the fact that she was too old to deliver aircraft from factories to airfields, made her regretfully give up. She also crewed enthusiastically for her brother when he sailed to Scandinavia each summer.

As E. B. Balfour she wrote three detective novels with Beryl Hearnden. The most successful, *Paper Moon*, was translated into several languages.

In the late 1940s and early 1950s Lady Eve undertook extensive lecture tours in America, Australia and the Continent on behalf of the Soil Association. She also visited Israel as a guest of that country's Ministry of Agriculture.

In 1963 she moved to Theberton near the Suffolk coast, but continued to visit Haughley three times a week. She finally retired in 1984 although she cultivated a large organic garden until the end.

Last year, when she was 90, Lady Eve was the subject of BBC Radio 4's *Prophets Returned*, in which she discussed her life's work. Later she remarked: "I am just surprised to see that what I stood for all my life is no longer derided but more or less accepted."

Lady Eve was appointed OBE in the New Year's Honours List of 1990. She never married.

January 16 1990

PAUL POTTS

PAUL POTTS, who has died aged 79, was a bohemian poet and critic, best known for his anguished erotic memoir, *Dante Called You Beatrice*.

His talents were by no means inconsiderable, but Potts's output was undeniably exiguous. He preferred to haunt the pubs and clubs of Soho and Fitzrovia, where he discussed what it meant to be "a writer" and expatiated on the spiritual benefits of socialism. "Freedom," he would declare, "is a love affair with the whole human race, with all humanity, with everybody."

Dante Called You Beatrice (1960), though, was inspired by a much mourned inability to engage in less generalised love affairs. "I don't seem to have much talent for anything except perhaps for being hurt," Potts wrote. "I can never act – only react." He was similarly rueful about his professional life, noting that "I have found pawn-brokers much kinder than editors."

Despite manifest faults of mood and construction, the book makes moving and amusing reading. Its admirers have included Mr Michael Foot, and in the mid-1970s it was set as an A-level English text – an honour which Potts referred to as "a solitary feather in a rather dilapidated cap".

Paul Hugh Howard Potts was born at Datchet, Berks, on July 19 1911, to a Canadian father and an Irish mother. He was brought up in Canada but educated at Stonyhurst and was happiest when staying with his maternal grandmother in Co Mayo.

The adult Potts was clearly discernible in the boy. In his autobiography he described how he used to dispense bounty to the poor, on one occasion taking a joint of cold roast beef from the larder and giving it to a family of vegetarians.

In 1933 he came to London, where he immediately found a home among the Left-wing *literati*. He became a passionate supporter of such causes as Fenianism and Zionism. Poems began to dribble from his pen, and his first book of verse, *Instead of a Sonnet* (1944), was followed by articles in the "little magazines" of the day.

An early patron was Tambimuttu, the Indian litterateur and editor of *Poetry London*, who enjoyed a brief fame in the 1940s; and his cricle included the poets Dylan Thomas and Hugh MacDiarmid.

George Orwell was also a friend, and in a wireless broadcast once contrasted Potts with W. H. Davies. Davies, said Orwell, was "a proletarian, but he would not be called a proletarian writer: Paul Potts would be called a proletarian writer, but he is not a proletarian."

Potts was constitutionally incapable of leading a settled existence or earning a conventional living. On the outbreak of the Second World War he volunteered as a glider pilot and joined the Commandos, but his physical frailty intervened and he became the CO's batman.

After the war Potts went to Palestine to watch the Jewish state being born. He hoped to fight for it, but there is no evidence that he did so. His enthusiasm for both Ireland and Israel are celebrated in a meandering volume *To Keep a Promise* (1970) – though he later became disenchanted with Zionism. He followed this with *Invitation to a Sacrament* (1973), and five years later his poetry was republished with some new additions – the only one of his books that is still in print.

In his later years the indigent Potts lived largely on his memories, occasionally contributing book reviews to publications including *The Sunday Telegraph* and the *Tablet*. He was a notorious cadger of books from the offices of weekly magazines – though unlike most such cadgers he never pretended that he was going to review the book before he sold it. He also received a small gratuity from the Royal Literary Fund, and enjoyed intermittent handouts from his friends.

A big, untidy, handsome man with a bald patch and a broken nose, he continued to frequent the pubs of Islington, Fitzrovia and especially Soho, and was often to be seen at the "French Pub" in Dean Street. He was an habitué, too, of the Colony Room Club, though no favourite of its formidable châtelaine, Muriel Belcher, as he grew ever more argumentative, shabby and malodorous.

His irascibility, however, was never spiteful or malicious. Potts talked much of fairness and justice, and underlying his personal shortcomings was a genuine decency which complemented his equally genuine, if modest, literary gifts.

Potts's end was a characteristic one for a man who metaphorically wore an "Old Sohovian" tie (he was never known to wear a visible one): he died after setting fire to his bed.

January 30 1990

Laura Duchess
of Marlborough

LAURA DUCHESS OF MARLBOROUGH, who has died aged 74, was a lady of remarkable panache, capable of taking such varied roles as chatelaine of Himley and Blenheim, nurse, showjumper, *couturier* and author in her elegant stride without ever losing her sympathetic warmth and touching vulnerability.

Altogether Laura Marlborough was one of the most stylish and individual survivors of pre-war Society and maintained to the last the authentic atmosphere of a now vanished era. A friend of the Windsors, of Lady Diana Cooper, and the rakish set of aristocrats represented by the late Duke of Marlborough and the late Earl of Dudley (both of whom she married), she enjoyed a reputation as a *femme fatale*.

Although not a conventional "beauty", she possessed singular *chic* and "attack", wit, intelligence and a distinct quality of sex appeal – which inspired many men to behave in ways that in retrospect she found humorous. Her brother, the writer Hugo Charteris, used her looks and character for "Poppy" in his novel, *The Coat*: "Those big brown bedroom-eyes appealed with a look of waif-like experience that lay too deep for her own or anyone else's knowledge, a look such as haunts the eyes of a London chimp wrapped in the *Daily Mirror* and December fog."

In contrast to her sister Ann, the legendary political

hostess who married Lords O'Neill and Rothermere and Ian Fleming, Laura eschewed public "importance", preferring to lead a freer and more informal life. As their aunt, Kathleen Duchess of Rutland put it: "Of the two sisters, Laura was the one with the heart".

Besides being a noted gardener, she created, with innate good taste, delightfully *soignée* and comfortable homes and ran them with relaxed élan, most notaby Hertfordshire House, near Penn.

She was born Frances Laura Charteris on Aug 10, 1915, the second daughter of Capt Guy Charteris of the Scots Guards, himself a younger son of the 11th Earl of Wemyss and 7th Earl of March. Her mother, Frances, who died when Laura was 10, was a Tennant, a sister of Margot Asquith.

Thus her childhood was spent at the beautiful honey-coloured Cotswold manor house of Stanway, where with Charteris and Asquith cousins she took part in plays specially written by J. M. Barrie, and at Gosford in Scotland.

She married four times, first to the 2nd Viscount Long in 1933, when she was scarcely out of the schoolroom; they had a daughter. After a spell in New Zealand the marriage broke down and they were divorced in 1942. David Long was killed in action in 1944.

In 1943 Lady Long married Lord Dudley. During the Second World War she served as a nurse in Birmingham, and later set up a Red Cross Hospital at the Ward family seat of Himley Hall. She also had to entertain a great number of distinguished visitors, including Gen. de Gaulle, Lord Wavell and the Duke of Kent (shortly before his death on active service).

During these years Randolph Churchill was also in love with her. His last wife, June, recalled that Randolph wanted Laura by his bedside when he died.

After the war the Dudleys lived at Ednam Lodge near Sunningdale, where in a sensational and still unsolved burglary the Duchess of Windsor's jewellery was stolen in 1946. Laura Dudley launched herself on a new career as a racehorse owner and then as a fearless show-jumper, competing all over Britain and the continent.

Restless years followed the breakdown of her marriage with Dudley, during part of which she lived with the actor and songwriter Anthony Pelissier. She was now obliged to earn her living and landed a job with Christian Dior in London before opening a chain of dress shops, called Contessa, which prospered due to her inherent good taste and a natural flair for business.

The happiest years of her life were those spent with Michael Canfield, the American publisher, adopted son of Cass Canfield of Harper Row. The Duke of Windsor believed him to be the natural son of the Duke of Kent by an American girl.

Laura met Canfield in 1958, soon after the breakdown of his marriage with Lee Bouvier, younger sister of Jackie Kennedy. Some years Laura's junior, he was dubbed by William Douglas Home "The Adorable Canfield" – an inscription which now adorns his gravestone.

The Canfields created a fine garden at Herfordshire House and wintered in Barbados, but their idyllic marriage was shattered by his sudden death when flying home from America for Christmas in 1969.

Her later years were tinged with sadness. Eric Dudley, by then an unhappy tax exile, died six days after Canfield;

Hugo Charteris died in 1970 after a long battle with cancer.

In 1972 Laura married, as his second wife, the 10th Duke of Marlborough. "Bert" had known her since the 1930s and had always kept her photograph in his study, but her sojourn at Blenheim was of the briefest duration as the Duke died three months after their wedding.

The Duchess then took a house at Winkfield, where, in a fit of depression, she attempted suicide. Subsequently she was forced to spend some weeks in a pyschiatric home in Ascot.

But with characteristic resilience, she created a new life, split between her London flat in Montagu Square and a country house near Amersham, which eventually had to be sold when a motorway threatened to bisect its garden.

Television viewers were afforded a memorable vignette of the Duchess's style and humour when a documentary on the police featured a "stake-out" at the house after a tip-off about a burglary.

Some of the stuffier elements in Society were shocked by the Duchess's undeniably racy memoirs, *Laughter from a Cloud* (1980), though many less hidebound readers admired her refreshingly human candour. Out of the success of her book emerged a curious twilight romance.

The veteran historian, Sir Arthur Bryant, was chosen to speak at her Foyle's Literary Luncheon and soon afterwards they announced their engagement in the Court pages – though, in the event the marriage never took place. In recent years she had been writing an affectionate account of the animals in her life.

Ill health dogged the Duchess's last years, but she

continued to travel and spent several summers at the Hotel Cipriani in Venice. Her standards never lowered. Each year she bought a new collection of *haute couture* clothes, and her London flat was always filled with flowers.

February 21 1990

THE COUNTESS OF DERBY

THE COUNTESS OF DERBY, who has died aged 69, was the wife of the 18th Earl of Derby, the former Lord-Lieutenant of Lancashire and a prominent figure on the Turf.

Lady Derby herself took a passionate interest in racing, for which she had a sound instinct. The best horse to run in her name was her home-bred filly Tahilla, who won seven races, including the Sceptre Stakes at Doncaster.

Away from the racecourse, Isabel Derby lived life far removed from the vulgar attentions of the media. She carried out many duties in the North-West where she was an outstandingly diligent magistrate and honorary Colonel of the 319th (East Lancashire) Battalion of the Women's Royal Army Corps (TA).

But in 1952 she was involved in a much-publicised incident at the Stanley seat of Knowsley, when a footman went berserk with a Schmeisser gun (apparently acquired, with ammunition, for £3 and a pair of trousers) and fired

37 shots on the evening of November 5. Lady Derby was dining alone in the smoking room when the footman, smoking a cigarette, unexpectedly entered from the library.

Lady Derby rose from her chair and faced him, and then noticed that he was holding a machine gun which was pointed directly at her. The footman told her to turn round and then he shot her in the neck.

Leaving Lady Derby for dead, the footman next killed both the butler and the under-butler and wounded Lord Derby's valet and the French chef. The bullet which entered the back of Lady Derby's neck came out just below her left ear.

The footman was found guilty of murder but insane. The case caused a sensation, and one of its aspects which particularly absorbed the public in the austere post-war world was the amplitude of servants in the Derbys' employ. The then Prime Minister, Winston Churchill, is said to have remarked, "It's nice to hear of a house where you can still get a left and right at a butler."

But it was a terrible experience for Lady Derby and her staff – and certainly no laughing matter. In her memoirs Laura Duchess of Marlborough (*qv*) recalled how when she was travelling with Isabel Derby on the Golden Arrow the next year and a waiter in the dining car turned away from them, Lady Derby suddenly said in a ringing voice: "I suppose the bugger's going to shoot me now."

Isabel Milles-Lade was born on Oct 18 1920, the youngest daughter of Henry Milles-Lade, of Faversham, Kent, who was in turn the youngest son of the 1st Earl Sondes. In 1941 her brother succeeded to the Earldom of

Sondes, and the next year she and her sisters were granted the style and precedents of the daughters of an Earl.

In 1948 Lady Isabel married the 18th Earl of Derby in Westminster Abbey. The ceremony was attended by King George VI and Queen Elizabeth, Princess Elizabeth, Princess Margaret and other members of the Royal Family.

Lord Derby's father, Lord Stanley, a Minister in Neville Chamberlain's administration, had died 10 years earlier (in the lifetime of his own father, the 17th Earl, the celebrated statesman known as the "King of Lancashire").

The loyal Lancastrian's toast was, "God Save the Earl of Derby and the King!" At one stage the Stanleys enjoyed sovereign rights over the Isle of Man and in the early 19th century the brilliant Edward Stanley (grandson of the 12th Earl, who instituted the Derby at Epsom) declined the throne of Greece with the observation: "Don't they know I'm going to be Earl of Derby?"

In 1949 Lord and Lady Derby opened Knowsley, which had been enlarged and improved by the 17th Earl in 1912, to the public. After the shooting incident, the Derbys carried out a further reconstruction of the great house to the designs of Claud Phillimore.

Then, in the 1960s, Lord and Lady Derby decided to move to a new house in the vast park at Knowsley, a wonderfully rural oasis amid the urban sprawl of Liverpool. This neo-Georgian building was also designed by Phillimore and excited the interests of 1960s sociologists by having no fewer than 10 servants' bedrooms.

The Derbys, who were a notably close couple, continued to maintain a remarkably grand way of life into the last decade of the 20th century while upholding the best aristocratic traditions of courtesy and concern for others; their loyal staff were utterly devoted to them.

Isabel Derby was a lady of great vitality and humour; direct and of decided views but with no "side" to her.

Lady Derby is survived by her husband. There were no children of the marriage.

March 22 1990

ARTHUR LUNN

ARTHUR LUNN, who has died aged 93, served in Fortnum & Mason for nearly 60 years and built up a list of customers – or "friends" as he liked to think of them – that embraced many crowns and coronets.

The original Mr Fortnum was a footman to Queen Anne. Given his start by the perk of selling off candle-ends, he then set up as a grocer with a shopkeeper friend called Mason. Nearly three centuries later Fortnum & Mason are festooned with Royal Warrants; and Lunn was the man with whom the royal shoppers liked to do business.

"Where's little Mr Lunn?" the King of Norway would ask, and Mr Lunn would duly appear to assist in the choice of Christmas presents. Queen Elizabeth the Queen Mother was another customer. Lunn could remember her arriving with Queen Mary and a host of retainers soon after he had been taken on at the shop. It was the beginning of a long acquaintance, and in 1980 the Queen

Mother invited him to Clarence House for her 80th birthday party.

As for the Queen, Arnold Lunn never actually *served* her but, as he said, "I've smiled at her, you know." Over the years he honed the technique of receiving royalty in the shop: two steps backwards at the regal approach, then one step forward and "At your service, Your Majesty."

Lunn never became complacent about his job, but years of dealing with monarchs left him difficult to impress. When the Crown Prince of Jordan issued an invitation to stay at his palace in Amman, Lunn turned him down like the proverbial bedspread. "At my age I don't like travelling," he said. "Anyway, I like it here. But I didn't want to hurt his feelings, and I was glad I could tell him that during the war I saw Amman in the distance."

Arthur Lunn was born at Bourne, Lincs, on Sept 12 1897 and educated locally. In 1914 he volunteered for the Army and, initially too young for active service, became a stretcher-bearer in the Medical Corps.

Later he served with the London Regiment in Egypt, Palestine, the Dardenelles and France. Although twice wounded, in 1919 he ended up with the forces occupying Germany.

Afterwards Lunn returned to Bourne, where he married a local girl before leaving to take up a job in a grocery shop in Finchley. By 1930 he had his own shop in Streatham, though this failed – partly as a result of Lunn's generosity in affording credit during the Depression.

There followed three years at Agar's in Manchester, after which Lunn, already a Fellow of the Institute of

Grocers, was invited to don the morning-coat (crimson during the festive season) and pin-stripes that dignify the Fortnum's assistant.

Things were difficult at first, but fortunately the Marchioness of Londonderry – "such a lovely lady, beautifully gowned" – was on hand to offer some timely encouragement. In those early days, Lunn recalled, he would serve perhaps a dozen account customers a day, whose purchases would all be delivered. None of the items displayed anything so vulgar as a price tag, so the assistants had to remember them all.

During the Second World War Lunn acted as a fire warden in Piccadilly and was on duty when Fortnum & Mason was firebombed. He was deafened, his clothes were torn, and he lost his glasses – though these were later found intact on a pile of rubble.

The post-war years brought a different kind of shopping. In the 1980s Lunn would deal with perhaps 90 customers a day, who all paid cash and took their goods away. But, he insisted, the essence of his job never changed – to make shopping a pleasure for the customer.

The esteem in which Lunn was held by his customers was regularly demonstrated. One woman summoned him to the deathbed of her father, who handed him a sealed envelope containing £50 in recognition of his years of service. Another customer, whose wife had been much cheered by Lunn ringing up to tell her jokes on her deathbed, presented a gold tie-pin as a keepsake. Lady Docker used to kiss him – "A lot of ladies do. I love being kissed."

Occasionally Lunn, who performed in amateur opera, put his singing talent to good use in the shop. Italian women were liable to find themselves regaled with arias expressive of their fatal beauty.

As Lunn proceeded triumphantly into his ninth decade Garry Weston, the Canadian owner of the store, asked if he had ever thought of retirement. "Oh no, Sir," the ancient retainer replied, "I'm far too old to retire."

In fact Lunn theoretically retired on at least three occasions, but he was always persuaded to carry on and never actually left. On his 90th birthday he was made a "Freeman" of Fortnum's, which meant that he was allowed to report for work as and when he thought proper. He had been expecting to attend work on the day that he died.

Lunn's charm and cheerfulness were the outward expression of an inner goodness that sprang from deep religious conviction. He was heavily involved in Church affairs, and during the 1930s ran a mission at Acton.

He is survived by a son.

April 8 1990

VISCOUNT BARRINGTON

THE 11TH VISCOUNT BARRINGTON, who has died aged 81, may have had the endearingly eccentric appearance of a peer from the pages of P.G. Wodehouse but underneath was a multi-faceted man of considerable accomplishment and unwavering principle.

In his younger days, as Patrick Barrington, he was a poet, publisher and puppeteer of delightful wit and ingenuity. His *Songs of a Sub-Man*, a collection of comic verse originally written for *Punch*, has become a classic of the *genre*.

An adept adaptor of Victorian and Elizabethan metre, he combined fantastic invention with metrical clarity to inspire such trills as:

I had a duck-billed platypus when I was up at Trinity,
For whom I soon developed a remarkable affinity
He used to live in lodgings with myself and Arthur Purvis,
And we all went up together for the Diplomatic Service . . .

In later years Barrington became a leading figure in the "pro-life" movement. He was a dedicated opponent of abortion legislation, and drafted the original aims and objects of the Society for the Protection of Unborn Children, of which he was chairman. He was also a founding member of the committee of the Human Rights Society, working to ensure that euthanasia did not reach the statute book.

Barrington was a passionate champion of the right to life of both the young and the old; it was, in his view, the same principle at risk. He played a lively part in debates in the House of Lords, and was contemptuous of the feminist argument that "A woman has the right to do what she likes with her own body."

He said: "The only maxim of that kind that is, I think, a more pernicious one would be that a *man* has a right to do what he likes with his own body. Of course he has not. He has not the right to rape a young girl; he has not the right to mug an old lady; he has not the right to assault a referee on the football field."

His ceaseless campaigning made him one of the best-loved characters in the House. Many of Barrington's *dicta* in the Chamber have passed into legend. There was, for example, an exchange with the Methodist peer Lord Soper, who had said: "I am at this moment responsible for 14 pregnant girls."

Barrington observed: "Unlike the noble Lord Soper, I am not responsible for 15 illegitimate girls . . ."

"I meant that I visit them," interrupted Soper.

"I beg the noble Lord's pardon," said Barrington.

In moving an amendment to the Nullity of Marriage Bill in 1971, Barrington absorbed the House by recalling how, in the 1930s, a male servant in his sister's employ, who was understood to have changed sex before, announced that he was changing sex again. "He left with the cook-housekeeper and they went as a married couple, but as to who was which I cannot say," said Barrington. "I understand they were both interchangeable."

But perhaps the most memorable occasion was during a debate on the Abortion Bill, when Barrington uttered the immortal words: "Like most of your Lordships, I was born." He did not explain to a curious House how the remainder of Their Lordships had originated.

Patrick William Daines Barrington was born on Oct 29 1908, the only son of Bernard Barrington, the merchant banker (a partner of Sir Lawrence "Jonah" Jones, who paints a perceptive picture of him in his evocative memoirs *Georgian Afternoon*) and a grandson of the 9th Viscount Barrington.

Young Pat – or "Pip" as he was known to his family – was educated at Eton and Magdalen College, Oxford. On coming down from the university he dabbled in diplomacy for a spell as an honorary attaché at the British Embassy in Berlin; but his unstoppable flow of conversation and untidy appearance did not find favour with the formidable Ambassador, Sir Horace Rumbold.

Barrington was called to the Bar by Inner Temple but found the ideal outlet for his humorous wordplay as a contributor to *Punch* in the 1930s. Among hundreds of sentimental love ditties, which bore such titles as *My Love is a Theosophist* and *I Sent My Love a Coconut*, perhaps his most celebrated was *Take Me in Your Arms Miss Money-penny-Wilson*, which concluded:

> *Cold, cold, cold is the melancholy mould,*
> *Cold as the foam-cold sea,*
> *Colder than the shoulder of a neolithic boulder,*
> *Are the shoulders you show to me.*
> *Cruel, cruel, cruel is the flame to the fuel,*
> *Cruel is the axe to the tree,*
> *But crueller and keener than a coster's concertina,*
> *Is your cruel, cruel scorn to me.*

At the outbreak of the Second World War Barrington enlisted in the Royal Artillery. He cut an unlikely figure as a soldier, but it was typical of him to make many lasting friendships in the ranks before he received a commission.

Like the true aristocrat he was, Barrington always treated everyone the same; he was as happy to discuss his views on life with a cabbie as with a Fellow of All Souls.

Subsequently his gift for words led to a more appropriate contribution to the war effort at the decoding centre at Bletchley. Besides his official duties he kept his fellow boffins amused with revues and entertainments of his own devising.

After the war Barrington worked in publishing —

becoming one of the early partners in Weidenfeld & Nicolson – and toured with his own puppet show of the Nativity, for which he not only wrote the script and music but made and manipulated the puppets, as well as engineering extraordinarily effective *coups de théâtre*.

In 1960 he succeeded his uncle in the viscountcy and took the Liberal Whip in the House of Lords. He first became involved in "pro-life" work when he heard the Earl of Longford speaking against Lord Silkin's Abortion Bill in 1966.

"Is this a Catholic show?" he asked Lord Longford afterwards. "Or are heretics allowed to join in?"

As chairman of the Society for Protection of Unborn Children, Barrington was instrumental in recruiting to the cause such luminaries as Malcolm Muggeridge and Alan Bourne (the central figure in the key "Bourne Case" of 1938, after which risk to medical health was accepted as grounds for legal abortion). He was also a trustee of the charity Human Rights.

Barrington exemplified his own principles in facing his final illness – which cruelly deprived him of the power of speech – with characteristic courage and forbearance.

He never married; the succession to the title was not established at the time of his death.

Sir Malcolm Pasley writes: Patrick Barrington was indeed a wonderful man. Not only was his mind as full of wonders as Aladdin's Cave, but he always retained a sense of childlike wonder at the mystery and sanctity of human life.

This made him especially good with young children,

to whose serious amusement he devoted himself with infinite care and patience. Arranging a puppet show, constructing a geometrical figure out of cardboard, or inventing a special song to illustrate a piano lesson were just as important as preparing a speech to the House on a subject dear to him.

He will no doubt be most widely remembered for his humorous verse, which secured him a lasting place in a great English tradition. Every poem he ever published ought to be tracked down and treasured.

He was a master of gentle and amiable burlesque, and sometimes he turned his banter against himself:

> *I'm only a Second Trombone*
> *But one of these days you'll find*
> *Some hint of the passionate human thoughts*
> *That burn in a trombone's mind.*
> *They're thoughts that would stultify a bassoon*
> *And stagger a clarinet;*
> *But they're only a Second Trombone's, girls*
> *And nobody knows them yet.*

Patrick was so steeped in poetry that it became part of his daily life. His method of timing a boiled egg, for instance, was to recite a fixed number of the quatrains of Omar Khayyam.

He could easily have recited the whole lot, for he seemed to have the entire corpus of English poetry at his command. Feed him a line from Browning, and he would simply go on until asked to stop – and sometimes a bit further.

He was a man of many talents, particularly artistic

ones, all of which he used generously to give delight, and
sensitive guidance, to others. Sustained by a strong
religious faith, he was the most selfless, the least worldly-
wise of men. All those who knew him have been left very
much the poorer.

April 16 1990

MRS VICTOR BRUCE

MRS VICTOR BRUCE, the dare-devil aviatrix, racing-
driver and speed-boat pilot, who has died aged 94, made
her mark on the 20th century by breaking records in the
air, on land, and at sea.

Indeed her death deprives *Who's Who* of one of its
most remarkable entries: *"Travelled furthest north into
Lapland by motor car; holds record for Double Channel
Crossing, Dover to Calais, by motor boat; holder of 17 World
Records, motoring, and of 24-hour record; single-handed drive,
covered longest distance for man or woman, 2164 miles, in 24
hours; Coupe des Dames, Monte Carlo Rally, 1927.*

*"Flying records: first solo flight from England to Japan,
1930; longest solo flight, 1930; record solo flight, India to
French Indo-China, 1930; British Air refuelling endurance
flight, 1933. Holds 24-hour record by motor boat, covering 674
nautical miles, single-handed, 1929; first crossing of Yellow
Sea.*

*"Show jumping, 1st Royal Windsor Horse Show, 1939.
Order of the Million Elephants and White Umbrella (French
Indo-China). Fellow, Ancient Monuments Society. Publications:*

The Peregrinations of Penelope; 9000 Miles in Eight Weeks; The Woman Owner Driver; The Bluebird's Flight; Nine Lives Plus."

The only daughter of Lawrence Petre, squire of Coptfold Hall, Essex (a grandson of the 11th Lord Petre), she was born on Nov 10 1895, and christened Mildred Mary. Her mother, a Shakespearean actress, was American, and her great-grandmother fought off Indians across the plains in the 1849 California gold-rush.

Young Mildred was educated at the Convent of Sion in Bayswater and spent most of her holidays riding ponies and her brother's motor-cycle on the family estate. In 1926 she married Victor Austin Bruce, fourth son of the 2nd Lord Aberdare; they had a son.

Bruce shared her taste for adventure, and, before their marriage was dissolved in 1941, he accompanied her on many of her expeditions.

In 1927 the Bruces undertook a 6,000-mile tour through Sweden and Finland, and then penetrated 270 miles north of the Arctic Circle, where they planted a Union Jack after "running out of road".

Driving the English-built, six-cylinder saloon car was hard work, as the road was rarely straight for more than 20 yards, but Mrs Bruce remained at the wheel throughout the journey.

Standing barely five feet tall, the petite and vivacious Mrs Bruce never wore overalls or slacks, always a blouse and skirt and a string of pearls. "Don't call me a women's libber," she snapped at one interviewer late in life. "I don't really approve. I was a girl among five brothers and I've always tried to remain feminine."

After the Lapland trip, she went on to break numerous land records, and became a frequent participant at Brooklands, where she raced against such legendary drivers as Malcolm Campbell and Henry Segrave.

In the 1927 Monte Carlo Rally she drove for 1,700 miles over ice-bound roads through fog and blizzards from John O'Groats. On arrival, after 72 hours non-stop driving, she fell asleep at the wheel.

Next, in December 1927, she took turns with her husband to drive 15,000 miles at 68mph in 10 days and nights round the Montlhéry track near Paris. They suffered frost-bitten fingers, but broke 17 records.

The 24-hour record came in 1929, when she drove a motorcar single-handed for 24 continuous hours on the Montlhéry track. During that time, she covered more than 2,200 miles at an average speed of 90mph – she maintained that it would have been 100mph had she not taken a hurried swig from a Vichy water bottle which someone had inadvertently filled with petrol.

When she finished she was delighted to find that she had also broken the world record for the greatest non-stop run by a single-handed driver. The British Racing Drivers' Club made her a life member.

In the same year, Mrs Bruce entered the Monte Carlo Rally again, this time setting off from Sundsval, on the border of Lapland. But hardly had she begun the 2,250-mile trip, than her car went out of control while descending a steep hill, dashed against some rocks, and turned half-way over a precipice. One rock also penetrated the floorboard and the springs and bodywork were smashed.

Mrs Bruce hitch-hiked the 20 miles back to Sundsval, where she found a garage and brought out 14 men with a breakdown truck. The car was fitted with a new body and springs within 24 hours, and Mrs Bruce was the first competitor to arrive in Monte Carlo: "Going slowly always makes me tired."

Meanwhile, she had become an ardent devotee of the motor-boat and hydroplane, and soon held the record for the Channel crossing from Dover to Calais by motor-boat. In August 1929, she also broke the record for the return journey, crossing to Calais and back in 79 mins 24½ secs.

"In the future when I want to cross the Channel," said Mrs Bruce, "I shall use my speed-boat in place of the Channel steamers, which are push-carts by comparison."

But in spite of her reputation as an accomplished record-breaker on both land and at sea, eyebrows were raised in aviation circles when, in 1930 while window-shopping in Burlington Gardens, Mrs Bruce bought a two-engined Bluebird IV for £550.

Soon curiosity gave way to horror when it emerged that, despite slender solo experience – only 40 hours – she was secretly planning a solo flight to Tokyo and on around the world home.

Mrs Bruce, having equipped the cockpit with a Dictaphone to record her impressions, set out from Heston on Sept 25 1930 and arrived in Tokyo two months later. She had suffered a series of incidents necessitating repairs en route: her plane had overturned in Persia and she had been lost for a while after a forced landing in mountains near Istanbul.

Mrs Bruce's return was one of the aviation events of the century, for Amy Johnson and Winifred Spooner, together with a bevy of men flying Bluebirds, had crossed to Paris to escort her home.

Next day she arrived officially at Croydon where the Fulham boy scouts and girl guides (of which she was patron), turned out a guard of honour. The attendant publicity helped her found her own aviation company, Air Dispatch, which operated from Croydon.

The Dictaphone recordings of this and other flights were later compiled into a travelogue, *Round the World by Air and Steam*. Her record solo flight from India to French Indo-China included a near-fatal spell over the Annamitic range, which she described as follows:

"The time is a quarter-past four. I managed to make a kind of landing in a clearing in the jungle, and from what I can make out I am somewhere within 20 miles of a little place on the border of French Indo-China.

"It has been a terrible experience. If only I could reach some place and there is somewhere to land, I will be safe, as my petrol will not hold out much longer. Shall not dictate any more. Too worried.'

The moment came when she had to risk all and descend. She put the head of her machine down and swept through thousands of feet of cloud, giving out the message: "If I happen to be killed this will be my end, so goodbye. I have done the best that I can, but I am lost, and therefore if I come through it will be by the grace of God."

Soon afterwards, in an article in the *Star* entitled "What it Feels Like to be the Husband of a Famous Airwoman", Victor Bruce related a comment he had overheard: "That's Victor Bruce. Would you let your wife fly round the world by herself? He must be a funny sort of chap."

"Well, I don't know these people," he continued, "and I'm not sure that I want to. But they evidently don't know my wife!"

In 1932 Mrs Bruce broke the record for the longest distance covered over water in 24 hours, 694 miles against the liner *Berengaria's* 691. Her circuit included the lightship *Solent*, which she roared around every six minutes until the keepers were dizzy.

The next year, equipped with a single-seater Miles Satyr, and a Fairey Fox bomber destined for scrap which she bought for £12.10s, she joined a flying circus. "I got so used to turning upside down," she wrote in her autobiography, *Nine Lives Plus* (1977), "that I was surprised if a whole year went by without a mishap."

After the development of civil aircraft Mrs Bruce ran a company for the air dispatch of newspapers, a passenger service to Paris, and signed up the first air hostess, Daphne Vickers.

In 1937 she took on a contract for Army co-operation, night-flying planes in searchlights as target practice for the Territorial Army. In an effort to fill her spare time by day, she also bought a pony, and in 1939 was first in the open jumping class at the Royal Horse Show at Windsor.

During the Second World War, she spent eight months operating an air ferry service to France, and then ran a factory at Cardiff repairing crashed RAF planes.

Latterly Mrs Bruce lived at Bradford-on-Avon, Wilts, surrounded by parrots and motor-cars. In spite of living dangerously – so that already in 1930 *The Daily Telegraph* had prepared her obituary – she had achieved her childhood ambition of "making a million". But she said that it was not the money, but "the fuss" that she loved best of all.

Accordingly, in her mid-seventies she returned to the track to test-drive the new Ford Capri Ghia Saloon; and then at the age of 81, after 37 years out of the air, made a spectacular airborne comeback, demonstrating that her pioneering spirit was undiminished.

As part of a flying refresher course, she looped the loop in a Chipmunk two-seater plane over Bristol. Sweeping away from the airport in her 1938 Phantom III Rolls Royce, she exclaimed: "What a lark! It's knocked 50 years off my life."

May 23 1990

"KIM" DE LA TASTE TICKELL

"KIM" DE LA TASTE TICKELL, the outrageously flamboyant landlord of the Tickell Arms at Whittlesford, near Cambridge, who has died aged 73, was a legendary figure in East Anglia.

Joseph Hollick de la Taste Tickell was born in 1917 and educated at Marlborough. He dabbled with a variety of professions, as well as amateur theatricals, and then settled down to run the Tickell Arms, near the family home of Whittlesford Manor.

Clad in 18th-century knee breeches and silver-buckled shoes and styling himself squire of the village, he presided over a hostelry which became a cult among the *jeunesse dorée* and fashionable dons of Cambridge University.

To his regulars Tickell was Cambridge's answer to John Fothergill, whose Spread Eagle at Thame was once a magnet to Oxford undergraduates; to others he seemed more like the Basil Fawlty of the Fens. "I'm not having south London garage proprietors and their tarts in here!" he would screech at startled patrons, "*Out, out, out!*"

Tickell had many categories of "insufferables" – especially left-wingers, blacks and "modern" women. In 1962 he barred from his pub anyone wearing a CND badge. "They stand for everything I detest," he explained. "They are disloyal to the Crown, despise law and order and cause a great deal of trouble ... I won't have Communists in the place either."

The same year he became engaged in controversy over a local Christmas decorations factory. He felt that its female workers lowered the tone of the village – "factories attract the wrong sort of girl!" – and refused to serve them.

When he accused them of "shameful language and disgraceful behaviour" a group of them confronted him, claiming that their language was as nothing to that heard outside the Tickell Arms at closing time. "Have you ever heard me use bad language?" asked Tickell.

When the girls all chorused "Yes!" he said: "I only use good old English words like damn, blast and bloody. You never hear me using four-letter Lady Chatterley words." A woman among them called out "I've heard you say 'Get off my *fucking* grass!'" and the cry went up "Debag him!"

In 1970 Tickell found himself charged with malicious wounding and possession of an offensive weapon. He had ordered a barefoot young American woman to put on her shoes, and later was alleged to have slashed at a man in her party with a carving knife.

He then called for the various mediaeval weapons that decorated his walls – "Give me my mace and my halberd!" – and ran from the inn shouting "I will take on any bugger who disapproves of the way I run my house!"

Tickell appeared in court sporting a pink carnation in his buttonhole and with an eye-glass on a ribbon round his neck. He apparently made a good impression, was acquitted of both charges, and remained unapologetic and unrepentant.

Decked out in opera cape and silk scarf, he was an avid supporter of the Arts Theatre, Cambridge.

"Kim" Tickell bore his long final illness with the same exemplary courage that he had shown during his service in the Second World War. He was unmarried.

June 5 1990

DENYS WATKINS-PITCHFORD

DENYS WATKINS-PITCHFORD, best known as the author "BB", who has died aged 85, had no contemporary equal as a writer, illustrator and compiler of books about the English countryside for readers of all ages.

His most celebrated books were *The Little Grey Men*

(serialised on television in 1975) and *Brendon Chase*, both long established as classics of children's fiction; but almost a dozen of his others are ranked as high in their more specialised fields. *Confessions of a Carp Fisher*, for instance, is one of the best-loved fishing books of the 20th century and two of his shooting books, *Tide's Ending* and *Dark Estuary*, are also treasured works.

He contributed regularly to the *Shooting Times* for more than 50 years. His pseudonym of "BB" was derived from the size of shot he used to shoot geese.

Denys James Watkins-Pitchford was born on July 25 1905, the second son of a country clergyman, the Rev Walter Watkins-Pitchford, who wrote several operas which were performed on the wireless. The Pitchfords claimed a connection with Pitchford in Shropshire, one of the most bewitchingly romantic places in England with its ancient church, timber-framed manor house and a ford where pitch can be seen on the surface of the water.

Young Denys was raised at Lamport, Northampton-shire, in one of the loveliest rectories in England. At the age of four he incontrovertibly saw a gnome.

At the age of 36 he wrote the greatest book about gnomes in the English language, *The Little Grey Men*. Its stature was immediately recognised and it won the Carnegie Medal in 1942.

As a child Watkins-Pitchford was sickly and also suffered the defect of being born without collar-bones; but there was compensation. Illness meant that he never had to go to school and lack of collar-bones gave him the grip of a bear.

Much of his time was spent exploring the countryside with gun, rod, snare or butterfly-net; a zest for the chase fuelled with poetic meaning by his delight in such books as W. H. Hudson's *Far Away and Long Ago*, Richard Jefferies's *Wildlife in a Southern County*, Ernest Seton's *Wild Animals I Have Known* and J. W. Fortescue's *Story of a Red Deer* – though in the fullness of time he was to consider Llewellyn Powis the supreme master among English writers on natural history.

For Watkins-Pitchford, Man, at his most natural, was a hunter, and it was as a hunter that a man best understood nature. This zest for the chase never left him; even in old age he shot and fished with the excitement of a boy, though by then blind in one eye and dependent on dialysis.

A childlike excitement and wonder, untinged by adult sentimentality, distinguish all his books and pictures; enhanced as they are by a profound sense of history in general and a knowledge of the wild based on sensual experience.

This experience first expressed itself in a talent for drawing and painting. He studied at Northampton School of Art, won a travelling scholarship to Paris, continued as a post-graduate at the Royal College of Art and ended as assistant art master at Rugby School, a post he held for 16 years.

Here he was not without effect (Denys Lasdun, the architect, was perhaps his star pupil) but he was not happy teaching. Nonetheless the period contributed significantly to his later success.

His first publication, an anthology of sporting literature, *The Sportsman's Bedside Book* (1937), was gleaned from the Temple Library; and *Brendon Chase* (1944), the story of three public-schoolboys who live for a year as outlaws in an English forest, must owe almost as much to Rugby as does *Tom Brown's Schooldays*. He also benefited from the encouragement and example of his fellow bird-artist and fellow art-master, Talbot Kelly.

Although he was to become most famous as BB the writer, the painting and drawing Watkins-Pitchford did in his own name were always the mainspring of his activity and style. He wrote like a painter, his eye for visual accuracy being the chief distinction of his prose.

His texts were inseparable from the (usually) black-and-white illustrations, whose "moonlight witchery" so enhances their romantic charm.

As a painter of birds in the landscape he was undoubtedly the match of any of his contemporaries, but it is in these illustrative vignettes and drawings in scraperboard that he is at his most personal and characteristic. In fact he may well have been the first artist to adopt scraperboard for fine-art use, the technique having previously found favour only with commercial artists.

His humour and engaging sense of mischief could also find pictorial expression. It was only a chosen few who were let into the secret that the beautiful Thorburn watercolour in his sitting-room was a Watkins-Pitchford "forgery".

The two sports which most stirred his visual and poetic imagination were carp fishing, which he can be said virtually to have invented, and goose shooting – his passion for which is acknowledged by his choice of pseudonym. Both are solitary occupations, affording the sportsman hours of meditation and observation; and both are undergone at the most secret times of the day in mysterious, beautiful and even dangerous places.

They are memorably commemorated in three standard works: *Confessions of a Carp Fisher* (1950), *Tide's Ending* (1950) and *Dark Estuary* (1953). To these books must be added a dozen or so that have continued in print, among these the lastingly popular anthologies such as *The Countryman's Bedside Book* (1941), *The Fisherman's Bedside Book* (1945) and *The Shooting Man's Bedside Book* (1948).

His works of fiction included *Wild Lone: The Story of a Pytchley Fox* (1938), *Manka, The Sky Gipsy: The Story of a Wild Goose* (1939) and *The Pool of the Black Witch* (1974), a novel but widely regarded as the best of all introductory books to fishing. In the 1960s he began the popular Bill Badger series for children.

Altogether Watkins-Pitchford had nearly 60 "BB" books published and illustrated at least 30 by other authors. This considerable opus was achieved despite a far from easy personal life; apart from being dogged by ill-health, Watkins-Pitchford had the bad luck to fall heir to a family curse.

The curse had been laid on his father who, as a young man on a pilgrimage to the Holy Land, made the mistake of refusing alms to a beggar. The beggar swore that the then unmarried clergyman's first-born son would die before manhood, and also the first-born son of his second son.

And so it transpired: Engel Watkins-Pitchford died as a schoolboy and Denys Watkins-Pitchford's second son, Robin, at the age of eight. A further blow fell in 1974 when his wife, the former Cecily Adnitt, died before her time – in his opinion from inhaling a pesticide that was being sprayed on the field adjoining their garden. He met these misfortunes with typical fortitude.

Saddened by the destruction of pre-motor car England, Watkins-Pitchford was particularly proud of the work he did to help preserve the rare Purple Emperor butterfly.

Each year he would collect as many Purple Emperor eggs as he could and then cultivate them on protected bushes in his garden. When they were hatched he would release them into the wild.

In his later years hardly a week would pass without someone arriving at his beautiful old house in the Northamptonshire countryside. Always kind and attentive to visitors, he was particularly pleased when a party of Japanese arrived unannounced – all fans of his children's books.

Watkins-Pitchford was appointed MBE in 1989. He is survived by a daughter.

Until the end he stayed true to the words of an old Cumbrian gravestone with which he prefaced all his books:

> *The wonder of the world*
> *The beauty and the power,*
> *The shapes of things,*
> *Their colours, lights and shades*
> *These I saw.*
> *Look ye also while life lasts.*

September 11 1990

HELLE CRISTINA
HABSBURG WINDSOR

HELLE CRISTINA HABSBURG WINDSOR, a familiar
figure in the Anglo-Portuguese world who has died in
Lisbon aged 100, was, even by the standards of pretend-
ers, one of the more bizarre aspirants to the blood royal.

She claimed to have been born at the Court of Spain
in May 1890 as a natural child of the future King George
V of Great Britain and Queen Maria Cristina of Spain,
widow of King Alfonso XII and daughter of Archduke
Karl Ferdinand of Austria. "I was born on the steps of the
throne," she used to say. "So awkward for her mother,"
observed one Lisbon wag.

By her own account, Helle Cristina was ferried as a
baby to Malta, where an Englishwoman put her on a ship
headed for the East. The "royal lovechild" was thus
transported to Smyrna, where she was brought up by a
certain Dr Salerio. After a two-year sojourn in a convent
on the Greek island of Tinos, Helle Cristina, now in her
late teens, boarded a ship for Marseilles, from where she
followed the railway line to Bordeaux, and eventually
crossed the border into Spain.

She spent some time working in music-halls before
marrying Roberto Cunat, whom she described as the
southern "regent" of a large industrial firm. She was said
to have had two sons by this marriage, although in later
years she never revealed where they were.

Mrs Habsburg Windsor, as she styled herself, liked

to recall meeting her mother in adult life: "She was with her son, King Alfonso XIII, and she looked so happy. I was glad for her because I could imagine the sorrow of being separated from her only daughter." (Helle Cristina was apparently unaware that her mother had in fact had two daughters by King Alfonso XII.)

"I never spoke about my father with my mother. We had no opportunity. Besides, I think we were both so transported that we never thought of speaking, just of being together. It was an occasion."

She also remembered meeting her father – as well as her half-brother, the Duke of Windsor – on several occasions. He was willing, she said, to do anything for her. What he did is unclear.

Soon after the outbreak of the Second World War, Mrs Habsburg Windsor arrived as a refugee in Lisbon with neither papers nor passport, though her *Cartao de Residencia* declared her to be British.

It was at this time that she divulged her origins. Nobody took any notice, but her conduct fast made her a thorn in the side of the British Embassy; she would appear uninvited at numerous official functions, claiming to be a representative of the British Government. She was also a regular worshipper at St George's Church, and more than once occupied the British Ambassador's pew, declaring in a guttural German accent that she took precedence.

Mrs Habsburg Windsor, who spoke several languages and had journalistic experience in Egypt, was frequently taken for a spy – although nobody had any idea for whom she might be working. Ostensibly she made her living by teaching English. She was eventually banned from the premises of the British Hospital, where she was accustomed to sit for hours in the waiting room.

September 16 1990

BETTY MCKEEVER

BETTY MCKEEVER, the Master of the Blean Beagles who has died aged 89, won a place in the *Guinness Book of Records* for having been the longest serving Master of a beagles pack, and was a legend in Kent for her attachment to Edwardian sporting tradition.

She was born Jean Bethel Dawes at Kemsdale House, Faversham, on Feb 26 1901, daughter of William Dawes, a prominent figure in shipping, who inherited Mount Ephraim – the family seat since the 18th century.

Young Betty became Master of the Blean Beagles at the age of nine, on the understanding that she looked after them entirely on her own. This condition she abundantly fulfilled. Indeed there was nothing she could not do for them – stitching them up when they were cut, feeding them, mucking them out, and so on.

In 1931, she married Thomas McKeever. The couple settled at Waterham Farm, near Faversham, where Betty gradually built up a pack of 17½ couple, which she took out regularly twice a week, across what she called her "enormous country", around Dover, Sandwich and Sheppey.

Besides being a Master of the pack, Mrs McKeever

was a considerable farmer and livestock breeder, and a fine shot; in her younger days she also used to take her horses to Ireland to race – sidesaddle.

Invariably adorned in tweeds and pearls, she had an encyclopaedic genealogical knowledge of local people and what they did.

A naturally sociable figure, she would organise convoys of coaches to ferry fellow enthusiasts to the Derby and the Grand National.

Betty McKeever was also a redoubtable *raconteuse*, and held robust views on a number of matters; she was especially concerned by what she regarded as the modern girl's inability to run: "I think there is something wrong with their shoeing."

She continued to take an energetic interest in her beagles until her death, latterly following the pack in a golf buggy.

September 22 1990

FELIX HOPE-NICHOLSON

FELIX HOPE-NICHOLSON, who has died aged 69, was a bachelor dandy of the old school and the owner of More House, Tite Street, Chelsea, a remarkable family home which had remained more or less unchanged since the 1890s.

Most of his life was spent in this mysterious and labyrinthine mansion, its five floors and many dusty passages crammed with family portraits, bric-à-brac, dolls' houses, religious paraphernalia and Stuart relics, including pieces of Charles I's coffin and James II's heart.

More House – which Felix Hope-Nicholson never attempted to modernise – was built in the neo-Tudor style by the painter John Collier in 1882 and acquired 10 years later by Felix's maternal grandmother, Mrs Adrian Hope, a fashionable portraitist who was often employed by Queen Victoria. Adrian Hope – the son of Col William Hope, VC – was secretary to the Great Ormond Street Hospital and acted as guardian of the two sons of his neighbour in Tite Street, Oscar Wilde, during the latter's imprisonment.

Charles Felix Otho Victor Gabriel John Adrian Hope-Nicholson was born on July 21 1921. His father, Hedley Nicholson, the son of a mackintosh manufacturer, was a brilliant grammar-school boy who had won a place at Christ Church, Oxford, and had been called to the Bar before marrying into the Hope dynasty, scions of the Earls of Hopetoun (subsequently Marquesses of Linlithgow), and adding their name to his own.

Felix's mother, Jacqueline, who died in 1972, was a most erudite and accomplished woman, who in later life acquired the air of a Queen-in-exile and used to stop the traffic in the King's Road with her annual pageant. She claimed responsibility for introducing her cousin by marriage, Una Lady Troubridge, to Radclyffe Hall, author of *The Well of Loneliness*.

Young Felix was educated at Summerfields, Eton and Christ Church. During the Second World War, in which he served as a private in the infantry, he became an *habitué* of the decadent downstairs bar at the Ritz Hotel in Piccadilly.

He would recall that he and his Oxford friend Roddy
Lambton were known in the bar as "the Boys" and that
the regulars included an officer in charge of posting at
the War Office who "was known as 'Colonel Cutie'
because he called everybody 'cutie' ... He had an
insatiable mania for meeting young second lieutenants".

Hope-Nicholson also recollected such notorious occasions as the time when the drunken Paddy Brodie (said to
have partly inspired Evelyn Waugh's character Miles
Malpractice) approached the bar "having mistaken it for
the *pissoir*"; and when Aircraftsman Brian Howard (part-
model for Waugh's Anthony Blanche and Ambrose Silk),
on being asked his name, number and station by an
outraged senior RAF officer in the bar, said, over his
shoulder, "My name is *Mrs Smith*".

Eventually, as Hope-Nicholson recalled, the Ritz bar
became "too queer for the authorities . . . The War Office
managed to have it shut for 'repairs' and thus effectively
closed it down." Hope-Nicholson was sufficiently *louche*
in his own right to merit being banned from a local
Chelsea pub, the Pier Hotel.

In his maturity, Hope-Nicholson became a more
formidable figure, magisterial in appearance, wise, witty
and wonderfully droll. His dedication to genealogy and
his excessive fondness for the Graham Monteith tartan –
which he had made up in waistcoat, dressing-gown,
cushions and curtains – caused those who did not know
him to dismiss him as a snob; but he remained open-
minded, affectionate, generous to those in need and
entirely devoid of bachelor touchiness.

He continued the family tradition of taking in
lodgers. This had begun in his childhood when Cdr Mary

Allen, head of the women's police force, resided at More House and wore her jack-boots at breakfast.

Among the colourful flotsam of characters who passed through the house over the years were the ballet critic Richard Buckle, Clement Freud, Nancy Cunard, the young Antony Lambton, Peter Quennell, Lady Isabel Milles-Lade (later Countess of Derby – *qv*), and a certain Miss Huntley, a former governess to the Spanish Royal Family, who had a mania for mending household linen. The house also provided a haven for Augustus John's mistress, Mavis Wheeler (the "Beautiful and Beloved"), before and after her imprisonment for shooting her lover Lord Vivian in 1954.

In his later years Hope-Nicholson held court lying on a sofa in the pale green ante-room beside his first-floor studio. In spite of some infirmity, he continued to attend mass at the Brompton Oratory each Sunday and some years ago announced with glee that he had purchased a commodious grave space for himself – "the size of a first-class *Wagon-lit*" – in the Brompton Cemetery.

He remained at the centre of a huge circle of friends, cousins, nephews and nieces. Many will remember his annual "Crib" party, held on the Feast of Epiphany, and attended this year by the grandsons of both Oscar Wilde and Augustus John. There were also the cod dinners in his basement kitchen, an historic room with an open range and plate-rack suffering from a rare fluffy disease which Rentokil's expert had never seen before.

More House was latterly "discovered" as a film and television location. Several scenes for the BBC2 drama *Portrait of a Marriage* were shot there – and the house was used for Simon Gray's television play, *Old Flames*, starring

Simon Callow and Stephen Fry, whom Felix found to be a cousin of the Hope-Nicholson family.

He is survived by his sisters Lauretta, who married the painter Jean Hugo, and Marie-Jacqueline Lancaster, author of *Brian Howard: Portrait of a Failure*. Felix Hope-Nicholson hoped that More House might be preserved as a permanent museum.

September 23 1990

ARTHUR MACKINS

ARTHUR MACKINS, the amateur weather forecaster who has died aged 82, frequently rivalled the Meteorological Office with his prognostications, based not on satellite intelligence, but on phenomena including anything from volcanic eruptions, comets and sea temperatures to the length of spiders' threads.

Mackins was employed as a clerk in the foreign department of Cox's & King's branch of Lloyds Bank in Pall Mall, but devoted more than 50 years of his life to his hobby, and by the time of his retirement to Bognor Regis had begun to claim a 90 per cent success rate.

His most notable coups included the accurate prediction of October temperatures in the 80s in 1969, a baking July following a miserable June in 1971, and a long hot summer after snow had stopped play at a cricket match at Buxton in 1975.

Mackins was regularly consulted by newspapers from all over Europe, British television and radio, companies such as Wall's ice-cream, an assortment of show organis-

ers, barbecue hostesses, nervy brides and even, on one occasion, a tremulous L-driver about to take a test.

Known as Britain's "fair-weather friend", Mackins was sometimes criticised for being overly optimistic in his forecasts. He admitted to having received the odd poison-pen letter — including one anonymous, type-written postcard complaining of a wrong prediction and curtly advising him to pack it in.

A tailor's son, Arthur Mackins was born in London within the sound of the Bow Bells on June 26 1908 and educated at St Aloysius's School, Highgate. His interest in the weather began in his early teenage years, motivated largely by his enthusiasm for cricket.

After school he joined Lloyds Bank, where, after his official retirement in 1973, he continued for a further five years on a part-time basis, commuting to London by train from Bognor Regis.

Unimpressed by the Meteorological Office's sophisti-cated methods, Mackins believed that the weather went in cycles, and over the years he collected meteorological records dating back to the 1920s, which, together with analysis of sea temperatures, provided the basis of his most trusted predictions.

Spiders' webs, he said, could be of assistance in short-range forecasts. "If a spider makes a long single thread across a corner then it will be dry the next day. If it's only a short one then rain is likely." And the arrival of Halley's Comet, he claimed, was a fairly sure-fire indica-tion of a scorching summer.

Believing himself to be a typical Englishman, Mack-ins saw nothing odd about his obsession with the weather. For some years he wrote for newspapers in America, advising readers on the periods in which they could be guaranteed good weather for a holiday in Britain. He also regularly presented a forecast for the cricket season on BBC Radio 2's sports programme.

He wrote a book, *Prophet of the Sun*, a mixture of meteorological commentary, anecdotage and history, which was with a publishing house at the time of his death.

Mackins is survived by his wife, Iris, a son and a daughter.

September 27 1990

BEATRICE "TILLY" SHILLING

BEATRICE "TILLY" SHILLING, who has died aged 81, was not only a notable acro engineer, responsible for remedying a defect in the Rolls-Royce Merlin engine during the Second World War, but also a renowned racing motor-cyclist.

In the 1930s she stormed round the Brooklands circuit and was awarded a coveted Gold Star for lapping the track at more than 100 mph on her Norton 500. "Tilly" Shilling was once described by a fellow scientist as "a flaming pathfinder of women's lib"; she always rejected any suggestion that as a woman she might be inferior to a man in technical and scientific fields.

In 1940, when Hurricane and Spitfire pilots encountered a life-or-death carburettor problem, she was already a highly regarded scientist at the Royal Aircraft Establishment at Farnborough. The problem which landed on her desk in the carburation department was this: pilots were obliged to turn on their backs in combat to dive because the "negative-G" of simply putting the nose down resulted in starving the engine, causing it to splutter or cut out.

This was a critical defect since the Daimler-Benz engine powering enemy Me 109s permitted Luftwaffe pilots to perform the manoeuvre unhindered. Miss Shilling came up with a simple stop-gap device – which cost less, as it happened, than a shilling.

Nicknamed "Miss Shilling's Orifice", it was a metal disc about the size of an old threepenny bit, with a small hole in the middle. It was brazed into the fighter's fuel pipe, and when the pilot accelerated in a dive the disc stopped even momentary starvation of the Merlin engine. By March 1941 Miss Shilling's Orifice had been installed throughout Fighter Command, sufficing until replaced by an improved carburettor.

A butcher's daughter, Beatrice Shilling was born at Waterlooville, Hants, on March 8 1909 and after working as an electrician and electrical linesman she took an engineering degree at Manchester University.

In the 1930s she was recruited as a scientific officer by the RAE and began on a small salary doing fairly menial work. Even as a senior member of that establishment she was renowned for rolling up her sleeves and getting her hands dirty – shopworkers respected the fact that she could braze a butt joint between two pieces of copper with the skill of a fitter.

When she married George Naylor, whom she had

met at aerodynamics night-school classes, colleagues presented her with a set of stocks and dies. It was said that she turned her own wedding ring on a lathe in stainless steel.

After the war she shone in charge of investigations at Farnborough – such as a probe into aquaplaning by aircraft taking off or landing on wet runways. These occurrences raised particular public alarm when an Elizabethan airliner crashed on take-off in slush at Munich, killing most of the Manchester United football team.

Her investigation of the related problems included conducting a series of trials for the Engineering Physics Department to assess braking performance on an experimental high-friction runway surface in conditions of heavy rain. She summoned a convoy of bowsers to spray water on the concrete, while a wingless naval Scimitar ran up engines as if for take-off.

Miss Shilling shared her passion for speed on wheels with her husband, and visitors to their home were astonished by the variety of motor-cycle parts scattered around. In the 1950s she successfully raced her 1935 Lagonda Rapier at Silverstone, her skilful engine-tuning producing a speed of more than 100 mph.

She also participated in sportscar racing at Goodwood, and another of her pastimes was pistol shooting.

She was appointed OBE in 1948 and retired in 1969, after 36 years at Farnborough. She is survived by her husband.

November 18 1990

TREVOR KEMPSON

TREVOR KEMPSON, who has died aged 58, was the doyen of muckraking journalists.

Hard-nosed but charming, he brought a stern moral line to his duties as chief investigative reporter on the *News of the World*. "I abhor political hypocrites and gangsters," he declared, "and it's my personal crusade to get them."

His greatest coup was to bring about Mr Antony Lambton's resignation from the Ministry of Defence in 1973. One Saturday afternoon Kempson was at the *News of the World* office working on his exposure of Bernie Silvers, the Soho vice king. Two men (one of them Colin Levy) arrived at the newspaper claiming to have some film and a tape-recording of a Government minister in bed with a prostitute – Levy's wife, Norma. Kempson replied that he had heard something to that effect, so they each wrote down the name and swapped slips of paper: both read "Lambton".

The noises on Levy's tape were meaningless, and the film was of a kind which could only be developed by the manufacturers. Levy took Kempson home to Maida Vale, where he introduced him to Norma as an insurance man. When Lambton telephoned to make his next appointment, Kempson fixed up his own recording device and secreted a photographer called Brian in the bedroom wardrobe.

"I am determined but not vicious," he said of his

methods. "It's a game of cat and mouse, and I want to be the cat."

In the early 1970s he worked on the Janie Jones scandal, which involved sexual bribery in the record business. He also exposed the drug-taking of Ian Botham and Mick Jagger; both threatened to sue for libel, but could not because of his evidence. Kempson took pride in his thoroughness and accuracy, and boasted that he had "never misquoted anybody".

He was a close friend and confidant of a number of senior police officers, and of such criminals as the Kray brothers, the Richardson gang and the Great Train Robbers. He paid regular visits to Ronnie Biggs in Brazil; and when Charlie Wilson was murdered in Spain earlier this year his widow rang up Kempson to give him the story.

Undaunted by threats against him and his family, he claimed that: "There's only one criminal who hates me, and that's because I hate him for turning against his gang. They should stick to their code."

A notable consumer of whisky and cigarettes, he loved to hold court in the pubs of Fleet Street, pouring out colourful anecdotes; he always wore a chunky gold bracelet given him by Jayne Mansfield.

Trevor Edward Kempson was born on April 1 1932 and educated at Merchant Taylors', where the sort of newspapers he was interested in were forbidden. When he asked for the *People* at the local shop the woman behind the counter refused him, so he bribed her with an entire month's sweet ration.

The young Trevor thus discovered the crime reporting of Duncan Webb, the man who coined the phrase, "I made my excuses and left." He was enraptured: "Even then I thought that that was what I wanted to do."

In 1952, after National Service as a military policeman, he accordingly joined Laxton's, the Reading news agency. Eddie Laxton eventually made him a partner, but in 1962 Kempson took a salary cut to join the staff of his beloved *People*, which he left four years later for the *News of the World*.

Despite the nature of his stories and the characters he was obliged to deal with, Kempson never subscribed to the foot-in-the-door school of journalism: "I've learned that the way to get the best out of people is to be kind and gentle."

It is reckoned that during his career he must have employed his hero's catchphrase about making his excuses more frequently than any journalist alive. He often paid quite large sums of his newspaper's money for the services of prostitutes, but maintained that he never availed himself of them – "Because there's a saying in Fleet Street: 'You don't fuck the story.'"

Kempson married, and had three sons.

December 8 1990

DAME VIOLET DICKSON

DAME VIOLET DICKSON, who has died aged 94, was a celebrated, indeed an awesome, figure in Kuwait, where she lived for more than 60 years, and where she remained for several weeks after the Iraqi invasion in August 1990.

During her 60 years in Araby – half of them as a

widow – Violet Dickson knew many of the chief actors in its history, among them King Abdul Aziz ibn Saud of Saudi Arabia, King Faisal of Iraq, four Kuwaiti rulers, and many tribal sheikhs. She moved with equal ease among western diplomats and travellers such as Bertram Thomas, Gertrude Bell, Freya Stark, Wilfred Thesiger and Ian Fleming.

Dame Violet's knowledge of Kuwait, and in particular her unparalleled grasp of the feuds and rivalries festering among the kingdom's 600-strong royal family, made her an indispensable resource for incoming British ambassadors and visiting notables.

Her 80th birthday party, held in a tent in the embassy compound in the summer of 1976 was a major event in the life of the British community, and the heavens laid on an almighty thunderstorm for the occasion.

Yet, for all her prestige, Dame Violet continued to occupy the modest seafront house that had been her home since her arrival in 1929, when she had been carried ashore in a sedan chair with her husband, Col Harold Dickson, the political agent and later the local representative of the Kuwait Oil Company.

In the 1950s she looked on regretfully as neighbouring properties were demolished to make space for the concrete commercial temples of modern Kuwait. Her own house was eventually dwarfed by these monstrosities; a cool and dark oasis amidst that blazing heat, it was built of sun-dried mud strengthened with coral rock, with ceilings supported by mangrove poles, and a spacious verandah overlooking the Arabian Gulf.

Here, even in extreme old age, Dame Violet would hold court over a classic English tea. Attempts made after her husband's death in 1959 to persuade her to move into a more comfortable and modern abode were doomed to failure, even though it was rumoured that the current ruler Sheikh Jaber Al Ahmad Al Sabah – now in exile – had offered the hospitality of his palace.

But Dame Violet was not content to stay in the town of Kuwait; she made frequent ventures into the desert, both to visit her Bedouin friends – she was an *habituée* of tribal weddings – and in pursuit of new botanical and entomological specimens.

As long ago as 1933 she was sending dried flowers back to Kew; and in the same year the Natural History Museum supplied nets, killing bottles and other equipment to assist her quest for desert insects, especially grasshoppers. A plant – *Horwoodia dicksoniae* – and a beetle – *Julodius speculifer dicksoni* – were named after her. In 1955 she published *The Wild Flowers of Kuwait and Bahrain*, which carried her own illustrations.

Dame Violet was a mountainously large, sturdy-legged woman, who talked in a surprisingly small, sharp voice. She spoke Arabic in a Bedouin dialect, though she never learnt to read or write the language. She was an intensely practical peson of simple tastes, never bored, and wholly without intellectual pretensions.

The same artlessness was evident in her appearance; the hair was scraped back into a bun, the feet were thrust into ankle socks and flat shoes, the torso enveloped in a huge shapeless dress, and the whole surmounted by a little cotton sun-hat.

During the Second World War she donned a shabby coat and skirt made by a Kuwaiti tailor out of a piece of man's suiting.

Dame Violet was dismissive of women and made no secret of her preference for male company. This distaste for her own sex, she happily admitted, was often reciprocated, notably by certain Arab princesses, who hid in the cupboard during her visits to their palace.

Though Dame Violet was a good listener, and rarely offered gratuitous advice, her conversation could be robust. She nicknamed one of her favourite desert flowers "the donkey's penis", and shocked an earnest scholar at an embassy dinner party by explaining that the Arabic word for a sea urchin meant "the female vulva".

Her patrician manner made her a revered figure among the middle-class expatriates who came to the Gulf. To the end she did her best to ignore the oil-rich city which had grown up around her, continuing to shop in the *souk* and to patronise the Central Post Office, in spite of the proliferation of local shops and post offices across the city.

She returned to England every summer and – courtesy of Swiss Air – paid annual visits to Switzerland, where she had spent part of her youth. Kuwait, though, had become her spiritual home; she faced life with a wry and deadpan humour and seemed to have gained an almost Islamic acceptance of whatsoever the fates afforded.

Violet Penelope Lucas-Calcraft was born on Sept 3 1896 at Gautby in Lincolnshire, where her father was a land agent in charge of the local estates belonging to the Vyners of Newby Hall in Yorkshire. As a child her special delights were collecting butterflies and birds eggs, pastimes interspersed with the trapping and skinning of moles.

Young Violet was educated at Miss Lunn's High

School, Woodhall Spa, and at Les Charmettes at Vevey in Switzerland, from which she returned with some difficulty on the outbreak of the First World War.

In 1915 she showed her independent spirit by going to work at Smith's bank in Lincoln. Three years later she was posted to Cox's bank in Marseilles, and it was here that she met her future husband when he came in to inquire if he had any mail. A week later the decisive Captain Dickson – then serving in the Indian Army – sent Miss Lucas-Calcraft a telegram proposing marriage.

Violet accepted without hesitation, and in the autumn of 1919 the couple were married by special licence in St Thomas's Cathedral, Bombay. After a brief honeymoon at the Taj Mahal Hotel, Violet Dickson found herself swept into the inhospitable conditions of Arabia.

Her married life began in Mesopotamia and Captain Dickson – son of the consul-general in Jerusalem, grandson of the physician to the British Embassy in Istanbul and great-grandson of the physician to the Ottoman Pashalic of Tripoli – soon instilled in his wife his enthusiasm for the Near East, and especially for the Arabs of the desert. Their two children, who were given Arab names – Saud for the son, Zahra for the daughter – were brought up to think of boiled locusts as a special treat.

After Mesopotamia, the Dicksons lived and worked from 1923 to 1924 at Quetta in Baluchistan, from 1924 to 1928 at Bikaner in Rajputana and from 1928 to 1929 at Bushire in Iran, before in 1929 Captain Dickson was appointed political agent in Kuwait.

When the Dicksons arrived in Kuwait – then a small, dusty town with unsurfaced roads – the entire European community numbered only 11 souls. Moving into the dilapidated mud house on the harbour, they were obliged to repair its walls with their own hands.

Rats were exterminated by scattering barley on a white sheet and shooting the rodents by moonlight with a .410 shotgun.

Violet Dickson's social sway owed much to her husband's long and intimate friendship with Sheikh Ahmad, Emir of Kuwait, who died in 1950. Such was the trust which this ruler placed in the Dicksons' judgment that one evening over dinner he sought Violet's help in finding a suitable wife.

Somewhat hesitatingly, she mentioned a beautiful girl whom she had met on one of her forays into the desert. The recollection proved fortunate, for the marriage which the Sheikh subsequently contracted proved extremely happy.

Dame Violet liked to recall how, in 1937, her husband had found Kuwait's most productive oilfield after dreaming about a beautiful girl rising alive from a tomb. Rather more credit, however, might seem due to the native woman who interpreted this masculine reverie to mean that oil would be discovered in an area far removed from contemporary wells, near a solitary sidr tree.

The Dicksons enjoyed a close friendship with the celebrated adventurer H. St John Philby, and during a visit to London in the summer of 1957 they entertained Philby and his son Kim — cleared 18 months earlier by the Foreign Secretary, Harold Macmillan, of being the Third Man — to dinner at the Hyde Park Hotel in Knightsbridge.

Dame Violet's somewhat disappointing autobiography, *Forty Years in Kuwait*, was published in 1971. Her services to Anglo-Kuwaiti relations were recognised by her appointment as MBE in 1942, as CBE in 1964 and as DBE in 1976.

She is survived by her two children. Saud has been High Commissioner in Anguilla, and Zahra Freeth an author, runs a stall in Colchester antiques market.

January 1 1991

MAJOR DONALD NEVILLE-WILLING

MAJOR DONALD NEVILLE-WILLING, raconteur and inveterate mythomane, who has died aged 89, was variously an actor, dancer, soldier, hotel manager and night-club impresario.

A diminutive, dapper figure, invariably sporting a red carnation, "the Major" had a knack for popping up in the most unlikely places. In one of the most sensational divorce cases of the 1930s, for example – between Edward James and Tilly Losch – Neville-Willing appeared as a star witness, having noticed the naked lover through an open door.

As Beverley Nichols once said of him, "He elevated the tricky profession of publicity into genius." In this field he enjoyed a triumphant spell as entertainments manager of the Café de Paris in the 1950s, and the *artistes* he represented at one time or another included Richard Burton and Elizabeth Taylor.

The son of a Manchester cotton manufacturer, Donald Neville-Willing was born in 1901. His father, he liked to say, never recovered from a prep-school report which said of young Donald, "Good at everything, but excels at sewing."

He was despatched at the earliest opportunity to the Dutch East Indies, where it was hoped he might excel in more manly accomplishments: but "Donnie" remained, as he put it, "one hundred per cent effeminate" and returned to Britain as soon as he was able.

He found congenial work in a Cochran revue at the London Pavilion, and appeared in the cast list of *On With the Dance* in 1925. Later in the 1920s he went to America, where he checked into the George Washington Hotel in New York. Finding himself unable to pay his bill, he offered to arrange the flowers as part payment, was co-opted on to the staff and within a year was assistant manager.

During the Second World War – which he described as "the best thing ever to happen to English homosexuals" – Neville-Willing attempted to join the Home Guard, but by dint of securing two ambulances from rich Americans he was sent to Cairo with the Ambulance Field Service. There he was interviewed by General "Jumbo" Wilson, who granted him a commission after inspecting his fingers when drinking a cup of tea. "Good Boy! You don't hold your *pinkie* out."

"You won't have to do any fighting," the General reassured him. "We'll put you on the General List. You'll be a gaberdine swine." Thus established as the oldest second lieutenant in the Army, Neville-Willing helped set up rest camps on the North-West Frontier and was Jack Hawkins's assistant in organising entertainments in Bombay for "the Forgotten Army". It was his proud claim – and a true one – that he introduced Hawkins to his future wife.

The Major landed his job at the Café de Paris in 1952, when it was still a *chic* night-club, celebrated for its oval dance floor (copied from the palm court of the *Lusitania*) and the spectacular double-staircase down which Marlene Dietrich made her memorably slinky descent.

In 1957 he announced that he would stage *Cinderella* at the Café de Paris, with a cast drawn from the "Princess Margaret Set", who had previously appeared in a charity performance of *The Frog*. But soon afterwards the club closed because it did not make money, and the Major left the West End for Liverpool, to join Sam Wanamaker's New Shakespeare Theatre Club – a short-lived association which ended with a good deal of bad blood.

Neville-Willing then became John Heyman's manager at World Film Services; he later worked for Christopher Stamp when he managed The Who pop group; and yet another of his roles was as road-manager of a provincial tour by Norman Hartnell, the dress designer, on which he kept the girls in order.

For 35 years the Major was based in a small house in Kinnerton Street, Belgravia, the lease of which was given him by Hermione Gingold. He was unmarried.

Hugo Vickers writes: I am unlikely to forget my first sight of the Major. In 1984 there was a service of dedication of a stone for Noël Coward in Westminster Abbey. At the end of it Lady Diana Cooper was leaving the Abbey on the arm of her son, John Julius.

Suddenly a little man scampered forward, took her arm and escorted her down the aisle, bowing and waving to the congregation like a marionette – a curious antic, at the end of which he appeared anxious to accompany Lady Diana into her car. Lady Diana was left asking: "Who d'you suppose he was?"

Weeks later the indomitable Major was relaying his own version: "Her son called me over. He said: 'Donny, help me with my mother.' Well, she is 92. Lady Diana Manners . . . she's the Duchess of Something now. I've known her all my life. We walked down the aisle and we were photographed by everyone, and people rang up and said, 'Donny who were you with?'"

Inevitably the Major was a man more alluding than alluded to. There is, for instance, no mention of him in Noël Coward's diaries, yet the name "Noël" was seldom off his lips. All his life the Major was an uninhibited raconteur of his exploits – even if he trimmed veracity in cavalier fashion and incorporated as many famous names into his stories as possible.

The hotel he was associated with in New York before the war was by all accounts a pretty louche one. The Major had an unerring eye in selecting suitable guests and was a familiar figure at the quayside, touting at the gangways of the transatlantic liners.

During these years he frequented a particular brothel and would leave his manservant to give indication where he could be found by answering calls, "Mr Neville-Willing has gone to his club." He would announce to complete strangers, however, that he eschewed sex entirely and was "a kiss-and-cuddle person" – he was accordingly known in some cirlces as *"Never-Willing."*

He claimed that during the Wall Street Crash of 1929 the air was filled with the sound of falling stock-brokers, and that after each crunch on the pavement he would check to see if it was from his hotel or the one opposite. So he said.

It was in New York that Neville-Willing had all his teeth extracted. In mid-session the dentist got cold feet and declared, "A proper extractor must do this job", so he was sent off in a taxi, with eight teeth loose. In the midst of further agony, the new dentist said: "Look what this is doing to my hands. The veins are all swelling. I shall have to stop!"

Neville-Willing was rather disappointed in the false teeth he ended up with, and considered them a liability on amatory excursions – "I'm unlikely to be successful if the moon is bright," he complained.

Out in Bombay during the war Neville-Willing ran into Cecil Beaton at the Taj Hotel. The photographer described him in his diary as "like a kind old Jewish matriarch. Has been exceptionally useful to me, arranging special passes and doing odd chores."

Neville-Willing introduced Beaton to the Beach Candy Swimming Club, where the troops went to cavort; arranged a meeting with the Indian dancer Ram Gopal; and ended by packing Beaton's suitcase for him – "mothering me to the last".

Neville-Willing returned to England transformed as "the Major". The actor John Merivale recalled meeting him in London during the war, and his slight irritation at having to salute him; Noël Coward went further and dubbed him "Major, baby". The Major then went to Holland to assist with the restoration of civil liberties.

Few of his colourful tales would have passed muster with those fact-checkers employed by American magazines – he was wont to end interviews with the worrying phrase: "I'm glad you're checking and you know what I say is the truth. I'm honest."

But the Major was entertaining company, and always held his own. Like many of his sort he had a book of racy memoirs up his sleeve, which never found the favour of a publisher. By any but show-business standards he might be deemed a glorious fraud, but without such men the world would be a dimmer place. He would have loved the giant wreath that Elizabeth Taylor sent to his funeral.

March 10 1991

SIR RUPERT GRAYSON, BT

SIR RUPERT GRAYSON, 4th Bt, who has died aged 93, claimed to have dedicated himself "unselfishly and wholeheartedly to extracting as much pleasure from life as it had to offer."

This endeavour entailed much globe-trotting, as well as careers as Guardsman, King's Messenger, seaman, writer and publisher. In every circumstance "Rupe" Grayson manifested a talent for survival: it was said of him that even if – unlikely contingency – he had tried to drown himself in the Thames he would have been washed up alive in the Grill Room of the Savoy.

Wyndham Lewis used Grayson as the model for a grotesque character named Captain Humphrey Cooper Carter in his 1932 satire *Snooty Baronet*. "Humph", possessed of a colossal chin, was "absolutely like a big carnival doll – all costard and trunk, no legs to speak of." At the time Grayson made legal noises about some passages in the book, but when, at the end of his life, Lewis's caricature was read to him again, he simply roared with laughter.

Rupert Stanley Harrington Grayson was born on July 2 1897, the second of six sons – there were also six daughters – of Lt-Col Henry Mulleneux Grayson, a Liverpool shipping magnate who was Tory MP for the Western Division of Birkenhead after the First World War, and created a baronet in 1922.

Rupert's childhood home was Aberduna Hall, near Mold in North Wales; later the family settled down in a house called Ravenspoint on Tre-Arddur Bay in Anglesey. Here the Graysons constituted almost a separate community; as the children married, so houses and cottages proliferated for their accommodation.

It was from his father – known as "HMG" within the family circle – that Rupert Grayson inherited his epicurean leanings. Henry Grayson was considered the best-looking member of the House of Commons, and was reputed to have been the only one returned without ever making a single election speech. On polling day, after he had been elected with a 10,000 majority, a shrill voice sounded above the triumphal hubbub: "I wouldn't mind 'avin' a kid by you, Mister!"

Young Rupert was educated at Harrow, and then served with the Irish Guards in the First World War in which he was twice wounded. The same shell that inflicted the first of these injuries, lodging a splinter in Grayson's hand for the remainder of his life, killed Rudyard Kipling's son John. Kipling invited Grayson many times to Bateman's, his house in Sussex, treating him almost as a surrogate son.

Another consequence of the war was that Grayson, impressed by the devotion of the Irish soldiers to their ancient faith, became a Roman Catholic — in sharp distinction to his father, whose English Protestant God reflected the appropriate ideas about the British Empire, cricket and banking.

In 1919 Grayson married Gertrude Lawrence's cousin Ruby Banks, who had been the model for Raphael Kirschner's war-time pinups, but beyond the initial romantic idyll the union did not prosper. In 1925 he went to sea as a deckhand on what he called "bug-ridden tramps" in Latin American waters. After much experience — not least that of "the uncontrolled sexual hunger of the primitive woman" — he finally jumped ship in New York, which meant that his discharge papers were stamped "Voyage Not Completed" — a phrase which he adopted as the title for his first book of reminiscences, published in 1969.

Fortunately Grayson felt a compulsion for memoir writing. "I've always believed a man writes his autobiography because the tombstone is no longer in fashion and in his conceit he wants to record that he once existed." His second volume, *Stand Fast, the Holy Ghost* (1973), was, in his own parlance, a corker, written in a rollicking style.

It describes with comic relish the high life Grayson pursued on the Riviera and elsewhere after his return from sea. From a base provided by Louis Drexel, a scion of the Philadelphia banking clan who had married his sister Nancy, Grayson mixed merrily with a constellation of 1920s socialites, ranging from Duncan Orr-Lewis, the playboy millionaire baronet and Grenadier, to Scott and Zelda Fitzgerald.

The creator of Gatsby did not impress. "With his odious manners and great talent as a writer," Grayson wrote of him, "he was a money snob ready at the drop of a hat to raise his own hat to the rich."

For Grayson the ethics of Lotus-land found quintessential expression in the figure of Babe Barnato, a Bentley car buff and compulsive pleasure seeker, who was the first of the playboys to cease wearing hats. "He estimated it saved him a thousand a year in cloakroom tips," Grayson recalled.

Meanwhile Grayson had begun to write thrillers, notably the *Gun Cotton* series, "the James Bond of the Twenties and Thirties". A family publishing house, launched around 1930, also enlisted his energies in the role of literary talent scout. Before the Second War brought its demise, Grayson & Grayson had published luminaries as varied as Mauriac, O'Flaherty and Edgar Lee Masters.

In the mid-1930s Grayson spent nine months in Hollywood, consorting with the stars and taking "sneak-shot" photographs of their off-duty doings. He also composed music for films. Back in London, he resumed his old way of life, "a delightful sort of literary vagabondage", as he called it.

With the outbreak of the Second World War, he volunteered for a post which he had briefly filled when recovering from his wounds at the end of the First World War, that of King's Messenger for the Foreign Office, responsible for bags diplomatically exempt from frontier inspection. Grayson was supposedly the Messenger to whom a customs officer remarked: "I think, sir, your pouch has been roughly handled – some of its secrets are leaking out the bottom."

Afterwards, glorying in his lack of a fixed address, Grayson devoted his time to sampling the pleasure spots of the world. He used the Queen's Elm pub in Fulham Road as a London postal drop, and would occasionally hold court there, complete with an album of snaps illustrating his expeditions.

His restlessness was another legacy of childhood, for Sir Henry had peregrinated widely, with his brood in tow. "Our friends," recalled Grayson, "were the Pullman porters, seamen and waiters; our playrooms the decks of ships, passages of great hotels and corridors of international trains."

Many of Grayson's autumnal years were spent in Denia, on Spain's Costa Blanca, where his wit, charm, splended irascibility and cavalier sense of dress endeared him to Spaniards and expatriates alike. In his *Who's Who* entry he listed as his club the Tropico – a modest café in Denia, where a plate of paella costs 200 pesetas and egg and chips a mere 125.

But Sir Rupert's output as an author – he wrote some

20 thrillers — prove that he was no *flâneur*. In 1950 Michael Denison read extracts from his third volume of memoirs, *Cloak Without Dagger*, on Radio 4's *Book at Bedtime*.

Grayson succeeded his nephew in the baronetcy in 1987. He married, secondly, in 1950, Vari Colette, daughter of Major Henry O'Shea of the Royal Dublin Fusiliers. Another nephew, Jeremy Brian Vincent Harrington Grayson, born in 1933, succeeds as 5th Bt.

Sir Rupert recently announced in the Tropico that he intended that his last words should be "What time is the last flight?"

April 7 1991

FRANCES FARQUHARSON OF INVERCAULD

FRANCES FARQUHARSON OF INVERCAULD, wife of Capt Alwyne Farquharson, 16th Laird of Invercauld, who has died on the Isle of Mull, combined all the vitality and enterprise of her American roots with a deep respect for the "old world" to make a colourful career as a fashion journalist, before becoming one of the best loved characters of the Scottish Highlands.

She was born Frances Lovell Oldham at Seattle, America, around the turn of the century. Her father, Robert Pollard Oldham, was a company lawyer whose family, at Marietta, Ohio, could be traced back to Betty Washington, the only full sister of George Washington.

Her mother was Marybell Strickland, scion of a grand Bostonian family.

Frances grew up with a keen sense of history, and even as a little girl nurtured dreams of exploring the roots of European civilisation. Her mother died when she was still in her teens, and she had to take over the care of her younger brother and sister for some years. But while at school she began writing articles for local newspapers, saving the income with a view to paying her own passage to Europe.

Eventually her father helped her finance a trip, and entrusted her to the charge of a family friend who was sailing to Italy. After staying with an aunt in Rome, Frances travelled to Greece, Romania, Hungary, to Constantinople, Berlin, Paris and beyond, pursued everywhere by bouquets and proposals of marriage.

Gay, vivacious and tremendously talkative, she possessed an instinctive dramatic flair. She liked to dress up – particularly in Moroccan, Turkish and Spanish styles – and had no qualms about throwing together shocking pinks, canary yellows and vivid greens. Her great love was hats, and her outfits were invariably surmounted with an audacious head-dress – floppy or wide-brimmed hats, pill-boxes and (her favourite) amply upholstered turbans decorated with an orchid.

Frances wrote prolifically about her travels, and in Paris worked for some time in a *couture* salon. She had a strong memory, and never took notes when interviewing people for articles. She had, too, a remarkable facility for salesmanship – someone once remarked that she "could sell a straw hat to an Eskimo" – and soon after arriving in London she landed a job at *Vogue*, where she became fashion editor.

In 1928 she married James Rodney, a former RFC pilot who had won the MC in the First World War and was the second son of the 7th Lord Rodney. Five years later tragedy struck when a fire swept through the house in which they were staying, and Frances and her husband were forced to throw themselves from a second-floor window to escape. The ground was frozen, and she fell badly, fracturing three vertebrae in her spine.

Her husband ran back into the house to try to rescue those still trapped in the blaze; he was severely burnt, and died of complications in hospital soon afterwards. Frances herself was in hospital for more than two years, and never fully recovered her physical agility. As soon as she was able, though, she returned to work as fashion editor of *Harper's Bazaar*. She later became editor of the magazine, and in 1938 married for the second time, Capt Charles Gordon (dissolved 1948); they had a daughter, Marybell.

The Second World War found Frances crossing the Atlantic on a mission for the Department for Overseas Trade, to stimulate links between Britain and America. She spent six months there, doing hundreds of broadcasts and interviews, and was not content until she achieved her aim of seeing all the store windows on Fifth Avenue filled with prominent displays of British goods.

Soon after her return to Britain, she met Capt Alwyne Compton, who had been wounded while serving with the Royal Scots Greys in France (where he had won the MC) and was convalescing at his father's estate in Yorkshire.

They married in 1949 – in which year Capt Compton also assumed the surname and arms of Farquharson and was recognised Chief of the Clan. Frances embarked on a new life as the wife of a Highland Chief and Laird of Invercauld with characteristic determination, taking on the challenge of resuscitating a much encumbered and impoverished estate.

She developed a deep affection for the Scots, and in the course of the next three decades did much to foster local trade. She converted a deconsecrated church in the village into a theatre, which was inaugurated as the Invercauld Festival Theatre in 1952, and then converted a village hall into an exhibition centre for the sale of local handicrafts, including iron-works, ceramics, tweeds, glass blowing, jewellery and embroidery.

She also opened a women's clothes boutique, The Invercauld Speciality Shop, where Scottish lines of tartan and tweed had pride of place, and later followed this up with a men's shop, The Invercauld Sportsman.

Meanwhile she travelled all over Britain and further afield, armed with hand-looms and wool and promoting tartan. When asked on these journeys what she considered Scotland's best export, however, she took delight in responding, "the men". When it came to sartorial elegance, Frances used to say, Scots men provided her with her most virulent competition.

A talent for interior design went without saying. At Braemar Castle Frances spread her distinctive style liberally through many of the principal rooms, though she took great care to retain the indigenous period feel.

Pink remained her favourite colour throughout her life, and she daubed varying tones of it about her with superb confidence. Within weeks of her arrival at Invercauld in 1949 she had painted the entire exterior of a pagoda-style larder outside the kitchen in exuberant sugar-pink – "which looked marvellous," as her husband remarked, "against the snow".

Latterly Frances also persuaded her husband to receive paying guests at Invercauld House. With her charmingly softened American accent, her worldly, and yet also highly personal sense of humour, "Franzie" Farquharson proved an alluring hostess. She was buried at Invercauld in fitting style, with a brightly coloured bonnet adorning her coffin.

She is survived by her husband, and by her daughter.

April 28 1991

BARON ROLF BECK

BARON ROLF BECK, the Czechoslovakian-born industrialist, who has died aged 77, founded Slip Products, which specialised in motor accessories, and became known as the "Roving Baron" on account of the business trips he undertook all over the world.

A dark, sleek, persuasive personality, with a remarkable gift for languages, Beck was a natural salesman. He came to Britain before the Second World War with the idea of making Skoda motor cars in this country, with 51 per cent British parts and labour and 49 per cent Czechoslovakian parts.

Hitler upset this plan, but in 1939 the Baron created his own company, choosing the name Slip as being easy to pronounce in all languages. A year later he discovered Milex, a petrol economiser, and Dieslip, a fuel additive that attracted the attention of both the Admiralty and Ministry of War Transport.

The Government subsequently appointed Beck as an adviser on gas producer research, while Rolls-Royce made use of his talents to promote exports in America. After the war Beck made two transatlantic tours in this capacity, securing substantial orders; and he was particularly proud of having driven 740 miles in 10 hours – with only one arrest.

At home, Beck bought Layham Hall, in Suffolk, where his first wife kept exotic pets. In the Baron's absence on business, she found solace in the company of a white rat.

Guests at Layham, initially alarmed by this rodent, were generally won round by its docile character. The rat, when not sleeping on the Baroness's sleeve, would sit on her shoulder or nibble at titbits from her hand.

The Baroness also kept cats, labradors, guinea fowl, pekinese, several horses and a wallaby. Less successfully, she adopted an Indian sloth bear, named Bear.

In 1964 this animal suddenly went beserk and mauled its owner. The Baron, after stalking it through the mansion felled it with eight blasts from his shotgun.

After this experience he and his wife vowed that they would never again offer hospitality to wild animals; nevertheless, four years later his wife accepted a homeless five-foot-tall Malayan sun bear called Yogi at Layham.

This time the Baron was more cautious, and carried a cricket bat around with him on the estate in case of ursine aggression. But the bear seemed to be settling in splendidly: "It is such fun rolling around the place with him and taking him for walks," the Baroness enthused. "Yogi is perfectly sweet, and so *huge*, with enormous claws that could *destroy* you."

Within a month, however, disaster struck. Yogi ran amok throughout the house, causing nearly £500 of damage, after which he was swiftly despatched to a zoo at Cromer.

Rudolph Rolf Beck was born on March 25 1914. His father was Dr Baron Otto Beck, a successful industrialist in the Austro-Hungarian Empire and the Emperor Franz Josef's special envoy to Switzerland during the First World War.

Young Rolf was brought up on the family estates at Rohow, Czechoslovakia, where he acquired his first vehicle, a motor-bicycle, at the age of 11. He was educated at Theresanium Military Academy, before taking scientific and engineering degrees at Geneva, Zurich and Vienna Universities. As a young man, he was expert at sailing and skiing, and became a renowned amateur motor-racing driver, until he rejected the life of leisure to join the Skoda arms firm.

During the war, Beck made money from motor-car polish, and afterwards he embarked on several world tours to promote his own methods of saving oil. He believed that the new oilfields yielded crude oil containing too much sulphur, and evolved chemical formulae which, he claimed, not only enabled diesel engines and oil-fired furnaces to give greater power output, but also reduced engine wear.

In the late 1960s Slip Products fell on hard times, and in 1969 was in danger of going into liquidation.

Layham was put on the market, though fortunately not sold; and Beck subsequently managed to salvage his collapsing empire.

Latterly he continued to turn out new products, including Molyslip and Copaslip, a lubricant that prevented seizing, and in 1984, Molyslip 2001 – described by the Baron in *Who's Who* as "a metal treatment to be added to oil which considerably reduces engine wear, petrol and oil consumption, water and oil temperatures."

Beck married three times: first, in 1944, Elizabeth Fletcher; they had a son. He married secondly, in 1979, Countess Mariana von Rosen, daughter of Count Mörner of Bjorksund, Sweden; and thirdly, in 1990, Susan Cleland.

April 29 1991

VISCOUNT ST DAVIDS

THE 2ND VISCOUNT ST DAVIDS, who has died aged 74, was a canal boat enthusiast and much-loved figure among the children of Camden, where he founded the Pirate Club and was fondly dubbed "Pegleg" by its members.

Throughout his life he campaigned for the upkeep of the inland waterways and practised what he preached, living for many years on his yacht on the Regent's Canal.

Lord St Davids unexpectedly became a national figure in 1974, when his resignation from the Labour party was orchestrated by the Liberals for maximum political effect. Mr Jeremy Thorpe, then the Liberal leader, tantalised the press with hints of a grand defection to his ranks. But after 24 hours of carefully contrived mystery the unmasking of "Lord X" was widely regarded as an anti-climax.

"Lord *Who?*" was the initial reaction at Westminster and beyond. "Our darling Pirate King," replied the children of Camden Town, but no-one heard them.

At the time of his defection St Davids announced: "The mainstream [of the Labour party] used to stand for a classless honourable society. Now power is in the hands of the wild men who want to run Britain entirely for the trade unions."

Mr Harold Wilson, the Labour leader, was scathing about his resignation, saying: "It seems to me a case of Bertie Wooster rides again with a script from *The Pallisers.*"

St Davids indignantly pointed out that "Bertie Wooster was never a socialist. Damn it, I have been a socialist all my political life, and my voting record for the Labour party in the House of Lords is second to none."

St Davids founded the Regent's Boat Club – a floating youth club for boys and girls – almost by accident in 1966: "It began with youngsters asking to borrow my boats moored on the canal at the bottom of my garden. They told their friends and before I knew what was really happening we were in business."

A committee was formed, an old steel canal boat bought to serve as headquarters and a fleet built up around it, which grew to include motor boats, sailing boats, canoes and dinghies. Hundreds of local schoolchildren joined and spent their weekends and holidays happily paddling about in the water under the benevolent eye of St Davids.

It was funded from various sources, not least by boatloads of young pirates, gaily dressed in full regalia, who were despatched by the Viscount along the Regent's Canal with a brief to raid what they could where they could. The club was run on an extremely democratic basis, and children who misbehaved were allowed to choose between expulsion, confinement to the barge or "a smack on the seat".

The club ran for six years before St Davids retired from his position as warden because of staffing difficulties. A new venture, called the Pirate Club, soon succeeded it.

Jestyn Reginald Austen Plantagenet Philipps was born on Feb 19 1917. His father was the 1st Baron St Davids (later given a viscountcy on the recommendation of his friend Lloyd George); his mother, Lady Elizabeth Rawdon-Hastings, in whose favour the medieval Baronies of Strange of Knokin, Hungerford and de Moleyns were called out of abeyance in 1921.

Young Jestyn's paternal grandfather was the Rev Sir James Philipps, 12th Bt, of Picton in Pembrokeshire, several of whose sons became rich and influential through finance, shipping and other business, and three of whom became peers; Viscount St Davids, Lord Milford and Lord Kylsant.

The 1st Lord St Davids was a barrister, racehorse owner, financier and Liberal MP. The career of the 1st (and last) Lord Kylsant ended unfortunately with a term of imprisonment, incurred through infringing company law in what he felt to be in the interests of his shareholders; and the eldest son of the 1st Lord Milford, the present Lord Milford, rejected capitalism and became a Communist.

Young Jestyn was educated at Eton and Trinity College, Cambridge. He developed a taste for Left-wing politics and for being afloat at an early age. During the Spanish Civil War he broke his spine in a Basque cargo boat.

He inherited the Viscountcy of St Davids on his father's death in 1938 and joined the Labour party a year later.

During the Second World War he served in the Army as a batman to a padre and then as a petty officer in the Royal Naval Volunteer Reserve. Other youthful ventures included stints as a mate on a sailing barge and running pleasure boat trips from Paddington Basin to Uxbridge for seven shillings a day. But St Davids refusal to espouse the commercial spirit of his family resulted in his appearance in the bankruptcy courts in 1954, when he was forced to sell two of his three canal boats as well as the medieval Roch Castle in Pembrokeshire.

Undaunted, St Davids became an inveterate explorer of the canals of London and the Home Counties in his yacht, *Tortoise*. He also spent many happy hours playing with his model boats on the Round Pond in Kensington Gardens. He was, though, a formidable enemy of fireworks: he used at frequent intervals to introduce Bills in the House of Lords to regulate their sale and discharge.

He was an active figure in the House, both as a Labour peer and as an Independent. When the Peerage Bill was debated in 1963, St Davids spoke and voted against it on the grounds that it would be a mistake to extend the hereditary principle – although he admitted to feeling ungallant, as both his mother, Lady Strange of

Knokin, and aunt, the Countess of Loudoun, were hereditary peeresses in their own right.

But the Bill was enacted, enabling, among other
things, hereditary peeresses in their own right to take
their seats in the Lords. His 79-year-old mother duly
became the first to do so.

Lady Strange of Knokin and Lord St Davids were the
first mother and son to sit together in the Lords – albeit
on opposite sides of the chamber. In 1965 they marched
into opposite lobbies in the vote on the Earl of Arran's
Bill on homosexual reform. And when Lady Strange of
Knokin made her maiden speech – on the care of the
elderly – later that year, it was the first time in the
history of the House that a son was able to congratulate
his mother, "My noble relative".

His mother died in 1974, when he succeeded to the
Baronies of Strange of Knokin, Hungerford and de
Moleyns.

St Davids served on the committee of the House of
Lords Yacht Club. He had a notable collection of shells,
for which he had dived around the world.

He married first, in 1938 (dissolved 1954), Doreen
Guinness Jowett from Australia; they had a son and four
daughters. He married secondly, in 1954 (dissolved
1959), Elisabeth Woolf; and thirdly, in 1959, Evelyn
Harris.

The heir to the Viscountcy and the other titles is his
eldest son, Colwyn Jestyn John Philipps, born 1939.

June 13 1991

LORD VIVIAN

THE 5TH LORD VIVIAN, who has died aged 85, became a celebrity in 1954, when he was shot in the abdomen by Mavis Wheeler, the former wife of Sir Mortimer Wheeler and the former mistress of Augustus John.

Police were called to Mrs Wheeler's cottage near Devizes by ambulancemen, who had been sent there after a telephone call from a public kiosk at the end of a nearby lane. They had found Vivian lying on the ground some yards from the house. He also had a minor shot wound in the wrist.

Mrs Wheeler, who was immediately remanded in custody, intially denied any involvement in the affair. But at a second hearing she claimed that the shooting had been an accident: "I am devoted to him and he is devoted to me," she said.

When, after some weeks in a critical condition in hospital, Vivian began to recover, he admitted that he was "rather apprehensive about the future", since Mrs Wheeler had already threatened him with a gun on a previous occasion.

He also indicated that she had once attempted to commit suicide by cutting her wrists when they were both at the cottage. They had been living together for about six months.

Mrs Wheeler languished in Holloway prison until the end of August, when, almost a month after the shooting, she was called to trial, charged with attempted murder.

At the trial, which caused a sensation in the press and

continued at Salisbury Assizes for several weeks, it emerged that Vivian had been shot while he was endeavouring to climb through the window of Mrs Wheeler's cottage, but the two parties gave conflicting accounts of the precise course of events.

Mrs Wheeler said Vivian had pointed the gun at her "in fun", and that it went off when they both got hold of it. Vivian, who gave evidence from his hospital bed, claimed that she had shot him as he was re-entering the cottage by the window after a visit to the local George and Dragon pub – they had previously lost the key.

He was quite certain, he insisted, that Mrs Wheeler had not intended to kill him, but admitted that their relationship had for some time been complicated by Mrs Wheeler's fits of extreme jealousy. The principal problem, for both the defence and the prosecution, was that Vivian himself did not seem to be clear about what had happened.

He admitted to the court that during the time between his arrival at the cottage that day and the shooting that night he had drunk a quarter bottle of wine, three liqueurs, seven to eight glasses of sherry, three to four bottles of stout and "possibly two other drinks".

Vivian insisted that "some sort of accident must have occurred", and made no secret of his wretchedness at Mrs Wheeler being "pilloried" by everyone; he said it was quite untrue that she had broken up his marriage.

Mrs Wheeler was found guilty of maliciously wounding Vivian and sentenced to six months' imprisonment. Ten minutes after the sentence the couple were to be found, locked in the most unmurderous of embraces, in a cell beneath the courtroom.

Anthony Crespigny Claude Vivan was born on March 4 1906 into a long-established Cornish family. His father was the 4th Lord Vivian, who won the DSO in the First World War; his mother, Barbara Fanning, a former Gaiety Girl. His sister is Daphne Fielding, the author, formerly married to the Marquess of Bath.

Young Tony was educated at Eton and then sought adventure in Canada, where he became a call-boy in a Vancouver theatre. On his return to England he became assistant manager under Edward Laurillard at the Piccadilly Theatre. He also dabbled in musical entertainment – first as leader of a band called Tony Vivian and his Band at the Café Anglais, and secondly with another band at the Ritz Hotel.

On the outbreak of the Second World War Vivian enlisted in the Royal Artillery, but was invalided out in 1940. At the end of that year he succeeded to the peerage when his father died while out shooting near Bodmin.

He subsequently served as a special constable and as a war correspondent before becoming a theatrical impresario. Vivian went into partnership with the veteran showman Charles B. Cochran and for a while their company flourished.

Their first joint venture, *Bless the Bride* (1947), the A. P. Herbert and Vivian Ellis musical, ran for two and a half years at the Adelphi. But *Tough at the Top*, which replaced it, was a failure, and from then on Cochran Productions hovered constantly on the verge of financial ruin. Vivian plunged much of his fortune into it, and after the death of Cochran he found it increasingly difficult to make ends meet. In 1954, after a production of J. B. Priestley's *The White Countess* made a loss of £8,000, he closed it down.

All in all 1954 was a bad year for Vivian. Not long before being shot by Mrs Wheeler he had been arrested for being "drunk and indecent" at South Eaton Place. At Marlborough Street magistrates' court afterwards – where the charge was proved against him but he received an absolute discharge – Vivian caused some amusement by saying that his occupation was "a peer of the realm".

"That is a description," replied the magistrate, "but it is not an occupation, is it?"

"I beg your pardon, sir," said Vivian, "I thought it was."

In fact Vivian had hardly been a regular in the House of Lords. During his maiden speech in 1967, he apologised for the fact that, although he had taken his seat three months before the Coronation, his work as an impresario had prevented him from attending.

In the late 1950s Vivian embarked on a new, but hardly less ill-fated career in catering – first as manager of Charco's Restaurant in Chelsea, which soon burned down, and then as director of La Pavillon in Chelsea.

In 1962, after the police had been called in to investigate an incident at the restaurant in which a number of customers and a waiter were injured, Vivian announced his intention to leave "the smoke" of the city, and retire to a house five miles away at Norwood.

Within months, though, he re-entered the fray with a job as catering adviser aboard the Canadian Pacific liner, Empress of Canada, on a Christmas cruise.

He married, in 1930, Victoria, daughter of Capt H. G. L. Oliphant, RN; she died in 1985, They had two sons and a daughter.

The elder son, Brig Nicholas Crespigny Laurence Vivian, born 1935, now succeeds to the peerage.

June 27 1991

EARL ATTLEE

THE 2ND EARL ATTLEE, who has died aged 63, pursued a number of careers with varying degrees of success: in the Merchant Navy, in public relations, as a jewellery salesman and, more recently, as SDP spokesman for transport and maritime affairs in the House of Lords.

The only son of Clement Attlee, the Labour Prime Minister created an earl in 1955, Martin Attlee avoided politics in his early years, on the grounds that "one politician in the family was enough". He later described himself as a "right-wing Labourite", but left the Labour party in 1973. In 1981 he joined the SDP, and three years ago stood at Hampshire Central as SDP candidate for the European Parliament.

The same year he argued in the Lords that British interests could only be protected by pushing for a common currency and a central European bank, based in the City of London. He did not favour a United States of Europe, however, and thought members of the EC should be permitted "some quaint foibles". Britain, for example, should retain the mile and the pint.

In the Lords, Attlee was an active campaigner for the

disabled, and for stiffer penalties against drug traffickers. He once suggested that they should be forcibly "mainlined" with heroin, to "give them a taste of the living death they have been pushing".

He also confessed to the Upper House his own experience of drug use. On holiday in Portugal, he said he had been passed a cannabis cigarette at a party, and found himself "on a high". The Earl described how he fought the sensation, which he found very unpleasant.

Attlee "stumbled into the PR business", as he put it, after leaving the Merchant Navy in the 1950s and began his career as an account executive with Sidney Barton. He was assistant PR officer for British Rail's Southern Region at Waterloo from 1970 to 1976, when he was made redundant. He later ran his own company, Wilden Attlee PR Associates.

In 1971 he annoyed some of his more pompous colleagues in the trade by publishing an informative and humorous book, *Bluff Your Way in PR*, which was dedicated "to those clients I'd most like to handle — Brigitte Bardot, Miss World, etc."

Describing himself as "a very great male chauvinist", Attlee once wrote a short story for *Mayfair* magazine, and in 1977 announced: "I am writing the Great British Novel. It is about sex."

Martin Richard Attlee was born on Aug 10 1927, and educated at Millfield and Southampton University. He served in the Merchant Navy from 1945 to 1950 and for the next five years was an active member of the Honorable Artillery Company. He succeeded to the earldom on his father's death in 1967.

After losing his job at Waterloo he worked as a

Earl Attlee

jewellery salesman, selling chrome and gold-plated pendants and bracelets. He visited Saudi Arabia to sell identity talismans to the Saudi armed forces, but was forced to return when he discovered that Muslim law forbade personal adornments.

Attlee was appointed SDP spokesman on transport affairs in 1984, and four years later became SDP Deputy Whip in the Lords; he was also a member of the All-Party Defence Study Group.

He enjoyed every kind of challenge, and had an inventive streak. In 1985 he devised a process to prevent paint solidifying after the can has been opened – although the patent lapsed because he was unable to find a buyer.

Attlee also worked on ways to improve helicopter safety, and for a time could be seen running up and down his garden with a model helicopter on a stick – "My neighbours must think I'm mad," he said.

A keen supporter of various charities, Attlee was president of the National Association of Industries for the Blind and Disabled. In 1980 he celebrated Leap Year for the St John's Ambulance Brigade by playing leapfrog in Park Lane with Lords Redesdale, Marchwood, Ilchester and Kimberley.

The previous year, having fallen asleep one evening on an underground train and woken up at the end of the line, he made his way to a police station to inquire about late-night taxi services, and found himself roughly seized, bundled into a cell and charged with drunkenness.

The experience left its mark, and Attlee recently drew attention to "horrific stories of police arrogance, especially when it comes to picking up boys with public school accents". He was a prolific writer of letters to newspapers

— particularly to *The Daily Telegraph* — and a vigorous defender of his father's memory.

Attlee married twice: first, in 1955, Anne Henderson (divorced 1988), by whom he had a son and a daughter; and secondly, in 1988, Margaret Gouriet, an actress. He is succeeded in the earldom by his son, Viscount Prestwood (born Oct 3 1956).

July 29 1991

"DICKIE"
FELLOWES-GORDON

DOROTHY "DICKIE" FELLOWES-GORDON, who has died aged 100, was the companion of the redoubtable American hostess Elsa Maxwell and perhaps the last survivor of that hectic social whirl devoted to parties in London, Paris, New York and the Riviera.

Tall, with jet-black hair, the aristocratically Scottish "Dickie" Fellowes-Gordon cut a striking and elegant figure, and presented an extraordinary contrast to the mountainous Miss Maxwell. While some regarded Miss Maxwell, a legendary self-publicist, as ineffably vulgar, others professed to find her irresistibly funny. Eight years Miss Fellowes-Gordon's senior, she had an uncanny knack of picking up celebrities and of persuading rich social climbers to foot the bill for her lavish parties.

Miss Fellowes-Gordon, often disapproving of her friend's profligacy with other people's money, acted as a restraining influence on her wilder schemes. On one occasion she deterred Elsa from an ill-judged attempt to create a fake beach of rubber tar and sand on the rocks of Monte Carlo.

When they met in about 1912 Miss Fellowes-Gordon already possessed what Miss Maxwell described as "the beauty and sharp wit that were to make her one of Europe's *femmes fatales*, a role she attained without half trying'.

Ronald Bodley wrote of Miss Fellowes-Gordon that she had "one of the most lovely voices" he had ever heard. She once sang at the same party as Dame Nellie Melba, and Bodley could not decide between them.

He thought Miss Fellowes-Gordon might have achieved fame and fortune as an opera singer "had she not been blessed with a lazy temperament and enough money to live on without working'.

A scion of the lairds of Knockespoch in Aberdeenshire, Dorothy Fellowes-Gordon was born on Aug 3 1891.

Her ancestors included King George IV's physician, and the doughty Rear-Adml Sir Thomas Fellowes, who during his command of the gunboats at Cadiz from 1810 to 1811 is said to have slept every night in the *Watchful's* cabin — a hole seven feet long and three feet high — despite his considerable height and a girth which matched Miss Maxwell's.

Young "Dickie's" parents, Arthur Fellowes-Gordon accepted the American's familiar opening gambit, "I'm giving a little party tonight and I'd love you to come."

But while Miss Fellowes-Gordon treated what Miss

Maxwell called "the chi-chi pack shrilly pursuing notoriety after World War One" with Scottish disdain, her
looks and spirit did not fail to attract attention.

Their friendship took time to ripen. By the time they
met again by chance in London Miss Fellowes-Gordon
had had a row with her stepfather and was looking for
chambers of her own. She suggested to Miss Maxwell that
they set up house together. Elsa had no money, but
Dickie had plenty from her father's estate. "It's enough
for both of us," said Miss Fellowes-Gordon. "One of these
days you'll make a strike and the shoe will be on the
other foot."

Many years were to pass before this was even a remote
possibility, but Miss Maxwell noted, "Dickie and I hit it
off perfectly in our flat." For a great number of years Miss
Fellowes-Gordon   supported   Miss   Maxwell,   who
bemoaned her occasional inconvenient absences elsewhere.

When the First World War began the pair retreated
to a small inn at Marlow but this soon palled and in 1915
they sailed for America. In New York they furnished a
small apartment on Madison Avenue, and ate off a
wooden table with Woolworth utensils until Mrs O. H.
P. Belmont (Consuelo Vanderbilt's mother) generously
arranged a delivery of silver.

Their various activities included running a soda
fountain at the Allied Bazaar at Grand Central Palace.
On one occasion Miss Fellowes-Gordon sang at a party
given for Lucien Muratore and his wife Lina Cavaliere.

After the war the two women shared an apartment in
Paris near Montmartre, rented for $100 a year. Miss
Maxwell was out and about a great deal but "happy to
stay home occasionally and make a feeble gesture at

dieting on the meals prepared by Dickie, an excellent cook when the spirit moves her".

The pair frequently crossed the Channel. At a party in London given by Lady Colefax in 1922 Miss Maxwell picked up "a young man with an unusual, almost Mongolian countenance", and Miss Fellowes-Gordon duly paid his fare to Venice.

This was Noël Coward, then still trying to make his name. The three of them spent a fortnight together, after which Coward observed: "The life of a gigolo, unimpaired by amatory obligations, could undoubtedly be very delightful indeed."

He was to capture something of Elsa and Dickie's approach to life in his song *I Went to a Marvellous Party*:

> *Quite for no reason I'm here for the season,*
> *And high as a kite*
> *Living in error with Maud at Cap Ferrat*
> *Which couldn't be right*
> *Ev'ry one's here and frightfully gay,*
> *Nobody cares what people say,*
> *Tho' the Riviera*
> *Seems really much queerer*
> *Than Rome at its height.*
> *Yesterday night*
> *I went to a marvellous party . . .*

Miss Maxwell and Miss Fellowes-Gordon prevailed upon Coward to play the piano for them at a party given for Princess Helena Victoria, at which Ivor Novello and Gertrude Lawrence sang.

Elsa and Dickie were celebrated for their pranks. On one occasion Miss Fellowes-Gordon asked Duff Cooper if she might bring a rather eccentric Spanish authoress to dine – this turned out to be Hugo Rumbold, an incorrigible hoaxer, in disguise.

After the second World War Miss Fellowes-Gordon acquired an unpretentious farmhouse at Auribeau, 12 miles from Cannes. A millstone was converted into a low and notoriously unsatisfactory outside table, yet such were the jollifications organised there by Miss Maxwell that guests flocked from far and wide, travelling by winding back roads, to endure the discomfort.

Miss Maxwell's tricky friendship with the Duke and Duchess of Windsor began in 1947. Miss Fellowes-Gordon disapproving as ever, at first refused to meet them; she eventually succumbed to an invitation to the Windsors' Château de la Croe, though she went determined to dislike them.

But although Miss Fellowes-Gordon bridled when some of the guests curtsied to the Windsors she was impressed when the Duchess sensed this and firmly put out her hand, indicating that she did not expect a curtsey. Miss Fellowes-Gordon was also forced to concede that the Duke was "charming".

In 1959 Coward, dining in Paris with the Windsors, noted that "Elsa and Dickie not so good. Actually Dickie all right but Elsa thoroughly disagreeable and drunk with imaginary power. It was a sad day when she first began to write that idiotic [newspaper] column and still a sadder one when she was allowed on television. It has given her delusions of grandeur that are quite startling."

In 1961 Cecil Beaton observed Miss Maxwell at a Volpi ball in Venice, being assisted to the entrance "like a terrified buffalo . . . dressed in a gold-bead embroidery of a magnificence that should belong to a Calpurnia or a Volumnia".

Two years later Elsa Maxwell died in New York. Dickie Fellowes-Gordon led a quiet life thereafter.

Social historians, for whom she would have been a splendid source, assumed that she had died years ago, and she remained unconsulted by biographers – with the notable exception of Hugo Vickers.

In fact Miss Fellowes-Gordon came to live in London, spending her last days in Pimlico.

August 13 1991

"SADIE" BARNETT

"SADIE" BARNETT, a Cambridge legend, who has died aged 80, was one of the last of the great Dickensian landladies – and certainly the sole surviving private landlady in King's Parade.

She presided over the most splendid digs in the University at No 9 King's Parade, overlooking King's College Chapel and the Gibbs Building.

Mrs Barnett's social expectations of her lodgers were as traditional as the ambience of her rooms – and in this respect she was perhaps more of a Trollopian than a Dickensian figure. She would frequently ask Gonville and Caius College, from which she held the leasehold, to supply her with "proper young gentlemen". When Caius undergraduates became too *bourgeois* for her liking, she turned to Magdalene and Pembroke.

She greeted the representative of one noble family

with the words: "The last time we had a lord here, he hanged himself in room four." To another upon receipt of his Coutts' cheque at the end of his first term, she declared: "You're very modest, aren't you? You didn't say you was no *Hon.*"

In later years Mrs Barnett took in undergraduates from less exalted backgrounds, but she took a dim view of their career prospects when compared with their landed coevals'. "*Nah*, he's labour," she would say dismissively – though it was unclear whether by this she meant that he was destined for manual labour or was merely perceived as a supporter of the Labour party.

Mrs Barnett never entertained doubts about the rectitude of her grander residents. "He was such a gent," she once said, "When he was sick he was always sick out of the window."

One recent resident, Simon Sebag-Montefiore, set much of his fictional university memoir *King's Parade* (1991) at her house; but the publishers are said to have found the character based on Mrs Barnett beyond belief, and she was duly excised.

Mrs Barnett was always very proud of the achievements of her "boys", who latterly had included the historians Andrew Roberts and Michael Bloch. She regularly corresponded with her *alumni* all over the world, and would sometimes stay with them on her travels.

She was born Sarah Wolfschaut on Jan 3 1911 at Stepney, east London, the daughter of a Jewish fruit and vegetable trader in Aldgate.

Young Sadie was the seventh of 10 children and began life in the rag trade, as a dressmaker. At the age of

15 she met a waiter, Michael Barnett, whom she married in 1932.

They moved to Cambridge where Mrs Barnett began her career as a landlady. They separated during the Second World War but their childless union was never dissolved.

From the late 1940s Mrs Barnett enjoyed the lease-hold at King's Parade. Although *kosher* herself, she cooked breakfast of eggs and bacon for her lodgers, and had strict rules about women and hours of residence.

She regretted the passing of the more deferential under-graduates and after the upheavals of the 1960s felt sorely tried by her more high-spirited lodgers, who preferred an unsupervised existence.

Some claimed that Mrs Barnett was an unconscious exemplar of enlightened despotism, but in reality she was a maternal neo-feudalist who exercised great care over her wards. She could display an almost Plantagenet *"ira et malevolentia"*, which concealed a fundamentally good heart.

This fierce protectiveness manifested itself when the constabulary arrived to arrest one tenant after some under-graduate excess: "You leave him alone, he's not a burglar. He's not a murderer. He's one of my nice young men."

On another occasion, when some anti-"Blood Sports" campaigners, enraged by the sight of a brace of pheasants hung out of her window by one of her lodgers, sought to gain entry to the house, she gave them short shrift. "He can kill what he likes," she told them. "He's a *sportsman*, you know."

Attired in a quilted dressing-gown, Mrs Barnett would sit in her room for much of the day watching the trade test transmission card on BBC. "I am waiting for the Royals to come on . . . I know they will be on soon – Ascot and all that," she would say, whatever the season.

When some undergraduates tried to disseminate the "free Mandela" message to her lodgers, she showed them the door with the parting shot: "Who is this *Nelson Piquet* anyway?"

Mrs Barnett could always detect the tread of women's feet on the stairs and would display remarkable swiftness in bounding after them in order, prematurely, to enforce the official curfew.

She was intolerant of the ways of the Modern Girl and when introduced to two of the species at a tea party declared: "'*Pickle*' and '*Pooh*'? What sort of names are those? Get out of here, you brazen hussies! You're here for one thing – and for one thing only."

On one occasion she was found on her hands and knees outside the door, eavesdropping. Within, a lodger had a "punk" girl friend with dyed green hair, whom he hid under a blanket when Mrs Barnett suddenly entered.

Mrs Barnett poked the bedding with a broomhandle, thereby revealing the naked punk. She threw out the tenant, observing: "I wouldn't have minded if it was only the hair on her head that was green."

Sadie Barnett was an efficient landlady who was capable of great kindnesses to those in need – particularly foreign students, who for years afterwards would write her grateful letters.

But not for nothing did the university newspaper describe her as "King's Parade's Boadicean landlady".

August 15 1991

LT-COL HUGH ROSE

LIEUTENANT-COLONEL HUGH ROSE, an intrepid soldier and explorer, who has died aged 86, was the first European to climb the Kuh-i-Taftan, an active volcano in Persian Baluchistan.

Rose enjoyed a remarkably adventurous life, in which he saw service on the North-West Frontier, in Tibet, Aden, Persia, Egypt, Malaya and Borneo. Many of his experiences verged on the bizarre.

Hugh Vincent Rose was born on April 11 1905 and educated at Aldenham and Sandhurst. He had his first sight of military action at the age of nine in 1914, for his family were then living at Knocke-le-Zoute, where the Belgian infantry confronted the German Uhlans.

His family was evacuated from Zeebrugge by destroyer. Soon afterwards he told the whole exciting story to an old lady he met in the grounds of Farnborough Convent. Subsequently he learned that she was the Empress Eugenie.

Rose was commissioned in 1924 and was posted to the 3rd QAO Gurkha Rifles who were then in the Khyber and saw active service against the Afridis and Orakzais. In 1931, with two companions, he crossed the main Himalayan range by four dangerous and little used passes – each more than 18,000 ft – to explore and sketch, for the Survey of India, an unmapped area called Hoti, on the British border land of Western Tibet.

There he discovered an unknown pass across the Zaskar Range into Tibet but heavy snowfalls trapped his party, one of whom had a badly poisoned knee, at 14,000 ft. As the only skier in the expedition, Rose then crossed into Upper Kumaon, covered 18 miles by moonlight to the village of Gonsali and returned the next night with food and stores carried by two Kamet porters.

Thus fortified, the party crossed into Tibet and thence home by the Niti pass. All three were then severely reprimanded for overstaying their leave and for crossing into Tibet without official passes.

In 1932 Rose was seconded to be personal assistant to the Resident and Chief Commissioner of Aden. Shortly after his arrival the Emperor Haile Selassi and King Alfonso of Spain turned up at the same time to stay at the Residency.

At the subsequent banquet Rose had to decide whom to place on the Resident's right, a ruling Emperor or a non-reigning King married to a British princess. He decided in favour of the Lion of Judah and as a result was made a Chevalier of the Ethiopian Order of Menelik II.

Although Socotra was part of the Aden Protectorate it had never been visited until reports were received that the Sultan was flying the Italian flag. The Resident, the political agent and Rose thereupon sailed for Temerida, the capital, in HMS *Penzance* which, on arrival, trained its guns on the palace and invited the Sultan on board.

The Sultan was received with due ceremony before being ordered to entertain the ship's company ashore for a week and to provide 30 camels and guides for the exploration of the interior. Although the coastal Arabs were prosperous merchant traders, the Aboriginals in the interior were given to witchcraft and cannibalism.

The party then went on to Mukalla, where the Sultan

laid on a Guard of Honour. Although dressed as Boy Scouts this guard turned out to be the Sultan's slaves. The party's next assignment was to fly in three Wapiti aircraft to Shibam in the Hadramaut, which had also never been visited. The object was to stop a civil war between the Fahdli Sultan of Shibam and the Seyyids of Tarim and to rescue an English peer's son who was feared lost in those parts.

On their return journey, having ended the war and found the peer's peregrinating son, Rose had to share the rear cockpit of the Wapiti with a wild Arabian Oryx destined for London Zoo.

Shortly afterwards, when spending 10 days leave in British Somaliland. Rose suddenly came face to face with a black-maned lion and its mate. Both were on the point of charging him when his life was saved by a village marriage procession which suddenly emerged from the bush with ululations and drum beating.

Rose's next appointment was at Meshed, in northeast Persia, as Vice-Consul. There his chief task was to organise the escape of White Russians across the border, 70 miles away.

He also helped to organise espionage, which included the robbing of a safe in the Soviet Embassy. Subsequently he was appointed Vice-Consul at Zaliidan in the south, where he collected numerous archaeological specimens.

Here he discovered that the 12,000ft-high Kuh-i-Taftan, though an active volcano, was blanketed in snow, and also lay in a prohibited military zone where the new Shah was fighting rebel tribesmen. As he descended, Rose encountered some black-tented nomads whose white-bearded patriarch had a goat killed in his honour. On returning to Zahidan, however, Rose learned that his hirsute host was the chief rebel and that in consequence questions were being asked about Rose in both the *Majlis* (Persian Parliament) and the House of Commons.

Rose was then transferred to South Waziristan, on the North-West Frontier of India, as assistant political agent. Rose's predecessor – and indeed his successor – were murdered, a fate which Rose only narrowly escaped, being shot at several times. On another occasion, when trying to discover the whereabouts of the elusive Fakir of Ipi, Rose's small party was ambushed and nearly wiped out.

The headquarters of the agency was at Tank, where, assisted by the Nawab who provided the horses, Rose founded a tent club, as pig-sticking associations were known.

In 1935 Rose attended the Staff College at Quetta. Subsequently he held various staff appointments, but during the Second World War he served with his battalions in the Middle East, at one time as acting CO.

After this he became GSO1 in Aden and then Commander of the Mewar Infantry in Egypt. After the war he commanded the 4th/1st Gurkha Rifles in Malaya and also took over 33 Brigade. His last active service command was with the 1st/3rd Gurkha Rifles in Calcutta during the traumatic period of Partition.

In 1950 Rose came out of retirement to act as deputy director of operations against Coptic and Muslim terrorists in Eritrea. There he introduced the "Ferret Force" system, later adopted by Gen Templer in Malaya.

In 1952 Rose obtained a Colonial Office appointment as State Home Guard Officer, Perak, Malaya, and from there, in 1954 went to Singapore to work with the Joint Intelligence Committee, Far East. His final appointment was Deputy Defence Secretary, North Borneo.

At the end of this contract he returned to England and floated a property company in South Kensington and a firewood business in Devon.

Apart from his polo, pig-sticking, shooting and ski-ing (which he continued into his eighties), Rose was a competent squash player who represented the United Services and Army and Navy clubs, and an enthusiastic yachtsman.

Rose published a book of poems and contributed to various journals, including *Blackwood's Magazine* and *The Times*. He was a Fellow of the Royal Geographical Society.

His first marriage, to Barbara Allcard, was dissolved. They had a son (Maj-Gen Michael Rose) and a daughter. Rose married secondly, in 1954, Susan Sclater; they had a son.

September 13 1991

SIR EWAN FORBES OF CRAIGIEVAR, BT

SIR EWAN FORBES OF CRAIGIEVAR, 11th Bt, doctor, magistrate, landowner and farmer, who has died aged 79, was embroiled in a three-year dispute during the late 1960s to establish his claim to the baronetcy.

For Sir Ewan had been registered as a girl at his birth and went by the name of Elizabeth Forbes-Sempill until

1952 when – by that time a much-loved GP in his native Aberdeenshire – he re-registered his birth and changed his name to Ewan Forbes-Sempill.

He was born on Sept 6 1912 and baptised Elizabeth as the third and youngest daughter of the 18th Lord Semphill, head of the Forbes-Sempill family, a long-established Scottish dynasty holding a 15th century Barony and a Baronetcy of Nova Scotia, created in 1630.

Young "Betty" (as she was known) was educated at her home by a tutor after having refused to go away to a girls' school. Her girlhood was dominated by general gender insecurity. Sir Ewan was later to remark that he thought "everyone realised my difficulties but it was hard in those days for anyone to know what to do."

The greatest ordeal came towards the end of the teenage years, when Betty Forbes-Sempill was taken to London "to go through with that ridiculous convention, the coming-out season". She "hated every minute of it" and longed to return to her horses and dogs in Scotland.

The recalcitrant Betty was sent abroad – where she attended Munich University – before her dearest wish was granted and she returned to Scotland. There she recruited a team of Scottish country dancers from Donside. They were dubbed the "Dancers of Don" and delighted audiences all over Scotland. Miss Forbes-Sempill was also a talented harpist and clarsach player.

On the death of her father, the 18th Lord Sempill, in 1934, both the barony and the baronetcy passed to her elder brother, who entrusted the management of his Fintray and Craigievar estates to his sister.

Miss Forbes-Sempill's little beige van – "Betty's Covered Wagon" – containing produce from the farms and game from the moors was a familiar sight in the neighbourhood. She left the fashionable world of London far behind as she took to speaking and reciting in broad Scots. Her usual attire at this time was a mannish kilt – although she eschewed the masculine fashion of turning down her stockings.

During the Second World War she went to Aberdeen University to study medicine, and after graduating in 1944, worked for a year as a senior casualty officer at the Aberdeen Royal Infirmary.

In 1945 she took up practice in the Alford district and it was from this point onward that Elizabeth Forbes-Sempill looked and behaved liked the man she knew she really was. Her practice was one of the largest in north-east Scotland and "the Doctor" (as she became generally known) was tireless in her efforts to reach her patients. In the winter months she often had to travel through 10ft drifts of snow to reach isolated hill crofts – hazardous journeys which she undertook in an ex-Army caterpillar-tracked bren-gun carrier specially procured for the purpose.

Dr Forbes-Sempill went about her change of gender in the quietest possible manner. She applied to the Sheriff of Aberdeen, and acquired a warrant for birth re-registration.

Then, on Sept 12 1952, there appeared a notice in the advertisement columns of *The Press and Journal*, Aberdeen, which stated that henceforth Dr Forbes-Sempill wished to be known as Dr Ewan Forbes-Sempill.

The patients at his medical practice were loyal and supportive when sought out by the press. "The doctor has been telling us for some time of his intended announcement. We admire his courage in taking this step," said one. And the 100-year-old Mrs Isabella Grant waxed lyrical in his praise: "the doctor's a fine craitur [sic] – I wouldn't change for anything."

Dr Forbes-Sempill himself was extraordinarily candid: "It has been a ghastly mistake," he told one reporter. "I was carelessly registered as a girl in the first place, but of course, that was 40 years ago . . . The doctors in those days were mistaken, too . . . I have been sacrificed to prudery, and the horror which our parents had about sex."

Some three weeks later the doctor announced that he was to wed Isabella ("Pat") Mitchell, his housekeeper. It was a fairly quiet ceremony.

On the death of his brother, the 19th Lord Sempill, in 1965, the barony passed in the female line to the 19th Lord's eldest daughter. It was assumed that the baronetcy would passed to Ewan Forbes-Sempill, but his cousin, John Forbes-Sempill (only son of the 18th Lord Sempill's youngest brother, Rear-Adml Arthur Forbes-Sempill), challenged the succession to the baronetcy.

The case was taken to the Scottish Court of Session. The court ruled in favour of Ewan Forbes-Sempill, but when his cousin continued with his challenge the dispute was taken to the Home Secretary, in whose office the Roll of Baronets is kept by Royal Warrant.

The Lord Advocate was consulted by the Home Secretary, James Callaghan, and eventually in December 1968, Mr Callaghan directed that the name of Sir Ewan Forbes of Craigievar (he had dropped the name of Sempill) should be entered in the Roll of Baronets.

The Doctor had given up his medical practice in

1955, after which he devoted himself to farming. He was appointed a JP for Aberdeenshire in 1969. In 1984 he published *The Aul' Days*.

There were no children of Sir Ewan's marriage. His cousin, John Alexander Cumnock Forbes-Sempill, born 1927, now succeeds to the baronetcy.

October 1 1991.

BILL DRISCOLL

BILL DRISCOLL, the journalist who has died aged 67, belonged to a Fleet Street tradition that disappeared even before the newspapers had left "the Street of Shame".

An old-fashioned Irishman who lived to regret that his compatriots were becoming sober and serious, Bill Driscoll (or Derek O'Driscoll as he sometimes styled himself) tended to fantasise about his own history. Those meeting him for the first time were impressed to hear of his aristocratic Prussian ancestry, of how he had fought on both sides in the German-Russian war — between careers as a mining engineer and the first mate of a rice ship, plying the South China Sea.

When his friends became better acquainted with Driscoll, or O'Driscoll, the family story turned out to be a little less exotic. His father, who had been described as a professor of logic at Heidelberg University, had in fact originated from West Cork and worked as a printer in Fleet Street.

Bill Driscoll variously claimed Skibbereen and Heidelberg as his birthplace: in fact it was Peckham, south London, on Sept 21, 1924. He did however, hold an Irish passport.

Although Driscoll was a man of considerable erudition, where he had acquired his education proved hard to establish. A similar uncertainty attached to his military service. His mastery of the German language had, he claimed, led to a spell as Ribbentrop's jailer before the Nuremberg trials, but other versions had him fighting in the last battle of the Ardennes and being invalided out of the Army on the grounds of psychological unsuitability.

Driscoll worked in turn for the *Daily Mirror*, the *Daily Sketch*, the *People*, the *Daily Herald*, the *Daily Mail*, the *Daily Express*, the *News Chronicle* and the *News of the World*. He probably worked for most of the popular newspapers two or three times, generally as a crime reporter.

He had many of the qualities of a popular journalist – wit, inquisitiveness, a certain cunning – but he never could take his trade seriously. He was sacked from one paper for beginning a story about a Leicestershire murder with the words: "They called him the golden-haired Adonis of the Market Harborough smart set".

The great days of the crime reporter died out with the abolition of capital punishment. Driscoll moved into the gossip columns but found it hard to conceal his contempt for most of the showbusiness people he had to write about.

His disadvantage as a journalist was his aversion to putting words on paper. He enjoyed acquiring information, but despised the business of putting it into the newspaper.

Yet he had an eye for a story and made some unusual

contacts. He charmed the ancient Somerset Maugham and hit it off famously with the Rev Ian Paisley. He found his métier as a fixer or contact man with West German television.

On one occasion he turned up at the hospital bedside of a pregnant woman friend, accompanied by a female terrorist from the Baader-Meinhof gang. Driscoll wanted to know whether she knew of a "safe house" in Ireland for his friend. Her husband suggested Mountjoy Prison.

At one stage in Driscoll's career someone found him a job in Addis Ababa, where he disappeared for nearly a year, prefixed his surname with "O" and persuaded an Ethiopian friend to have all letters from the Inland Revenue returned to sender, "due to decease of addressee".

On his return to Britain he found himself, at any rate fiscally, dead. His periods of employment became increasingly sporadic. None the less friends ensured that his florid face was often still seen at London parties.

His anarchic behaviour, subject of so many anecdotes, delighted the regulars at El Vino. Over the years Driscoll, whose major claim to distinction was his own story-telling skill, achieved wider celebrity as a character in other people's stories – truly a raconteur's raconteur.

As an exponent and devotee of the oral tradition, Driscoll had an innate distrust of the printed word and a loathing for documents, particularly those with his own name appearing on them.

His marriage was dissolved. Bill Driscoll's lifelong

companion was Joan Kennedy, who stood by him for 40 years.

He had a daughter.

October 8 1991

LORD MOYNIHAN

THE 3RD LORD MOYNIHAN, who has died in Manila, aged 55, provided, through his character and career, ample ammunition for critics of the hereditary principle.

His chief occupations were bongo-drummer, confidence trickster, brothel-keeper, drug-smuggler and police informer, but "Tony" Moynihan also claimed other areas of expertise – as "professional negotiator", "international diplomatic courier" "currency manipulator" and "authority on rock and roll".

If there was a guiding principle to Moynihan's life, it was to be found on the wall of his office in Manila, where a brass plaque bore the legend, "Of the 36 ways of avoiding disaster, running away is the best."

Moynihan learnt this lesson at an early stage. The first time he ran away was in 1956, to Australia. There were two reasons for his flight. The first was to elude his father's fury over a liaison with a Soho night-club waitress.

The second was to escape his wife, an actress and sometime nude model; they had married secretly the previous year, and she had now taken out a summons against him for assault. Her father had made a similar complaint – "I regret to say I gave him a swift right uppercut," Moynihan announced from Australia.

The idea was that he should work on his uncle's sheep farm in the bush, but after five days he ran away to Sydney, where he made his debut as a banjo-player and met the Malayan fire-eater's assistant who was to become his second wife. The next year he returned to London, where he effected a reconciliation with his first wife and found a job as manager of the Condor, a Soho nightclub. The job did not last, and in 1958 he married the former fire-eater's assistant, by now a belly-dancer working under his management.

"Of course," Moyniham explained, "it means I shall have to become a Mohamedan first." To this end, at dusk each day he kneeled to the setting sun with a cloth draped over his head.

His father was displeased by the marriage, but Moynihan was unabashed. "Actually," he confided to a journalist, "I only see the old man when I'm a bit short."

Soon after the wedding he made his first court appearance, accused of the larceny of two bedsheets. He was found not guilty, but as he walked from the court he was presented with another summons, this one over a lease. It was time to run away again.

With his new bride, Moynihan moved to Ibiza to set up a nightclub; when this failed he left his partner to pick up the pieces and fled to the mainland, before returning home once more. His next venture was a coffee bar called El Toro, with a Spanish bull-fighting theme, at premises in Beckenham, Kent. But that, too, failed, so Moynihan set off with his wife on a belly-dancing tour of

Europe and the Far East. In 1961 the two of them converted to the Persian faith of Baha'ism: "It propagates Oneness of Mankind," Moynihan explained.

On their travels he occasionally challenged people to duels, but nothing came of these. An Italian declined to fight: "Moynihan's behaviour is founded on exhibitionism. It has nothing to do with gentlemanly conduct."

In Tokyo he challenged an American journalist who had disparaged his wife's dancing; the critic elected martinis or cold noodles as weapons. In 1960s London Moynihan cut a rather ridiculous figure in Kaftans, and worked for a time for Peter Rachman, the slum landlord, driving his maroon Rolls-Royce.

"I didn't really understand what was involved in those days," recalled Moynihan. "It was quite cruel. They had this big Alsatian dog that had been taught to soil the tenants' beds."

Moynihan later claimed that three years after Rachman was reported dead he met him at an hotel in Izmir, Turkey, where they had a drink together and reminisced about old times.

After he succeeded his father in the peerage in 1965 Moynihan took the Liberal Whip in the House of Lords, where he was principally concerned in arguing that Gibraltar be given to Spain. The House was not impressed. In 1968 Lord Boothby interrupted one of Moynihan's speeches: "My Lords, the noble Lord has bored us stiff for nearly three-qaurters of an hour. I beg to move that he no longer be heard."

Moynihan's business career and personal finances had meanwhile given rise to a number of misunderstandings. By 1970 he faced 57 charges – among them fraudulent trading, false pretences, fraud against a gaming casino and the purchase of a Rolls-Royce motor-car with a worthless cheque. To avoid disaster he fled once more, this time to Spain.

"I knew of my impending arrest 48 hours in advance," he claimed. "I'd been approached by a CID man who told me that for £50,000 the case against me would be dropped. Because I believe in God and England I told him to get stuffed." His extradition was sought from Spain, but he disappeared, to resurface the next year in the Philippines.

In 1968 he had married for a third time – another belly-dancer, this one a Filipino – and the new Lady Moynihan's family had a chain of massage parlours in Manila, where Moynihan remained for much of the rest of his life. At the Old Bailey in 1971 he was named in his absence as "the evil genius" behind a series of frauds. "This is a case of Hamlet without the Prince of Denmark," declared the judge. "The Prince figuring behind all these offences is Lord Moynihan."

As the 1970s wore on Moynihan found employment in the narcotics trade, as well as in fraud and prostitution. The first hint of this came in 1980, when he was named by an Australian Royal Commission as an associate of Sydney's "Double Bay Mob", engaged in the import of heroin from Manila.

No charges were brought, however, and Moynihan continued his life as a Filipino pimp under the patronage of President Marcos – "my drinking chum," as he called him. Marcos apparently shielded him from prosecution over the murder of a nightclub owner (who had married one of Moynihan's ex-wives). At one stage he ran a brothel within 100 yards of the British Ambassador's residence.

After the coup against Marcos in 1986, Moynihan's position became exposed, and the next year he was forbidden to leave the Philippines pending investigations of his links with drugs and prostitution.

Moynihan was thus vulnerable to pressure from Scotland Yard and the American Drugs Enforcement Agency to help them catch Howard Marks, a Balliol man who at that time controlled an estimated sixth of the global market in marijuana, and with whom he was already on friendly terms.

He approached Marks with a bogus offer to sell him an island in the Philippines, on which he could grow marijuana; and in return for his own immunity agreed to wear a secret tape-recorder to ensnare his friend. Marks was duly convicted in Florida, with Moynihan as chief witness for the prosecution.

The DEA gave him refuge and protection in the United States for a time, and hailed him as "a hero, one of the good guys". Marks saw things differently. "I feel terribly betrayed," he said, "He's a first-class bastard."

Perhaps the most charitable judgment of Moynihan was one offered by a friend: "Tony could never see wrong in himself, only in others. He thought he was just having harmless fun."

Antony Patrick Andrew Cairne Berkeley Moynihan was born on 2 Feb 1936, the eldest son of Patrick Moynihan, a barrister and stock-broker who succeeded to the Barony of Moynihan later that year.

Patrick's father, Sir Berkeley Moynihan, an eminent surgeon who introduced surgical rubber gloves to Britain from America, had been created a baronet during Lloyd George's final administration, and then a peer in 1929.

Young Tony was educated at Stowe and did his National Service with the Coldstream Guards; it was his last contact with respectability, and he was inclined to reminisce over it in his cups.

His father, the 2nd Lord Moynihan, died in 1965, financially embarrassed and facing charges of homosexual importuning. He had been chairman of the Liberal party executive from 1949 to 1950 but resigned from the party in 1963; his decision was announced by the Freedom Group, in which he was associated with Edward Martell.

Colin Moynihan, Conservative MP for Lewisham East and currently Minister for Energy, is the son of his second-marriage, and thus the half-brother of the 3rd Lord Moynihan. The two were never close, but in 1985 they fell out when Tony Moynihan announced that he intended to sell the Victoria Cross won in 1855 by their great-grandfather, Sgt (later Capt) Andrew Moynihan. Colin Moynihan is said to have raised £22,000 to pay off his errant half-brother.

In Manila, to which he returned after his sojourn in America, Moynihan lived in the suburbs in a heavily fortified house with a swimming pool, and had as his base in the city, a brothel named the Yellow Brick Road. "I just sit back and collect the money," he said. "The girls do all the work."

He frequently spoke of returning to England – "to clear my name," as he put it. "I miss things like decent roast beef and good newspapers, the civilised way of life."

In 1988 he claimed to have secured immunity from police prosecution, and announced that he looked forward to taking his seat on the Labour benches of the House of Lords.

Giving evidence at Marks's trial in 1989, Moynihan told the court that he had been appointed to the Order of Don Quixote by General Franco, whom he much admired. The court seems to have believed him, but no such order exists.

In *Who's Who* his recreation was listed as "dog breeding", but when pressed on this matter he strenuously denied it: "As for breeding dogs, I can tell you I don't. Like every Englishman I like dogs, but that's where it ends."

Moynihan is reported to have been married five times, and to have fathered various children. The heir to the Barony appears to be his son Daniel, born in February this year.

November 26 1991

MAJOR BETTY
HUNTER COWAN

MAJOR BETTY HUNTER COWAN, who has died aged 79, served with distinction in the Women's Royal Army Corps and then settled, with her old friend Major Phyllis Heymann, in Cyprus, where they were affectionately known as "The Cavewomen".

The sobriquet derived from their residence, Cave House, situated at Tjiklos, a circular plateau, 1,000ft up the Kyrenia Pass, which commanded a spectacular view of the north coast.

The Majors themselves favoured the nicknames "Wracks" and "Cranks", from the initials of their respective Army corps: Major Betty's WRAC, Major Phyllis's Queen Alexandra's Royal Army Nursing Corps.

Both Majors remained on duty throughout the worst EOKA troubles in Cyprus, and resolutely refused to budge from the place, even when the United Nations urged them to evacuate during the Turkish invasion of July 1974.

Because of its strategic location, on the edge of the key three-mile pass to Nicosia – for which there was some of the fiercest fighting of the Turkish campaign – Cave House became a focal point for both sides. In the mountains to the rear was the Greek-Cypriot National Guard, and ahead were the advancing Turkish hordes.

Major Betty, a proud Scot, and Major Phyllis, a feisty Yorkshirewoman, were in their element, and set about marshalling the multitude of refugees who were making their way up the hill, lured by a contingent of Finnish UN troops clustered in the vicinity of Cave House. During the thick of the invasion the Majors billeted the throng around a sheltered old water point, which was used for supplying the UN posts. They rationed what little water remained, and rallied the refugees to help fight the fires, which were devastating vast tracts of spruce and pine forest.

At one point some Turkish troops tried to take a short cut through the Cave House estate and were engulfed in the flames. One Turk, wounded in the leg by a bullet and badly burned, crawled within feet of the Majors' rosemary and lavender hedgerow and then shot himself.

"We felt fearfully sorry for him," said Major Phyllis, "but I think he did the right thing."

An Army officer's daughter, Elizabeth Hunter Cowan was born at Tunbridge Wells on Aug 12 1912 and educated at St Felix's, Southwold. Young Betty had a peripatetic childhood, staying with a variety of family friends in Britain.

She was a gifted musician, and had embarked on training to be an opera singer when the Second World War broke out. She began as a FANY – "an ancient animal," as she used to say, "now practically extinct" – and from 1942 did "a man's job" as deputy assistant director of supplies and transport in the War Office.

In 1947, by now a member of the WRAC, Major Betty went out to serve in the Egyptian Canal Zone. It was there, at British GHQ, that she met Major Phyllis Heymann.

That same year they went to Cyprus, where they fell in love with the estate at Tjiklos. Major Betty's task was to organise motor transport on the island, while Major Phyllis instructed the local military hospital in the latest vaccination techniques.

The estate was owned by a friend of Major Betty's, who invited them to return on their retirement in 1960, and fixed a nominal rent of £15 a month for their life tenancy. They remained, stalwart and inseparable, ever after.

After the end of the troubles the Finnish UN contingent stayed on at Tjiklos, and installed a sauna there. The Majors frequented the steamy bath-house at every opportunity, and were justly proud when the "Fin Con" presented them each with diplomas testifying to their having withstood temperatures of 112°F.

The Majors were dispirited by the sudden transformation, after the immigration of Turks from the south in 1975, of Greek Kyrenia into Turkish Girne. But things looked up again when Sabri Tahir, an old friend of British residents in the area, was appointed Mayor of Kyrenia.

In that capacity, the wheeler-dealing Turk — "the terrestrial rogue of business with many houses", as he was described by Lawrence Durrell in *Bitter Lemons* — began to hold court with his daughter every afternoon at his house, where he was able to explain the newly-named streets and shops to the Majors.

The two women also became friendly with Durrell, whom Major Betty described as a typical Kyrenian character: "Little men are often very aggressive, aren't they?"

By the mid-1970's more than half of the 800-strong British community had left, but, in spite of a lamentable shortage of gin, the Majors still enjoyed a stimulating social life. Each week they travelled to the British Council in the Greek south to watch a special matinée film, organised at their request to enable them to return home through the barricades before the 5pm Turkish curfew.

Besides birdwatching, they worked indefatigably to restore their estate to its former tranquil beauty, doing much to revive the many fields of cyclamen which had been destroyed in the fire.

After Major Phyllis died last year, Major Betty returned to live at a nursing home in Edinburgh.

December 31 1991

THE EARL OF SOUTHESK

THE 11TH EARL OF SOUTHESK, who has died aged 98, was the oldest member of the House of Lords and – although his name had disappeared from the official *Court Circular* list – he could also be regarded as the oldest member of the Royal Family.

In 1923, as Lord Carnegie, he had married Her Highness Princess Maud of Fife, second daughter of Princess Louise, the Princess Royal, who was herself the eldest daughter of King Edward VII and Queen Alexandra. Indeed, Charles Southesk was one of the last survivors of those who knew Queen Alexandra (died 1925), although on account of Her Majesty's deafness their conversation was limited.

The Carnegie wedding was a major royal occasion. The bride was given away by King George V. Beacons were lit from Inverness to the Firth of Forth, a distance of 100 miles, and all on land owned either by the family of the bride or bridegroom.

Princess Maud, then aged 30 and having already served for a decade as the devoted companion of her mother, suffered from asthma. Her friend Rafaelle Duchess of Leinster considered in her memoirs, that the Princess was possessed of "a rather pathetic, lonely, childlike quality . . . and a need for affection, and to be reminded that she was a royal princess". "Maudie's" marriage, according to the Duchess, "had been arranged for her".

There was a considerable disappointment in store for the bridegroom shortly after he had plighted his troth. The bride's father, the 1st Duke of Fife, had been in partnership with the 1st (and last) Earl Farquhar, a somewhat shadowy figure whose respectable claims to fame included being a personal friend of King George V and the man who introduced the Duke of York to his future bride, Lady Elizabeth Bowes-Lyon.

In Farquhar's extensive will he bequeathed the sum of £50,000 to Princess Maud, or to Lord Carnegie if he was by then married to her. Farquhar died a few months before the wedding and the couple's good fortune was made known to the public.

But when the will was proved Farquhar's spectacular debts wiped out the entire estate. Indeed, Princess Maud's mother, the Princess Royal, found herself liable for a considerable sum and had to sell some of her pictures at Christie's. Married life proved to be a saga of incompatibilities for the Carnegies. Princess Maud preferred the South, but was obliged to live on her husband's estates in the North. The Scottish air aggravated her asthma, and although she loved reeling, she often lost her breath.

Their only child, the Master of Southesk, was born in 1929 and eventually succeeded to the Dukedom of Fife in 1959 upon the death of his aunt Princess Arthur of Connaught, who had become Duchess of Fife by special remainder on the death of her father in 1912.

In the later years of their marriage Lord Southesk (as he became in 1941 on the death of his father, the 10th

Earl) and his wife appeared to spend little time together. Princess Maud lived mainly at Windlesham in Surrey and in 1945 succumbed to a fatal attack of asthma.

She was cremated at Golders Green and her ashes buried in Scotland, with her husband at the graveside. He was not present at the memorial service at the Chapel Royal attended by the Royal Family.

The Duchess of Leinster intimated in her memoirs that Southesk subsequently became something of an admirer of hers. She wrote that Princess Maud had had a premonition of her own death and had asked her several times to marry Southesk.

The Duchess recalled that "Charles was inclined to be restless, critical and cautious, but there was a great sweetness in him . . . He had even been called ungenerous, but I found him tender, generous and extremely patient and kind".

Despite what some interpreted as a coolness towards him in royal circles, Southesk was accorded a special place at certain occasions on account of his undeniable status as the widower of King Edward VII's granddaughter. For example, he walked in the funeral procession of King George VI in 1952; and in 1980 he sat near the front with the Royal Family at the special 80th birthday service for Queen Elizabeth the Queen Mother in St Paul's Cathedral.

Southesk was on good terms with the Queen Mother despite the fact that his kinsman James Carnegie of Finavon ("the swiftest of foot when running from the Battle of Sheriffmuir") had slain her ancestral great-uncle, the 6th Earl of Strathmore, in a drunken brawl at Forfar in 1728.

Charles Alexander Carnegie was born on Sept 23 1893, the eldest son of Lord Carnegie, who was in turn the heir of the 9th Earl of Southesk.

The earldom had been created in 1633 for the 1st Lord Carnegie, an Extraordinary Lord of Session, whose father was envoy to England at the time of Mary Queen of Scots. The 5th Earl of Southesk was attainted for his part in the Jacobite Rising of 1715, but the title was restored to the 11th Earl's grandfather in 1855.

Young Charles was educated at Eton and Sandhurst before being commissioned into the Scots Guards. He served in the First World War until 1917, when he became ADC to the Viceroy of India, Lord Chelmsford, for two years. In 1923, shortly before his own wedding to Princess Maud, he commanded the guard of honour at the wedding of the Duke of York to Lady Elizabeth Bowes-Lyon.

After joining the Reserve of Officers he concentrated on farming in Scotland. On the Elsick estate in Kincardineshire he began with a dairy stock of Ayshire cows and later added the breeding of pigs and poultry. King George V encouraged him with a gift of stock from Sandringham.

During the Second World War Southesk rejoined his beloved regiment, the Scots Guards. Afterwards he resumed farming, but was less fortunate in his other excursion into business – Carnegie Films, which went into voluntary liquidation in 1951 after completing just one production, *Dangerous Meeting*.

In 1952 he married secondly, Evelyn, widow of Major Ion Campbell and elder daughter of Lt-Col A. P. Williams-Freeman. Latterly they lived at Kinnaird Castle in Angus.

Southesk would occasionally favour readers of the correspondence columns of *The Daily Telegraph* with his views on public events. In 1965 he protested against the Archbishop of Canterbury's suggestion that force might have to be used in Rhodesia: "If the Archbishop upholds a practice that has proved futile in Africa, namely, universal suffrage, he should resign his office and stand for election by all members of the Church of England."

In 1974 Southesk noted that the "whole trend of violence has escalated because there is no penalty – like the cat and death" and advocated "just a shot, or the electric chair, to save more lives of innocent men, women and children"

During the Falklands conflict Southesk advocated the sale of the islands for £1 million a year for a decade: "The Argentinian flag could be flown below the Union Jack – starting halfway up the pole and then ascend yearly one-tenth of the remainder until it reaches the top."

In 1990 the name "Lord Carnegie" appeared among a list – which had mysteriously come to light – of supposed members of the Right Club, an anti-Semitic, German-sympathising organisation founded in 1939 by Capt Archibald Ramsay, MP. Questioned by a journalist, Southesk said that he had "never heard of the Right Club" and described Ramsay as "a very loyal, patriotic man".

Last year in *Country Life* Southesk suggested a scheme whereby the longer a family had occupied its seat the less inheritance tax it should pay. Thus the Carnegies, having owned Kinnaird for 500 years, might pay 2 per cent, other families on ancestral acres held for 300 years 4 per cent, and so on.

A tall, striking figure with a fine crop of white hair and bristling moustaches, Charles Southesk could appear aloof to strangers, though intimates attested to his charm. Even in his late nineties he still drove around the estate, climbed ladders and complained that he had more engagements than he could cope with.

He was appointed KCVO in 1926. The Earldom of Southesk and its subsidiary titles now pass to his son, the 3rd Duke of Fife.

February 18 1992

NESTA COX

NESTA COX, known as "the Nanny of Nanteuil", who died at Blois in France aged 92, was brought up to believe in the indestructibility of the British Empire, although in the event she herself proved the more indestructible.

"Nanny" Cox lived her life to standards of service, devotion and loyalty, which she never questioned and which saw her safely through the German occupation of France and membership of the French Resistance.

Nesta Ellen Cox was born at Thetford, Norfolk, on Dec 19 1899. She had no brothers or sisters and when she was orphaned at the age of three she was taken in by the family of an Anglican clergyman at Farnham.

After her training she started work as a 15-year-old nurserymaid but her exceptional gift for looking after children soon secured her an appointment as nanny. She spent four years with the family of a Royal Indian Navy Captain in Ceylon, where there was a white Rolls-Royce for the use of herself and the children.

Then, after an appointment in Gloucestershire, she moved to the house which was to become her home for the rest of her life, Château Nanteuil, near Huisseau-sur-Cosson in the Loir et Cher. She was issued with her *carte d'identité* in 1925, and became one of the legion of British nannies employed to bring up French children between the wars.

The house belonged to William Gardnor-Beard, member of a prosperous family of mine owners, and who had married Anne-Marie Denisane, great-niece of the Marquise de Perrigny. Mme Gardnor-Beard, a spirited young Frenchwoman, earned some notoriety on her honeymoon in Arcachon by publicly slapping the face of Mme Joseph Caillaux (the wife of Poincaré's finance minister and herself notorious for shooting dead the editor of *Le Figaro* after he had suggested that Caillaux was unpatriotic).

Mme Gardnor-Beard and Nanny Cox were both strong characters, but after a difficult few weeks they became firm friends and everyone in Nanteuil soon grew to love "N'neee".

Rather in the manner of the establishments portrayed in Anthony Powell's novel *A Question of Upbringing* and Terence Rattigan's play *French Without Tears*, the Gardnor-Beards had set up an informal tutoring course which attracted English boys and later girls, who were filling in time before university, the Army or the diplomatic service.

Among those who stayed at Nanteuil were Valerian Wellesley (now the 8th Duke of Wellington) and Jeremy Hutchinson (now Lord Hutchinson of Lullington, QC). It became one of the traditions of the house that anyone arriving from England should bring Nanny some tea, good tea in those days being unobtainable in the Loir et Cher.

The use of English was strictly forbidden at Nanteuil, except of course in the nursery. But since Nanny invited Gardnor-Beard's pupils to nursery tea, there was one period in the day when the rule could be broken.

As time passed, however, Nanny abandoned conventional English and tended to address all nationalities in a nursery *"Franglais"* of her own invention, which was spoken with little attempt at a French accent but which – thanks to her magical powers of communication – everyone understood. In return she had no trouble in understanding even Parisian *argot* when it came her way.

After the death of William Gardnor-Beard his widow married Comte Pierre de Bernard. On the outbreak of war in 1939 the majority of English Nannies working in France returned to England but Nanny Cox refused to abandon her post.

The Gardnor-Beards and their children had become her family and Nanteuil her home. After the fall of France in 1940 the house stood just north of the demarcation line and within the occupied zone.

Shortly after Dunkirk a message arrived that somebody outside wished to speak to Mme de Bernard. She and Nanny went out to find a former pupil, William Bradford, now an officer in the Black Watch who had escaped capture and was trying to make his way back to England.

He had swum the River Loire in the mistaken belief that Nanteuil was in the Vichy Zone. There were German troops quartered on the house at the time but the de Bernards managed to help Bradford on his way. He later rose to command the 51st Highland Division.

It was in this manner that the de Bernards joined the Sologne Resistance. They, and Nanny, were recruited by Col Buckmaster's *Réseau Adolphe* which later became part of the much larger "Prosper Network".

Nanny's first task was to help Anne-Marie de Bernard interview the often dubious "English" men or women, who claimed to have been sent from London. The network eventually received Yvonne Rudellat, the first woman agent sent by Special Operations Executive into occupied territory.

Despite the proximity of German troops, the park of Nanteuil was used to conceal arms and radio transmitters parachuted by the RAF. On one occasion the RAF even parachuted supplies of tea for Nanny, who regularly assisted the de Bernards in supporting sabotage and passing on RAF aircrew.

When the Prosper Network was broken by the Abwehr in June 1943, the de Bernards were arrested by the Gestapo at Orléans and subsequently deported. Nanny Cox was left in sole charge of the children and the house.

It was a difficult as well as a frightening time for her, but she made as little of it as anyone possibly could — only saying later that she had always kept a copy of the *New Testament* with her in case she, too, was picked up.

After the war both Pierre and Anne-Marie de Bernard returned from the concentration camps, although with their health broken. Mme de Bernard re-opened the school at Nanteuil and the English pupils re-appeared, still bearing their packets of tea.

Nanny Cox, though entitled to hold the *carte de resistance*, never applied for one; she never considered that she had done anything worth remarking. Nor did she bear ill-will towards the Germans, remembering that many of the ordinary soldiers had behaved correctly. She regarded the war and the occupation of France as an episode of extremely bad behaviour which was now closed.

Nanny Cox enjoyed occasional visits to England but otherwise never left Nanteuil. She lived to look after the children of her original children and then the children of those children. It was not uncommon for visitors to see old – sometimes very old pupils of the school at Nanteuil returning to the house and being moved to tears on finding Nanny Cox still there, largely unchanged.

If, for the first time in 67 years, tea is not served at 4 o'clock sharp at Nanteuil this week, Nanny's spirit still watches over the house. At her request her ashes have been scattered beneath an oak tree in the park.

March 2 1992

"TEASIE WEASIE" RAYMOND

"TEASIE WEASIE" RAYMOND, the flamboyant hairdresser, who has died aged 80, was the leading *coiffeur* of his generation.

Raymond had a bland egotism that provoked and charmed in equal measure, and he took his calling seriously. He saw himself as an artist, a philosopher and a psychologist. "I can tell a great deal about a woman from her hair ... The Duchess of Windsor's hair, for instance, is very assertive. It is not 'easy' hair. It is *dogmatic*."

Raymond had a calm brown face, gold-capped teeth and the hands of a mechanic. At the time of his first success he dressed in loose-sleeved satin shirts, tight trouserings and sandals, and painted his toenails and fingernails scarlet.

He later abandoned this costume, but was always a snazzy dresser, favouring tartan dinner jackets, gold lamé catsuits and blue carnations. Such attire proved perfectly acceptable in his salons, with their silk ceilings, but was greeted with less enthusiasm on the Turf, where he was a successful owner (he twice won the Grand National, with Ayala in 1966 and Rag Trade 10 years later).

In 1968 Raymond was refused admission to the Royal Enclosure at Ascot. The next year he was allowed in, and for more than a decade he startled the racegoers – and horses – with morning suits in such colours as orange, brown and a shade he called "nipple pink", until in 1983 Ascot officials took the unprecedented step of asking him to reconsider his wardrobe. He complied.

"I have *never, never*, publicised myself," he once protested, to general incredulity. His most profitable publicity – and his ubiquitous sobriquet – derived from his appearances on a television programme called *Quite Contrary*, on which he uttered the memorable line, as he held up a lock of hair, "A *teasie-weasie* here, and a *teasie-weasie* there." Mr Teasie Weasie was born.

"Teasie Weasie may be a rotten name," he once said, "but the man behind it is not what he is purported to be."

Raymond Pierre Carlo Bessone Raymond (he added the second Raymond later) was born in 1911. He furiously denied that his birth had occurred in Brixton, and insisted instead on Normandy.

He earned his first pocket money making false beards and moustaches in his father's barber shop, which was in Soho, but soon decided there was no future for him in the family business. Competition for jobs was fierce, and for a time he scraped a living as a wrestler in the Blackfriars Road, until landing a job at a barber's in Deptford.

Young Raymond suffered at Deptford. For most of his customers hair-washing was a bi-annual operation, and curling the ripe strands with a hot iron was too much for his delicate stomach.

A few years later he won the Grand Prix for hair-styling and permanent waving at the International Exhibition in Paris. In 1936 Raymond opened his own salon in Grafton Street, Mayfair, and 10 years later a second one in Albemarle Street; others followed, in Cardiff, Bournemouth and Birmingham.

By 1955 Teasie Weasie shampoo sachets were selling a million a week, enabling, as he put it "all those women who can't come to me to get at least a little bit of me".

Raymond had always been interested in politics (he used to do Mrs Attlee's hair), and in 1968 he stood as a Liberal in the Bournemouth council elections. He was not elected, and later that year announced his intention of standing at the next general election, as an Independent Liberal, having fallen out with the party over its policies on nuclear weapons and Europe.

In 1964 he toyed with the idea of becoming a monk and went to receive instruction from "a wise man" in Morocco, having made some startling confessions in the *News of the World*: "Brutality and violence have loomed large in my career," he recalled. "I ripped off her tutu, a short and fluffy skirt."

A few weeks later, however, he was seen at the Venice Lido with Rosalie Ashley, an actress some 30 years his junior. He told reporters he was "cleansed of evil thoughts" and was on his way to Rome for an audience with the Pope.

In 1972 Raymond reappeared on television, playing a hairdresser called Monsieur Fabrice in *Crossroads*. The next year he lost half his jaw, tongue and teeth to cancer of the mouth, but gallantly emerged from hospital as ebullient as ever.

Stung, perhaps, by imputations of effeminacy, Raymond threw himself from an early age into the role of man of action: flying, parachuting, ski-ing and big-game hunting. He upset his neighbours in Eaton Place by displaying his trophies on the balcony railings of his flat.

Raymond was appointed OBE in 1982.

After his first marriage was dissolved, he married Rosalie Ashley. He had three daughters by his first marriage, one of whom predeceased him.

April 2 1992

JAMES CRESPI

JAMES CRESPI, who has died aged 53, was a legendary character at the Old Bailey.

A consummate legal eccentric, Crespi was a brilliant performer at the Bar but quite insouciant of his gifts. Even when he had left a brief in a taxi or restaurant, his prodigious memory enabled him to recall every detail of the case, in much the same way as he could recite copious chunks from Gibbon's *Decline and Fall of the Roman Empire*.

He was correct in law as a counsel, and as a recorder lenient in sentencing. In conversation he was amusingly inaccurate, and in gossip inclined to harshness.

Crespi had an anecdote or a quip for every occasion. In 1972, ignoring a policeman's warning not to walk outside the Old Bailey because of a suspected IRA bomb, he was blown off his feet. He liked to claim that it was only his obesity that saved his life. When a surgeon inquired if he had any allergies, he replied, "Lordy me, only to pain, my dear fellow." And when a lady called to visit him in hospital, a nurse had to restrain him from flinging off the sheet to stand up for his visitor.

Caesar James Crespi was born in 1928 and educated at Cambridge. Young Caesar grew up to bear a strong resemblance to his Roman namesake – at least as Shakespeare saw him, "mighty, bold, royal, loving". He was better known, though, as James.

Called to the Bar by Middle Temple in 1951, he lectured at Aberystwyth University before entering criminal practice in the chambers of Fred (later Lord Justice) Lawton. He was a brilliant advocate, but his forte was more in holding court in El Vino the Fleet Street wine bar.

According to Crespi, the wine waiter at Simpson's would greet him with a clenched fist over his breast and the words "*Ave*, Mr Crespi!" He disdained to book for dinner at Rules: ignoring the queue of American tourists, he would prod the *maitre d'hôtel* with his umbrella and say, "Do ask our colonial brethren to wait their turn."

Most taxi drivers knew him so well that they did not have to ask his address – though one novice cabbie, taking Crespi to the Savoy for his favourite breakfast of kidneys, noticed the wing collar, mistook him for a waiter and set him down at the staff entrance.

Crespi's girth made it impossible for him to walk far, and he would even take a taxi from Norwich Crown Court to the Old Crown Hotel opposite – a distance of no more than 150 yards.

July 8 1992

ALBERT PIERREPOINT

ALBERT PIERREPOINT, who has died aged 87, was Britain's leading executioner for 25 years, but later campaigned for the abolition of the death penalty.

Short and dapper, with mild blue eyes, a pleasant singing voice and a fondness for cigars and beautiful women, Pierrepoint was fascinated by bar tricks with coins and matchboxes – which were in plentiful supply at the oddly-named Help the Poor Struggler, a pub he kept in Lancashire. While employed as a hangman he never spoke of "t'other job", and he hated the thought of any impropriety, unseemliness or vulgarity connected with his craft, which he viewed as sacred. After his retirement, however, he spoke of it freely – notably in his autobiography *Executioner: Pierrepoint* (1974).

"Hanging must run in the blood," he explained (his father and an uncle were both hangmen). "It requires a natural flair. The judgment and timing of a first-rate hangman cannot be acquired."

Pierrepoint was undoubtedly a first-rate hangman: "I hanged John Reginald Christie, the Monster of Rillington Place," he wrote, "in less time than it took the ash to fall off a cigar I had left half-smoked in my room at Pentonville."

During his career he hanged more than 400 people – his record was 17 in a day ("Was my arm stiff!"). In 1946 he went to Vienna, where he ran "a school for executioners"; the British authorities had sentenced eight Polish youths, but refused to hand them over to Austrian hangmen, whose methods were brutally unscientific. Pierrepoint hanged the youths at the rate of two a day, and stayed on for a fortnight to give further instruction.

He recalled only one awkward moment in his career. "It was unfortunate. He was not an Englishman. He was a spy and kicked up rough."

In 1956 Pierrepoint resigned, incensed at the meanness of the Home Office, which had granted him only £1 in expenses, and began his campaign against capital punishment.

"If death were a deterrent," he wrote, "I might be expected to know. It is I who have faced them at the last, young lads and girls, working men, grandmothers. I have been amazed to see the courage with which they take that walk into the unknown. It did not deter them then, and it had not deterred them when they committed what they were convicted for. All the men and women whom I have faced at that final moment convince me that in what I have done I have not prevented a single murder."

Albert Pierrepoint was born on March 30 1905 at Clayton, a district of Bradford in the West Riding of Yorkshire, and brought up in Huddersfield and Manchester. His father, Harry, had been an executioner for 10 years, and his uncle for 42. Young Albert was nine when he first conceived the ambition to become an executioner.

When he moved with his mother to Manchester, he spent half a day at school, and the other half working in the local mills, a practice which the law then allowed boys over the age of 12½.

Six months later, he left school and started work as a piecer at the mills. In 1926 he found another job as a horse-drayman at a wholesale grocers, and by 1930 had become a motor-drayman. It was then that he wrote his first application to the Home Office to be included in the list of official executioners, but there were no vacancies.

A year later Pierrepoint was invited to an interview at Strangeways Prison, where he was disappointed to learn that he was the tenth applicant to be interviewed, his chagrin only slightly lessened when he noticed that the previous applicant was clearly drunk. None the less he was accepted.

After a week of intense training by the prison engineer, Pierrepoint was placed on the list of approved assistant executioners – subject to his attendance at an execution to test his nerve.

The first execution he attended was not, however, authorised by the Home Office, but by the Irish government. Tom Pierrepoint (Albert's uncle and then the chief hangman) was contracted privately, and was allowed to select his own assistant. He chose his nephew. Pierrepoint's first British execution was at Winson Green Prison in Birmingham, where the executioner, once again, was his uncle. The role of assistant involved pinioning the condemned man's legs and getting off the trap as fast as possible, but it was the gravity of the occasion that was the real test.

It was 1940 that marked the turning point in Pierrepoint's career. After acting as assistant to an executioner who had been less than competent, he was asked if he would be prepared to be head executioner.

His first execution as principal hangman was that of a gangland murderer at Pentonville in London, and further engagements soon followed.

In 1943 he was sent to Gibraltar to execute two saboteurs. During the Second World War there were 16 spies convicted in Britain, and Pierrepoint hanged 15 of them (the 16th was reprieved).

He always maintained that there was no glamour in taking the lives of others and he abhorred all publicity, so he was displeased when Gen Sir Bernard Montgomery announced from his headquarters in Germany that Pierrepoint received a £5 note in an envelope, with a slip of paper reading simply "Belsen".

At the end of the war Pierrepoint became a publican. His pub attracted ghoulish sightseers by the coach-load, but he denied press reports that he ever discussed "t'other job" with his customers. He did admit, though, to having hanged one of them, a man convicted of the murder of his mistress.

He hotly denied, too, the existence of a sign reading "No Hanging Round the Bar", though several people claimed to have seen such a sign – among them the late Diana Dors, the actress, who also claimed that Pierrepoint had sung amorous songs to her over the telephone.

In 1954 Pierrepoint himself was "sentenced to death" by the IRA for the execution of a terrorist in Dublin in 1944.

After his resignation, he settled down as landlord of another pub, the Rose and Crown at Hoole, near Preston, which he had taken in 1952, but the ghouls put him off pub-keeping, so he concentrated his energies instead on his small farm.

A keen fan of boxing, he was appointed a British Boxing Board of Control inspector in 1956.

Pierrepoint married, in 1942, Anne Fletcher.

July 13 1992

WILLIAM DOUGLAS-HOME

WILLIAM DOUGLAS-HOME, the playwright who has died aged 80, excelled at light, social comedy in an English tradition which took no account of theatrical fashion.

"Willie" Home's career in the theatre spanned more than five decades and he bore with good-humoured fortitude the slings and arrows of outraged dramatic criticism, and of the gallery – with which he was ready to tussle on first nights. Although his lightness of touch in drawing-room comedy sometimes brought accusations of careless craftsmanship, his plays nearly always attracted first-rate actors who appreciated his gift for dialogue. And if the story sometimes failed to carry conviction, his characters usually won enough sympathy.

Home's first unquestioned West End success was *The Chiltern Hundreds* at the Vaudeville (1947, and later filmed), which starred the veteran actor A. F. Matthews, who is said to have based his performance on the playwright's father, the 13th Earl of Home. Forty years on Home was still writing as individualistically ever, tackling such diverse characters as Augustus John, Field

Marshal Montgomery and Cecil Beaton, brought together in a conversation piece called *Portraits*.

If subversive elements could be detected in his comedies they derived from his instinctive and sometimes mordantly satirical humour, rather than from any hope of changing things. Yet he could write problem plays if he chose to.

One of his last plays, for example. *A Christmas Truce* (1989), reflected his preoccupation with the cruelty and absurdity of war by depicting the 1914 Christmas Day ceasefire on the Western Front, with its legendary football match and carol singing.

Although the play carried no explicit message, its story bore a striking parallel to Home's own experiences in the Second World War when, as a young officer he refused an order to attack Le Havre unless the French civilians were evacuated. He spent a year in prison for that demonstration of his conscience, and a few years later his spell inside inspired the play he thought his best, *Now Barabbas*.

A documentary piece, produced at the Fortune (featuring the young Dirk Bogarde), it drew compassionate attention to the plight of condemned murderers awaiting execution. And towards the end of his career Home brought out a frail but not altogether frivolous comedy about a priest required to marry a couple of young men.

Home's gift for respecting all his characters could be discerned in most of his plays – from the immensely popular *The Secretary Bird* (with Kenneth More, 1968) and *Lloyd George Knew My Father* (with Ralph Richardson and Peggy Ashcroft, 1972) to a wistful romantic comedy such as *The Kingfisher* (1977) with Richardson again and Celia Johnson.

Home's plays often showed a journalistic topicality, but his failure to charge these with the dramatic concerns of their era – especially those of the Angry Young Men – made his work anathema to the *avant-garde*.

The fact is that William Douglas-Home had no chips on his shoulder. He seldom explored characters deeply or surprisingly, preferring to stick to certain home truths. Although he often wrote about aristocrats, as in *The Reluctant Debutante* (the Cambridge, 1955, and later filmed) and *The Reluctant Peer* (Duchess, 1964), he did not view them with special favour. On the contrary, he used them as a subject for comedy.

To the serious-minded playgoer, however, most of his comedies seemed technically to creak, as if he had not put enough work into them, whether newly written or brought down from the shelf. But to most of his audiences – middle to upper-class and not anxious to be "disturbed" by or discover "significance" in a new play – the old-fashioned tone of William Douglas-Home's approach to the theatre was restful, well-mannered and refreshing in its courteous and untendentious aim. He never put any wrath into his writing.

If it did make political points – in, say, *The Reluctant Debutante*, in which a daughter rejects the rituals of the London Season, or *The Reluctant Peer*, derived from the author's brother, Sir Alec Douglas-Home, renouncing his earldom to become prime minister – it always made them good-naturedly.

What distinguished the playwright's career from

those of others, though, was an ability to keep his audience (and his head) at a time when so many around him were losing both. Since 1956 the Royal Court's regime had restored new writing to the British stage with a fervour that would never be repeated. But established dramatists outside its sphere of influence – Rattigan, Fry, and lesser talents who might have developed in later years – were driven from the stage by the vogue for "Kitchen Sink" theatre.

Much of the criticism directed against Home's plays had a snobbish flavour – Kenneth Tynan, for instance, would begin his reviews with such phrases as "The Honourable William tells us" – and Harold Hobson once wrote that "more critical injustice has been done to him than to any other British dramatist of our time."

Home was in any case undeterred. He went on writing not only to please audiences but also to please himself, and though his work could be uneven and sometimes slack, he never needed public funds to find his audience.

William Douglas-Home was born in Edinburgh on June 3 1912. His father, then styled Lord Dunglass, succeeded to the Earldom of Home six years later; his mother, the former Lady Lilian Lambton, was a daughter of the 4th Earl of Durham.

Of his father ("Charlie"), his third son recalled that he "made one of the two most memorable statements ever made on horse-racing when, one night at dinner in the early Thirties, he said, "The only certainty in racing is that you can't win a race unless you enter your horse in it."

His mother ("Lil"), a noted eccentric, had all her

teeth out at one go, without anaesthetic, then turned up for lunch quite untroubled; when her false teeth eventually arrived, they flew out of her mouth as she shook hands with an admiral.

Young William was educated at Eton and New College, Oxford, which he hated, remembering it as "a cold and gloomy and oppressive place . . . an architectural atrocity . . . I felt nothing but a lowering of spirit." He read history, was twice rusticated and took a Fourth.

Stage-struck, he then trained for the stage at the Royal Academy of Dramatic Art – where he was denounced by the Principal for having a voice "like a constipated bishop" – and shared a convivial lively flat in London with his old school friends Jo Grimond and Brian Johnston.

Home made his professional stage debut with the Brighton Repertory Theatre in 1937 and later that year arrived in the West End, playing Brian in Dodie Smith's *Bonnet Over the Windmill* at the New Theatre (now the Albery). His first efforts at writing plays were *Great Possessions* (1937) and *Passing By* (1940).

When his call-up papers arrived in 1940 Home replied, as he recalled in his memoirs, that "I was prepared to be conscripted, on the understanding, however, that, if my most strongly held political opinions should be challenged by the Government of Winston Churchill to a point beyond endurance, I was not to be relied on."

That point was reached on Sept 8 1944 when, serving as a tank commander with the Royal Armoured Corps, he disobeyed an order to attack Le Havre, which contained a large number of civilians, the German request for their evacuation having been refused. Capt Home told his colonel about his decision after driving round a turnip field 25 times to think it over.

The Army took no immediate steps against him. He then made the matter public by writing to the *Maidenhead Advertiser*, was court-martialed and cashiered the next month ("It's very rude to cashier someone," he complained) and sentenced to a year's imprisonment.

His brother Alec visited him in Wormwood Scrubs, but could not bear to look at him as he had grown a beard, so spent his visit discussing cricket with a warder. When his parents visited him in Wakefield Prison (to which he had been transferred) his mother felt that she should write to the governor "to thank him for having dear William to stay".

It was also during the war that Home embarked on his erratic political career. He stood, always unsuccessfully, in the Cathcart Division of Glasgow and at Windsor in 1942 as a Progressive Independent, at Clay Cross as an Atlantic Charter candidate in 1944 and then eventually at South Edinburgh as a Liberal in 1957. His brother Alec once asked him at breakfast, "What party are you in today?"

"I don't know," replied Willie, "I haven't read the papers yet."

Nancy Astor summed up Home's wartime career when she described him as "always fightin'". "Fightin' not to join the Army, fightin' to get out of it by fightin' to get into Parliament, then fightin' to get into prison."

Home's fighting spirit was again in evidence at the Aldwych Theatre in 1948, in his curtain speech at the first night of *Ambassador Extraordinary*. The play related how a diplomat turned up in Green Park from Mars with a message for the British foreign secretary about stopping wars. The gallery had booed it to the echo as the cast lined up on stage.

Despite the uproar Home went on and spoke to his audience. Looking up at the gods, he assured them: "I like heckling. Please go on. We have the night before us."

Although Home was best known for his light comedies, by no means all of his plays were based in the drawing room. *The Thistle and the Rose* (1949), for example, was drawn from events leading up to the Battle of Flodden; *The Queen's Highland Servant* (1968) dealt with the sentimental friendship between Queen Victoria and John Brown; and *The Dame of Sark* (1974, and later televised), with Celia Johnson, told of a brave woman's gesture of independence.

Home's love of racing was reflected in his riotous play *The Jockey Club Stakes* (1970). He himself had mixed fortunes on the Turf. His best horse was Goblin (L. Piggott up), which still holds the seven-furlong record at Newmarket.

Somewhat against his trainer's wishes, Goblin was subsequently entered in the Derby, in which it got off to a poor start. Home's sister Bridget, watching the race on television, thought that Goblin's tail had been caught in the rear gate of his stall, but in fact he had fallen asleep. In spite of this set-back Goblin finished 10th in a field of 25.

"The rest of my horses gave me great pleasure," Home recalled, "in their own non-winning ways." One of them was entered in a hurdle race at Wincanton, with Lord

Oaksey in the plate. "How did you find him, John?" asked Home as he rode in. "He ought to take up some other sport," replied Oaksey, "like golf."

Home was also a devout sportsman and once shot 100 pigeons from the lawn at the Hirsel, the family seat in the Borders.

He wrote several volumes of memoirs: *Half Term Report* (1954), *Mr Home, Pronounced Hume* (1979), *Sins of Commission* (1985) and *Old Men Remember* (1991). He also contributed some hilarious reminiscences to the old weekly *Field*.

Always a fund of jokes, and a brilliantly witty public speaker, Willie Home was the source and subject of hundreds of anecdotes that have passed into aristocratic folklore. He once smuggled a stuffed crocodile out of the Hirsel, and then took his mother and some other ladies on a walk. As the party crossed a bridge, Home's accomplice pushed the crocodile out into the stream, which Home then pointed out to his mother. "Good Lord," declared Lady Home, passing on unperturbed, "I didn't know they came so far north."

His brother Henry, the celebrated "Birdman" of BBC radio, once invited a senior Corporation executive to the Hirsel to witness his recording of an owl's hooting in the woods. But when the microphones were turned on a mortifying silence reigned – except on one, which gave out a wonderful owl's call. The recording was judged a great success, and was regularly used by the BBC's drama department as a sound effect when Juliet walked on to the balcony. Years later Willie Home asked his brother if he remembered "that owl". "Of course I do," replied the Birdman.

"It was me."

When his brother Alec was Prime Minister, Home used to telephone him and impersonate important people – Jack Kennedy and so on. The mild Sir Alec grew tired of this, and when a strong Scottish accent came on the line one day, claiming to be the Moderator of the Church of Scotland and asking the Prime Minister to address a group of women in an obscure part of the country, the Prime Minister gave a dusty reply to his brother and hung up. A puzzled Moderator rang back soon after.

Yet beneath the humour and the aristocratic *sprezzatura* there was a sensitive man of unfailing kindness and generosity.

In 1988, prompted by the controversy surrounding the wartime record of Kurt Waldheim, the Austrian president, Home sought a pardon: "I felt that if I had obeyed orders I could have been a party to what we now call war crimes," he explained (2,000 civilians died at Le Havre). But his request was refused by the Ministry of Defence.

Home married, in 1951, Rachel Brand, elder surviving daughter of the 4th Viscount Hampden and 26th Lord Dacre. The Barony of Dacre fell into abeyance on the death of her father in 1965, but five years later the abeyance was terminated in Mrs Home's favour, and she became Lady Dacre in her own right.

They had a son and three daughters.

September 30 1992.

LEN RUSH

LEN RUSH, who has died aged 83, was manager and custodian of the Royal Racing Pigeons from 1962 to 1983.

Stocky and red-faced, Rush described himself as "just an ordinary, humble sort of bloke". A non-smoking teetotaller, he was a carpenter, a special constable, a Methodist Sunday school teacher, and a pigeon-fancier from the age of 10.

Rush's charges were of the Delmotte-Jurion strain, descendants of the birds given to King Edward VII by King Leopold of the Belgians in 1886. Some of their forebears served in the two World Wars, carrying messages from trawlers, and in the Second War one of them won the Dickin Meal for avian gallantry.

medal

The move from Sandringham to the lofts in the garden of Rush's semi-detached house at King's Lynn was thus a break with tradition. It paid off handsomely, for he was a devoted trainer. Every day he rose at 4.45am, and half an hour later would be mucking out the birds, which he fed on a nourishing diet of maple peas, corn and cold water.

Most mornings Rush would then take a basket of pigeons to the local railway station, to be released from stations around Ely for practice flights. He would also put them on fishing boats in the Wash, to accustom them to flying over water.

"I love the birds," he explained. "Handle them from birth, when they are squeakers with hardly any feathers.

Talk to them – 'Hello, my old beauty! Hello my little peach!' This gives them confidence. They react like people all right. Race a cock yearling and they're as daft as a teenager – chase off after the first bit of skirt they see. The race seems to go out of their heads completely."

When Rush took over the job he had to start from scratch, breeding from the existing stock, which would have returned to Sandringham. Entered under the name of "Her Majesty, c/o 17 Kent Road, Gaywood, King's Lynn", and each with a ring stamped EIIR on one of its legs, the pigeons did the Queen proud in Rush's first season, winning seven first prizes.

Subsequent seasons were nearly as successful although the North Road Race (the Derby of pigeon-racing) proved elusive. In 1965 four of the Queen's birds were lost in that race. In 1972 they did not win any races at all, and more than half failed to return, which Rush attributed to changes in the ether.

During his stewardship Rush also did a brisk trade in royal squeakers (birds about 28 days old), which he advertised in the *Racing Pigeon* and dispatched as far afield as Calgary and Kansas City.

The Queen made some 17 visits to the lofts at King's Lynn, the first of which was nearly disastrous. Rush was so excited by the prospect that he entrusted his secret to a fellow Methodist. When the great day came, "I looked out of the window to see if the royal car was coming up the road, and saw this man and half Gaywood chapel gathered outside on the snowy pavement. He'd told them all!"

Fortunately the telephone rang, and Rush was

informed that as the roads were impassable the Queen would be coming the next day. "I just left them standing outside in the snow."

Rush retired in 1983. The Queen gave him 50 pigeons, and he set about racing under his own name.

His other ruling passion was soccer. He named his house "Highbury", and in the 1970s could boast that he had not missed a cup final since 1928.

He "had the luck", as he put it, "to be married to a woman with a feeling for birds". She predeceased him.

November 17 1992

MAURICE PEPPARD

MAURICE PEPPARD, who has died in his late eighties, was a legendary itinerant horse dealer in the Mendip Hills.

A fiercely independent spirit, Peppard lived alone in a caravan all his life. His material needs were minimal: bread and cheese, the light of a candle, a fire to sleep by.

This simple life kept him fit enough, even in his seventies, to slide under a barbed-wire fence or through an invisible hole in a thorn hedge, keeping up with his lurchers after a rabbit or hare. Many was the young traveller who learnt from "Pep" that money, possessions and luxuries are but the shabbiest of life's illusions, that the dirtiest of nights are the ones for catching rabbits — and he would sell you the dog for the job.

The youngest of 13 children, brought up in a railway carriage in a field by strict Victorian parents who took the pledge, Maurice Peppard was the black sheep. But his courage, ready wit and down-to-earth philosophy won him lifelong friends and admirers, even among those at the wrong end of his deals.

He was as brave with a horse as he was in adversity. Four times, as an old man, vulnerable and alone in his caravan, he was attacked and beaten by robbers at night. But his readiness for battle never deserted him and his strength pulled him through.

Pep's eye for a horse or a dog was undiminished by the increasing blindness of his latter years. He would have been proud of the cavalcade of fine, coloured cobs pulling flat carts and trolleys which drew him to his grave in Binegar Churchyard, beside his brother Bill – still remembered in those parts for horses like the Pride of the West and the Willoughby Gentleman. And he would have been gladder still at the deals struck in the yard of the Old Down Inn at his wake, where Irish musicians played travelling songs, and tales of Pep's craft and cunning were recounted among the throng.

How he sold his neighbour her own chickens, or his father a stallion as an in-foal mare under cover of darkness; how, as a lad, he escaped custody in South Devon and ran all the way back across country to freedom and the Mendips.

Maurice Peppard was well known for the subtle art of turning humour to advantage in a deal, often deploying light-hearted parables on the nature of human cupidity.

He would never have put himself on the side of the saints, though, and if you asked him about his next destination he was wont to reply: "Heaven I hope, but hell I'm afraid."

November 19 1992

SIR JOHN VERNEY, BT

SIR JOHN VERNEY, 2nd Bt, who has died aged 79, was a singularly engaging author, painter and conservationist with an outstanding record in the Second World War, when he won an MC, was awarded the Légion d'Honneur and was twice mentioned in despatches.

In the wartime SAS Verney was regarded as a courageous, congenial and reliable colleague. His comrades recall his first meeting with Blair Mayne, the Irish rugby international, heavyweight boxer and winner of four DSOs. Mayne was not pleased to see the casual young Englishman arrive in his regiment but greeted him civilly enough.

In the ensuing conversation the name Cromwell cropped up. Mayne growled, but Verney nonchalantly mentioned that Cromwell was a pretty sound chap. There was a hush in the Mess, and the others departed, not wishing to see the new arrival humiliated and probably thrown out of the window. When they tip-toed back half-an-hour later Mayne and Verney were chatting amicably.

In June 1943 Verney was chosen to command an attack on Sardinia, to divert German attention from the Allies' impending invasion of Sicily. With 30 others he squeezed into a submarine, which was forced to turn back by engine trouble 30 miles from its destination.

In what he later called a "moment of madness", he then volunteered to take the party in by parachute. Soon after landing they reached the German airfield at Ottana and blew up aircraft and petrol dumps with delayed fuses.

They bluffed their way across the island, pretending to the Italians that they were German and to the Germans that they were Italian, but before they reached the rendezvous point they were captured and sent off to internment in Italy.

Verney eventually escaped and after a long walk through the German lines made contact with an English regiment. He was first given a staff job but then rejoined the SAS and fought to the end of the war in Germany.

Going to the Wars (1955), his deft memoir, is rated by many as the best book to have come out of the war. It drew on letters he had sent his bride in England – a long-distance relationship they called "Holy Deadlock".

The sequel, *A Dinner of Herbs* (1966), returned in fuller detail to his adventures in Italy. As Anthony Powell observed in *The Daily Telegraph*, "Sir John possesses one extremely valuable – and rare – ability as a narrator in the first person; he has an unusually clear-cut view of himself . . . The all-important factor for the reader is that the author's personality is accepted from the first page."

A scion of the Verney Baronets of Claydon in Buckinghamshire, John Verney was born on Sept 30 1913. His father, Ralph Verney – a grandson of Sir Harry Verney, 2nd Bt of Claydon, a Privy Councillor and brother-in-law of Florence Nightingale – was Secretary to the Speaker of the House of Commons and himself created a baronet.

Young John was educated at Eton and Christ Church, Oxford. Nursing ambitions to be a painter, he entered the film industry and by 1936 was an assistant director. Then, to the surprise of his friends, he joined the North Somerset Yeomanry. "Perhaps you're an unconscious homo," one of them suggested.

In 1940 his regiment was sent to Palestine as part of the Cavalry Division. Verney fought in the Syrian campaign and then in the Western Desert, taking part in all the battles up to Alamein. After spending some time in hospital he volunteered for the SAS.

Verney's books included novels, traveller's tales, works for children and collections of light essays. He contributed to the *Cornhill* and other periodicals, and also produced annual editions of the amusing *Dodo Pad*. He was also a prolific painter and illustrator, and a decorator of furniture.

He lived for many years at Farnham in Surrey, where he was an Independent member of the town council. His slight figure, riding an ancient bicycle and wearing faintly disreputable clothes, was an everyday sight in and around the town.

Verney devoted himself to Farnham, defending its beauties against predatory shopkeepers and the demolition men; he rescued the derelict Maltings which became a thriving "cultural centre". In the early 1980s he moved to Suffolk, where he took a particular interest in the Gainsborough Museum at Sudbury, of which he was chairman for a time. John Verney was self-deprecating but never arch, modest but never dull. His literary comments sometimes betrayed anger, in every case well merited, but never malice. He was the antithesis of the "Scarlet Major".

He married, in 1939, Lucinda ("Jan"), daughter of Major Herbert Musgrave. They had two sons (the elder of whom died aged eight) and five daughters.

The only surviving son, John Sebastian Verney, born 1945, now succeeds to the baronetcy.

Craig Brown writes: Wearing his hat at a jaunty angle, his red-and-white spotted handkerchief billowing out of his old tweed jacket, Sir John Verney would potter around the village of Clare in Suffolk, buoying up everyone he encountered with his twinkling mixture of sprightly anecdote and old-fashioned courtesy.

At home, he would welcome one up to his studio with a cheery shout and the offer of a cigarette and a cup of coffee. There you would sit surrounded by his slightly mischievous, always witty, often saucy paintings, displayed higgledy-piggledy on canvas, paper and whatever spare furniture was at hand, chatting away as if lost in a cheery haven watched over by such patron saints as Uccello and Wodehouse.

Once, bumping into him in the butcher's one morning, I found myself invited back for a bowl of tinned figs. John was one of the few people I know whose presence could make even tinned figs seem thoroughly enjoyable.

His charming writings – and his blissfully dotty *Dodo Pads* – were similarly dedicated to the preservation of joy and irrelevance in a world he viewed as increasingly weighed down by the dread virtues of common sense and solemnity.

He once wrote of Edward Ardizzone's war drawings that, "in their tender and satiric fashion, they reaffirmed human values and showed the comic spirit everywhere bursting through the bonds of uniform, even in the midst of tragedy". Had he possessed an inkling of vanity, he might with justification have written the same of himself.

In my bedroom, there is a wall-cupboard painted by John. On the outside of the door there is a picture of me, sitting on my lawn, attempting to write, while in the corner of the garden three naked mallet-bearing ladies are tempting me away with the promise of a game of croquet. When you open the cupboard, there is a picture of my little daughter chasing the ladies away down the lane with the flourish of a mallet, forcing me to return to my work.

The whole work of art is funny, affectionate, mischievous, gentle and wholly delightful; in short, the mirror of its creator.

February 5 1993

JOHN MURRAY

JOHN MURRAY, who has died aged 83, was the sixth John Murray to head the publishing house of that name, founded in 1768.

His appearance — the loosely-knotted bow-tie, the slow, slightly percussive diction, the expansive gestures and a wonderfully expressive pair of eyebrows raised in benevolent surprise — changed little over the years. His was a pleasingly old-fashioned presence, but he was no amateur.

"Jock" Murray, as everyone in the business knew him, was immersed in publishing for some 60 years and considered it an occupation for a gentleman – a term he used precisely and without snobbery. To understand this one had only to see him in his green baize apron (inherited from a furniture removal man), setting up his stand at a book fair, mucking in with the fitters and craftsmen around him.

In an era of power squabbles and conglomerate imperialism, as the great names of publishing disappeared or suffered the indignity of reappearing as covers for lists at complete variance with their original character, Murray proved that small could be not only beautiful, but also prosperous and independent.

Tradition was always an important factor in his perception of the trade – but, as he put it, "I prefer to live up to our traditions, not on them".

His preference manifested itself in the steady evolution of the Murray list, each innovation established on a secure basis, as in the emergence of a post-war educational list that now accounts for half the firm's turnover. Among Murray's claims to be a real publisher, rather than a mere purveyor of books, was his reluctance to remainder a book or dispose of it by any means other than sales.

This policy proved rewarding on more than one occasion, when demand had dwindled to a thin trickle that would have led to pulping or discounting by the accountants who run the conglomerates. Murray's patience was justified by an eventual resurgence of interest and sales.

His authors included John Betjeman (for whose poetry he persuaded his rather reluctant grandfather to revive the firm's poetry list), Patrick Leigh Fermor, Osbert Lancaster, C. Nothcote Parkinson and Ruth Prawer Jhabvala, as well as Kenneth (later Lord) Clark. Murray's early enthusiasm for *The Gothic Revival* brought him all Clark's later writings, including the book of the *Civilisation* television series.

He regarded them all as members of an extended family, and the loyalty was mutual. When a writer on the Murray list was solicited by a marauding tycoon with a letter offering rich enticements it would be passed on to Murray, who would see the pirate off.

Murray was patient with slow authors, but could be courteously insistent when books became seriously overdue. A thrifty man himself, he restrained more than one of his authors – notably Freya Stark – from indulging in excessive spending on the strength of potential earnings.

None of his writers ever solicited his help in vain. On at least two occasions he put aside all his manifold business preoccupations to play the role of general factotum – once for Axel Munthe and once for John Betjeman, during a two-month illness.

Murray was delighted when someone described him as "the only publisher in whose company a failed author could sit at ease". I think that's the most wonderful recommendation," he said. "I'd like that in my obituary."

He was born John Arnaud Robin Grey on Sept 22 1909. He was a Murray on his mother's side, and his father, T. R. Grey, was also connected with the firm; he took the name Murray when he joined the family business as "slave and bottlewasher" in 1930.

He spent much of his childhood at the family house in Albemarle Street, which had been the publishing headquarters since before Waterloo. "During one of my holidays from school, when my grandfather was ill, Conan Doyle called in with new stories which we published as *The Casebook of Sherlock Holmes* in 1927. He treated me with such courtesy, as though I was a grown-up, asking me to let him know if anything more was needed, that I fell under his spell. If this is an author, I said to myself, what fun to be a publisher!"

His childhood hero was a butler called Barnes: "I admired the laying of the table, the serving, the cleaning of silver, the opening of bottles, and I struck a bargain that if he would teach me the mysteries of all these things I would let him play with the trains in my nursery. I thought the bargain was in my favour, and how right I was."

In later life he would note the consequences of his training as a butler:"I am afraid I embarrass American publishers when I help them on with their overcoats, since I always put my hand under the coat to pull the jacket down. They look around at me with the gravest suspicion."

Young John was educated at Eton, and during the holidays learned the craft of printer with Robert Gibbings, who ran the Golden Cockerel Press. "My main claim to fame," he modestly said of that apprenticeship, "is that I am the only publisher who has typeset in the nude. Unfortunately I hit the period when Gibbings was in his nudist phase, and as I was only 15 I found this embarrassing."

He went on to Magdalen College, Oxford, where he

became friends with Betjeman, and after serving with the Royal Artillery during the Second World War he returned to concentrate on the company's fortunes.

One of his first assignments was to be assistant editor of the *Cornhill Magazine* and *Quarterly Review*, two titles closely connected with the history of Murrays in the 19th century. As the great-grandson of John Murray II, Lord Byron's friend and publisher, Jock Murray, inherited a family tradition of service to Byron's memory. Having warmed himself as a child at the grate in which Byron's memoirs had been burned, his scholarly concern arose almost as an act of reparation.

With Peter Quennell he compiled the one-volume selection, Byron, a Self-Portrait (1950), and he was publisher of many works of Byronic scholarship and biography. None gave him greater pleasure than his close involvement with the editing of Leslie Marchand's 12-volume edition of Byron's collected letters. This drew on the firm's exceptional archive of manuscripts and relics, of which Murray was long the civilised and enthusiastic curator.

He kept Byron's boots, which he would polish from time to time, and in 1974 became involved in a curious drama when some of Byron's manuscripts were stolen from Albemarle Street and held to ransom for £200,000. The police advised Murray to raise the cash and set a rendezvous, and he duly turned up at Highgate Cemetery, where every grave-tidier, sightseer and grieving relation turned out to be a policeman: the thieves were caught and the papers recovered.

He was a prominent member of the Byron Society, and was for many years involved with the upper counsels of the Publishers Association. He was appointed CBE in 1975.

Jock Murray had an admirably equable tempermant. "Goethe wrote somewhere," he noted towards the end of his life, "that 'To be uncertain is uncomfortable, to be certain is ridiculous'. That applies to me with one exception, which is the Net Book Agreement. I'm rather bigoted about that and I only wish that the greedy boys would look more carefully at the reasons for it being started in about 1900."

He married, in 1939, Diana James; they had two sons (both of them publishers) and two daughters.

July 24 1993

JOHN BINDON

JOHN BINDON, who has died aged 50, was one of the most flamboyant London villains of his day, and turned his "tough-guy" persona to legitimate account as an actor in such television programmes as *Hazell*, *The Sweeney* and *Softly Softly*.

Possessed of a menacing physique and considerable charm, Bindon was a gregarious self-publicist who counted among his friends the Kray twins and Princess Margaret. Acquaintances were often frightened of him, but recall him as "screamingly funny".

When the Earl of Longford was engaged in his celebrated investigation into pornography, Bindon "flashed" at him outside the Chelsea Potter pub. He was justly famed for a party trick which entailed the balancing of as many as six half-pint mugs on one part of his anatomy.

He served several prison sentences, and in 1979 was accused of murdering an underworld enforcer in a club brawl.

A taxi driver's son, John Bindon was born in Fulham, London, in October 1943. He recalled his infancy as miserable (his mother used to keep him under the kitchen table) and said: "I've had this overwhelming urge to smash things up ever since I was a kid."

At the age of 11, he was charged with malicious damage. A few years later he was sent to Borstal for possession of live ammunition. Bindon made a living from such jobs as plucking pheasants and laying asphalt, before progressing to the antiques trade.

He was holding court one night in a London pub when Ken Loach, then filming *Poor Cow*, Nell Dunn's gritty story of working-class life, walked in. Noted for his use of amateurs, Loach thought Bindon "absolutely right" for the film. "The only thing out of character" said Bindon of his role, "is that I have to hit Carol White in one scene – and I never hit women."

The success of the film launched him on an acting career in which he played criminals. He held his own alongside Mick Jagger and James Fox in *Performance* and was a drug dealer in *Quadrophenia*. Bindon had no regrets about being typecast although he expressed a wistful desire "to play a priest sometime".

In 1968 he met Vicki Hodge, a baronet's daughter turned model, who introduced him to polite society. She invited him to Mustique, where Bindon claimed to have charmed Princess Margaret with his rough humour and Cockney rhyming slang.

The Princess denied meeting Bindon and was reportedly shocked to hear stories of their dancing together. His name was linked with a succession of women, including Christine Keeler, the former "Bunny Girl" Serena Williams and Angie Bowie, the wife of the pop star.

In the early 1970s Bindon dominated many Chelsea and Fulham pubs, where he was rumoured to run protection rackets. He could be gallant, but a close relationship was precarious. On one occasion a young man who offended him was reputedly driven in a car boot to Putney Common where Bindon made him dig his own grave before relenting. His innate anger was apparently only checked by the liberal consumption of cannabis.

Despite his substantial earnings – not entirely from acting – he was constantly in financial difficulties, and by 1976 he was bankrupt.

Two years later Bindon killed a gangster named John Darke during a struggle outside a pub in Putney. Badly wounded, he fled to Dublin, but returned to England for his trial, where the prosecution alleged he had been paid £10,000 for the killing.

The jury acquitted him after hearing that Bindon had gone to the aid of a man who had been knifed in the face by Darke. The actor Bob Hoskins appeared as a character witness: "When Bob walked in," Bindon recalled, "the jury knew I was OK."

His reputation as an essentially decent man had been enhanced when he was given the Queen's Award for

Bravery in 1968, for diving into the Thames in a vain attempt to rescue a drowning man – although Bindon allegedly boasted that he had been fighting with the man on Putney Bridge, had pushed him in and had dived in to save him only when he saw a policeman approaching.

In 1981 Bindon began a new career as a director of a company manufacturing hand-made shoes, but his impetuous personality continued to land him in trouble.

In 1982 he pleaded guilty to using a section of pavement as an offensive weapon against a "short and weedy" young man who had bumped into Bindon as he was celebrating his birthday.

In 1983 he was again declared bankrupt. A year later he appealed successfully against a conviction for threatening an off-duty policeman with a carving knife: "Now I won't have to play five-a-side football with George Best," he said.

In 1985 he was cleared of causing criminal damage to a restaurant in Earl's Court. Two years later he was charged with possessing an offensive weapon, and soon afterwards cleared of threatening to petrol-bomb the home of a mother of three.

His final days were spent in some privation and loneliness in the tiny Belgravia flat he had purchased in more prosperous times.

October 15 1993

"Joe" Carstairs

"JOE" CARSTAIRS, the motor-boat racer who has died in Florida aged 93, was the fastest woman on water in the 1920s, and in the 1930s became "Queen Joe of Whale Cay", the owner and ruler of an island in the British West Indies.

The daughter of a Scottish colonel and an American heiress, Marion Barbara Carstairs was born in London in 1900 and educated in Connecticut (her mother's fourth husband was Prof Serge Voronoff, "the monkey-gland surgeon").

She returned to Europe in 1916 and, claiming to be older than she was, drove ambulances for the Women's Legion in France. She also ran ambulances in Ireland during the Civil War.

On the death of her mother in 1920, Carstairs was due to inherit $4 million and several trust funds (her grandfather, Jabez Abel Bostwick, had been one of the founders of Standard Oil) – but only if she was married. She promptly married Count Jacques de Prêt, and left him at the church door.

Carstairs then settled in England, where she took up racing, established a boatyard at Cowes, had her arms tattooed and became a renowned party-giver and practical joker. The *Evening News* reported that she "can dance a Charleston which few people can partner".

"Toughie" Carstairs, as she was known, habitually wore trousers, reefer jackets and a beret – all made in Savile Row. In 1924 she won every race she entered, and by the late 1920s had taken almost every motor-boat trophy. In an effort to create a craft which could exceed 100mph, she built five boats named *Estelle* (after her mother). She broke several ribs when *Estelle IV* capsized in one of the trials.

With these boats Carstairs made three brave attempts to regain for Britain the Harmsworth British International Motor-boat Trophy, which Gar Woods had won for America in 1920. She did not succeed, but nonetheless established herself as the fastest female speed-boat racer in the world.

After the death of Sir Henry Segrave (who had lost his life setting a world water-speed record of 98.7mph on Windermere) Carstairs determined to break his record with *Estelle V*. Disappointed in that aim, she secretly backed Captain Malcolm Campbell's successful attempt at the land-speed record in 1931, to the tune of £10,000.

Carstairs had four silver-grey Rolls-Royces, and in the 1920s (with the Misses Molly, Betty and Bardie Coleclough and Miss J. MacKern) ran a Daimler hire-car company from Cornwall Gardens, London SW7. The clients they chauffeured around Europe included the Shah of Persia, and they led several expeditions to war graves on the Continent.

In the early 1930s Joe Carstairs took to travelling more widely. She ferried a large party to the Cocos Islands on a treasure hunt, surfed in Honolulu, shot game in Bombay, met cannibals in British New Guinea and fished for tunny in the West Indies.

From time to time she had announced her intention to give up racing because it was too expensive (she claimed to have spent £20,000 a year on equipment), and in 1934, complaining of impossibly high taxes, she finally sold her boats and shipyard and sailed for the West Indies.

She bought the island of Whale Cay for £8,000. "I am going to live surrounded only by coloured people," she said. "I am not even taking a motor car, for when I bought the island there were no roads. Now I am building roads and a residence, but my only means of transport will be two 10-ft dingies. The island is about 1,000 acres in extent and is nine miles long. I cannot say if I will ever return."

She built 26 miles of carefully signposted road, a lavish concrete-and-steel mansion, a wireless station, an electric plant, a school, a hospital, a boat-building shop, a refrigerator plant, a lighthouse, a church and a kennels. The total cost was £188,000.

When immigrants from neighbouring islands flooded in, "Queen Joe" was shocked at the lack of respect shown by many to the marriage vows. She accordingly instituted legislation whereby only couples who married in the church and lived respectably in the small, neat houses provided for them could remain on the island. Any moral lapse would result in banishment.

Carstairs encouraged the 500 islanders to eat more vegetables, forbade them to drink anything stronger than beer, banned voodoo practices and withdrew holidays if there was evidence of bad behaviour. The island was dotted with admonitory signs, such as "Notice: I eat brown rice in preference to white. Therefore, if brown rice is good enough for me and my household, it is good enough or even too good for the people. *M. B. Carstairs.*"

She did not welcome outsiders: four guards with

sawn-off shotguns were stationed around the island with instructions to shoot unauthorised visitors, and a watchman with a machete patrolled the interior. But in 1942 Carstairs was drawn out of seclusion when she rescued 47 survivors of a torpedoed American steamer.

She also built a deep-water harbour at Whale Cay for the use of the Royal Navy, and in 1944, without a word to her population, left the island to build warcraft in Florida.

By 1945 she was running a small steamship freight line to the Caribbean ports, and the next year she set up a chain of airports for private craft. She became an American citizen in 1951.

For the next 40 years she lived in Florida and Long Island, making occasional forays into New York in a Mercedes, equipped with a revolver.

January 26 1994

STANLEY GREEN

STANLEY GREEN, who has died aged 78, paraded Oxford Street for 25 years with a placard warning against the dangers of protein, and sold thousands of hand-printed leaflets (at 12p each) explaining why lustful feelings were induced by "fish, bird, meat, cheese, egg, peas, beans, nuts and sitting"

"Protein makes passion," he said. "If we eat less of it, the world will be a happier place."

Stanley Owen Green was born on Feb 22 1915 and

worked in the Civil Service before launching his campaign against lust in 1968. He had learnt from experience, he said, that "passion can be a great torment".

He produced his leaflets on a press in his small council flat at Northolt, west London: the tenants below often complained about the relentless thumping on printing days.

Until he qualified for a free travel pass, Green would bicycle to Oxford Street each day in his raincoat, cap and wire-rimmed spectacles. He recalled with pleasure that motorists reading the board on the back of his bicycle would toot their horns and wave. "I've known coaches pass," he said, "and everyone has stood up and cheered at me."

His own diet comprised porridge, fruit, steamed vegetables, lentils, home-baked bread and barley-water mixed with milk powder. He took his lunch in "a warm and secret place" near Oxford Street – "I think it is justified," he said, "because I am doing a public service and I need to be warm."

The campaign was not without its hazards. Green was twice arrested for causing an obstruction, and wore green overalls as protection against spit. But he held no grudges, explaining that people attacked him only because they mistook him for a religious man.

He liked nothing better than to distribute leaflets in Leicester Square on a Saturday night. He would home in on cinema queues, using such opening gambits as "You cannot deceive your groom that you are a virgin on your wedding night," and often sold 50 leaflets in an evening.

As well as inveighing against "love play", Green told

passers-by that to prevent drug-taking, promiscuity and vandalism they should spend more time talking to their children.

The Museum of London plans to exhibit Green's placard and a selection of his leaflets.

January 28 1994

LADY VICTORIA WEMYSS

LADY VICTORIA WEMYSS, who has died aged 104, was an Extra Woman of the Bedchamber to Queen Elizabeth the Queen Mother, her second cousin, and the last surviving godchild of Queen Victoria.

At her christening in 1890, in the private chapel of Windsor Castle (the room where the fire started 102 years later), Queen Victoria stood sponsor to this only daughter of her Master of the Horse, the 6th Duke of Portland, and his wife, Winifred, who later became Mistress of the Robes to Queen Alexandra.

Asked recently whether she remembered Queen Victoria, the sprightly Lady Victoria ("Vera" to her family and friends) replied: "Oh yes, very well. I remember going to Balmoral for her to see me, and sitting on my mother's knee waiting for her . . . I poked a hole in the yellow silk of the sofa. Then the Queen was wheeled in by her Indian attendant, and she presented me with a horse and cart and a doll.'

Lady Victoria had vivid memories of King Edward VII, who often came to shoot at Welbeck Abbey, the Portland family seat in "the Dukery" of Nottinghamshire;

of her aunt Lady Ottoline Morrell, the Bloomsbury hostess (of whom she would give amusing imitations); of the Empress Eugenie in the South of France; and of Archduke Franz Ferdinand, whose assassination triggered the First World War.

Her family stayed with the Archduke and his wife in Austria. "It was a charming house," Lady Victoria recalled, "a sort of *'Schloss'*, you know . . . and it was very comfortable and nice and gay, and we danced . . . Father asked them to come to shoot at Welbeck . . . They came in the summer and two or three times in the winter."

The Archduke nearly met his end at Welbeck rather than Sarajevo. "He was shooting," Lady Victoria recalled, "and the ground was slippery, and a cartridge went off and just missed him. It was terrible when he was shot in 1914. He had tried to do all that he could down in Bosnia and Hercegovina, but everything was so divided."

Lady Victoria Alexandrina Violet Cavendish-Bentick was born on Feb 27 1890 and spent much of her childhood at Welbeck, where her father had succeeded the legendarily eccentric 5th Duke of Portland 11 years earlier.

The 5th Duke, having been spurned in love by the Covent Garden singer Adelaide Kemble, adopted a highly individual sartorial manner. His trouserings were secured above the ankle by a piece of string, he hid himself beneath a vast coat and umbrella, and on top of his long brown wig he balanced a 2ft hat.

The staff at Welbeck were instructed to pay him no attention, but to pass him by "as they would a tree". He liked to stay in his bedroom, communicating through a letterbox in the door. Each day he would be posted a roast fowl; His Grace would lunch off one half of the bird and dine off the other. He undertook extraordinary subterranean building operations at Welbeck, which included an astonishing ballroom – said to be the largest room in Europe without supporting pillars – and miles of tunnels.

The 6th Duke took advantage of his predecessor's work, and entertained lavishly. A champion of the Turf, he used his considerable earnings from racing to build old people's homes, known as "the Winnings". His Duchess, Winifred, was much more than the beautiful hostess portrayed by Sargent, and took a special interest in the welfare of the miners on this vast private domain. The Portlands eventually moved to a smaller, modern house on the estate, and the Abbey later became a military college.

Among Lady Victoria's memories of life at Welbeck – where the figure on top of a fountain in front of the Oxford Wing represents her as a young girl – was a fire in October 1900, when she was woken at 3.30 am by the butler. "I think perhaps you'd better come downstairs," he said. The fire had started in her mother's maid's room. "In those days electric irons were rather a new idea," explained Lady Victoria, "and somebody had gone in – as a matter of fact to iron a blue sash and some clothes of mine – and they had left the iron on . . . Our own private fire-engine came bustling down, then the Worksop fire-engine, and fire-engines from all over; by half-past six they more or less had it under control."

The only fatality was Lady Victoria's wax doll, Netta, who melted. Her pet tortoise survived, swimming contentedly in the bath in the day nursery.

Until the First World War the family would travel to Worksop through an artificially lit tunnel built by the 5th Duke, which crossed the Welbeck lake via a causeway. "It was the normal route to Worksop in those days," said Lady Victoria. "My father gave strict instructions that on no account were motors to use the tunnel because it frightened the horses."

In his time the 5th Duke had a steel carriage which was drawn by horses through the tunnel to Worksop Station, where it was put on to the train for London; there it was met by more horses, and driven to his London house. Lady Victoria's family also used a tunnel (which she described as "rather unsafe") leading to the indoor riding school: "I remember the horses billeted there in the First World War suffered from melancholia gazing at the wall."

She stressed that she had "a blissfully happy childhood" at Welbeck in that Golden Age before the First World War. There had, she said, "to be nothing that was at all questionable. Father would have had a blue fit if it had been otherwise. Whenever there was anything that was doubtful one often thought, 'No, Father would not approve of that, because it's not quite straight.' Until I was 18, it was riding morning and afternoon, an egg for tea at 6pm and then early to bed."

Among her childhood companions was Lady Diana Manners (officially daughter of the Duke of Rutland but in fact the child of the celebrated philanderer Harry Cust), whom she remembered serving slap into the tennis net in the garden at Welbeck and reprimanding herself, "Come on now, Miss Cust!"

Lady Victoria's coming of age ball in the underground

ballroom was a grand affair, with guests including the King of Spain. But life changed dramatically in August 1914: "I remember everyone lining up at Father's study to say goodbye before going to the war." Lady Victoria saw family and friends, among them her husband-to-be, set out for the Front. The young men, she recalled, never spoke of the horrors when they were on leave from Flanders, remarking when questioned: "Well, I suppose I have seen a thing or two."

One evening in 1916, after dining at Hopetoun House, near Edinburgh, she heard the eerie rattle of chains outside in the Firth of Forth. The party went on to the terrace, and watched the Fleet weighing anchor and setting out for the Battle of Jutland; Lady Victoria remembered some of the ladies waving their underskirts to wish the men God speed. She remembered, too, that when the Fleet returned there were empty spaces in their formations at anchor.

During the war she worked in a munitions and aircraft factory at Chiswick, which she "enjoyed enormously".

In 1918 Lady Victoria married at Welbeck Capt Michael Wemyss, of the Royal Horse Guards, Chief of the Name of Wemyss of Wemyss, and a nephew of Admiral of the Fleet Lord Wester Wemyss, who, as the representative of the British Empire, had signed the Armistice at Compiègne less than three weeks earlier.

Lady Victoria provided the Duke and Duchess of Portland with their only grandsons, David, born in 1920, and Andrew, born in 1925. They lived on the coast at Wemyss Castle, Fife, in south-east Scotland. After the

Second World War, when many other families were reducing the size of their houses, the Wemysses embarked upon additions to their castle.

In 1937 Queen Elizabeth selected Lady Victoria as an Extra Woman of the Bedchamber, a position she held for the rest of her life. In 1953 she was appointed VCO.

Lady Victoria took a special interest in the Wemyss School of Needlework and in the Girl Guide movement. She also had a passion for farming, particularly sheep ("Rather appropriate for a Cavendish, really," she said, "that's how the family started, you know"). Her sheep won championships all over Britain, and towards the end of her life at least one champion was brought to her bedside for inspection.

She took an enthusiastic interest in the military college which took over her family seat. "I am always delighted to read the name of Welbeck in the passing out lists from Sandhurst in the *Telegraph*," she would say to the boys. "Good luck to you all – your master will be keeping me in touch and giving me all the 'low-down'."

Well into her 10th decade she would entertain the boys on their visits to perform at Edinburgh Festivals, and drive 50 miles into the city to see them. Lady Victoria was notorious for emerging at speed from the front gates of Wemyss Castle, paying scant attention to other motorists. She adhered steadfastly to her favoured position in the middle of the road, and would park her motor-car on the steps at Wemyss in bizarre positions of which only a helicopter would be thought capable.

She was a most generous hostess and always loyal to her friends, who came from many walks of life. The

Austrian Countess Elizalex de Baillet Latour referred to her as, "Dear Vera, the salt of the earth made up of the finest qualities and no faults."

A friend recently told her she had been an inspiration to all who knew her. Lady Victoria replied, "That's very kind, but I feel bound to say that I have made absolutely no effort."

She was not interested in publishing her memoirs, but would answer questions about her life from those who were interested; she once gave a memorable interview to the journal of "her" Welbeck College.

Capt Michael Wemyss died, after what Lady Victoria described as a "blissful" marriage of 64 years, in 1982.

May 10 1994

STAN GEBLER DAVIES

STAN GEBLER DAVIES, the journalist who has died in Ireland aged 50, was a Bohemian, wit and iconoclast.

Such was his contempt for the pieties of the modern Irish Republic that Davies stood as a Unionist candidate for the Dail. He also wrote a book debunking James Joyce, which did not endear him to his compatriots.

Though a dedicated carouser, Davies took great care over his light and seemingly effortless sketches and essays for such London newspapers as the *Evening Standard*, the *Spectator* and *The Sunday Telegraph*. This style of writing — the prose expression of the "crack" or "gas" of the pub — is a supremely Irish form, of which Stan Gebler Davies was a master.

He was born on July 16 1943. His Gebler grandfather was a Jewish musician from Bohemia, who moved to Dublin to play with Radio Eireann Orchestra, and his grandmother secretly had the infant Stan baptised a Roman Catholic, as a precaution against a Nazi invasion of Ireland.

As a result – as he often related – young Stan was bullied during his schooldays, by Catholics for being a Protestant, by Protestants for being a Catholic, and by both for being a Jew. But he was more than able to stick up for himself and took pride in his Jewish ancestry. His uncle, Ernest Gebler, a well-known author, married the novelist Edna O'Brien, known to her nephew by her first name, as "Aunt Josephine".

His father, Max Davies, a furniture manufacturer, took his family out to Canada in the 1950s, but as soon as he was old enough his son returned to follow the literary life in London and Dublin. His wit was soon in demand in Fleet Street.

But after 1969 the killings in Ulster removed much of the charm and fun from Irishness. And while many English journalists took the side of the Republicans, Davies loathed and denounced the IRA and its fellow-travellers.

So unfashionable were his views – at any rate until the 1980s – that he found it hard to find work on London newspapers, and turned instead to writing his book on Joyce, and pot-boiling thrillers under a pseudonym.

In the 1980s, though, Davies came to be seen as a forceful voice on Irish politics, as well as a graceful and funny chronicler of life in rural Ireland, with intervals at the Horseshoe Bar of the Shelbourne Hotel in Dublin.

He went to live in West Cork, not in the hope of tax exemption, but to flee the British Inland Revenue. He settled first at Kinsale, then further along the coast at Castletownsend, the site of the *Irish RM* stories. At the first literary festival in honour of Somerville and Ross, Davies was called on to arbitrate between the still quarrelling Anglo-Irish families of the book, and he much enjoyed the hunt that followed, to which they brought a fox in a sack, in case they could find no wild creature.

He then moved still further west, to a cottage near Union Hall, and close to his favourite town of Skibbereen. Like all newspapermen, he loved the story about the leading article which included the sentence, *"The Skibbereen Eagle* is keeping its eye on the Tsar of Russia".

It was in West Cork, an old Republican stronghold, that Davies stood as Unionist candidate in the 1987 Irish general election, in which he won 134 votes. Although he had embarked on this as a somewhat dangerous joke, he wanted to demonstrate to younger people that Ireland's secession from the United Kingdom was neither inevitable nor necessarily wise.

It was characteristic of Davies that while he was advocating reunion with Britain, he was at the same time returning to the ancient Catholic faith of Ireland. In London he was a regular at Mass at St Etheldreda's in Ely Place and afterwards at the lunches upstairs, presided over by Fr Kit Cunningham, an old friend and *ex officio* padre to Bohemia.

When Davies became ill with lung cancer and prepared to go into hospital for what he thought a hopeless operation, he wrote a number of farewell articles. But the operation succeeded – according to Davies because the hospital fed him intravenous vodka.

On his release a few days later the car that had come to fetch him was towed away, and he had to sit in a pub, with more vodka to kill the pain. When he recovered Davies had to face many jokes.

He married, in 1966, Janet Collis; they had a daughter.

June 24 1994

IAN BOARD

IAN BOARD, who has died aged 64, was the proprietor of the Colony Room, a Soho drinking club favoured by Bohemians, artists, homosexuals and assorted loafers.

He inherited the club in 1979 from his patroness, the legendary Muriel Belcher, on whose birthday he died. Perched on a stool by the door, clad in tasteless leisure-wear, his eyes protected by sunglasses, "Ida" (as he was known to his closest friends) would trade coarse badinage with his regulars. He had a kind side though, and could be extremely courteous to visiting mothers, whom he immediately enlisted as allies against everyone else.

Board was an heroic smoker and drinker – until recently he would breakfast on brandy, and he once consumed a bottle of crème de menthe at a sitting – and if his drinking destroyed his youthful good looks it also shaped and nourished his magnificent nose.

A labourer's son, Ian David Archibald Board was born in Devon on Dec 16 1929. His mother died when he was four, and he was brought up by a woman who, as he recalled, had "been bunged in the pudding club" by his father.

"Boards are very randy," he declared. "They all have strings of children. I think I'm the only poof in the family." There were seven full Boards and one half Board.

Young Ian ran away to London at 16 and returned to Devon only twice in later life. He managed to avoid National Service because he was a bed-wetter ("an hereditary affliction," he explained, "which runs in cycles of seven years"), as well as a conscientious objector and a homosexual.

He became a *commis*-waiter at Le Jardin des Gourmets in Dean Street, and it was there that he met Muriel Delcher, who had run away with her mother from Birmingham at 16, after being slapped by her father for wearing lipstick.

Muriel fulfilled the role of "a queens' moll" at Le Jardin, which was frequented by the likes of Noël Coward. She took a liking to Ian, calling him "gel" from the start, and when she opened the Colony Room Club – so called because her life-long companion Carmel came from the colonies – he joined her as barman.

At first the Colony clientèle were stockbrokers and City types, mostly "rich queens", but Muriel disapproved of any hanky-panky. Couples of either sex holding hands were told to "save it for the bedroom, dear".

One day Francis Bacon arrived, and he and Muriel immediately became friends. Bacon was on his uppers, and she gave him £10 per week to act as a "hostess", bringing people into the club.

By the 1950s the Colony had become the haunt of

artists, writers and actors. The only unforgivable sin was to be boring. Some, like Dylan Thomas and Brendan Behan, failed the test.

Tom Driberg, Johnny Minton, Terence Rattigan, the Hermiones Baddeley and ~~Hermione~~ Gingold, Frank Norman, James Robertson Justice, Lucian Freud, Joan Littlewood, George Melly and Craigie Aitchison were among the regulars.

In August Muriel, Bacon and Board used to holiday in the casino towns of the South of France. Bacon shunned the sun because it made his hair dye run. In the evenings, Ian and Muriel would watch him play roulette. It was in the days of currency restrictions, and they once found themselves stranded.

They decided to rob a rich acquaintance who was staying nearby. Board stood look out while Bacon shinned up a lamppost. Then they went to the casino where Bacon gambled the loot. He began to win at the tables, but as he did so his face slowly turned a frightening black (he had run out of hair-dye and had used boot polish instead). Having won their fares and more besides, Bacon shinned up the lamppost and replaced the stolen money.

Beneath its tough exterior the Colony had a heart of gold, and every year the club gave a party for disabled children.

Now that Board has fallen off his perch by the door, regulars must look to its next occupant, Michael Wojas. As Board noted, "People say Soho isn't what it was. But Soho never was what it was."

June 29 1994

INDEX

Allegro, John, 55
Anthoine, Julian "Mo", 144
Attlee, Earl, 241

Bacon, Sir Ranulph, 69
Balfour, Lady Eve, 158
Barnett, "Sadie", 249
Barrington, Viscount, 175
Beck, Baron Rolf, 229
Bindon, John, 315
Bland, Rev Michael, 84
Board, Ian, 333
Bonham Carter, Lady, 151
Breffny, Brian de, 125
Brennan, Dick, 75
Bromley-Davenport, Lt-Col Sir
   Walter, 149
Bruce, Mrs Victor, 181

Carnarvon, Earl of, 35
Carstairs, "Joe", 319
Chadwick, Len, 53
Clifford, Dorothy Lady de, 42
Clifford, Nerea de, 46
Cox, Nesta, 279
Crespi, James, 287

Daintrey, Adrian, 94
Damm, Sheila van, 40
Davies, Stan Gebler, 330
Derby, Countess of, 169
Dickson, Dame Violet, 209
Dill, Victor, 3
Douglas-Home, William, 293
Driscoll, Bill, 261

Elgin and Kincardine, Dowager
   Countess of, 137

Farquharson of Invercauld, Francis,
   225
Farrar, Lady Sidney, 32
Fellowes-Gordon, "Dickie", 244
Forbes of Craigievar, Sir Ewan, Bt,
   257

Gabbert, Michael, 77
George, Ann, 147
Glenconner, Pamela Lady, 132
Grant-Dalton, Sylvia, 66
Grayson, Sir Rupert, Bt, 220
Green, Stanley, 322
Griffiths, Catherine, 64
Guinness, Mariga, 127

Habsburg Windsor, Helle Cristina,
   195
Harty, Russell, 79
Hastings, H. de C., 6
Heywood, Very Rev Hugh, 25
Hoogterp, "Cockie", 113
Hope-Nicholson, Felix, 198
Hunter Cowan, Major Betty, 270
Huntly, Marquess of, 12

Isherwood, Lawrence, 134

Kempson, Trevor, 207
Koenigswarter, Baroness Pannonica
   de, 110

Langan, Peter, 121
Lunn, Arthur, 172

Mackins, Arthur, 202
Marlborough, Laura Duchess of,
  165
Marshall, Arthur, 117
McKeever, Betty, 197
Mee, Margaret, 106
Moynihan, Lord, 264
Murray, John, 310

Nagle, Florence, 100
Neville-Willing, Major Donald,
  215
Newborough, Denisa Lady, 23

Oakeley, Sir Atholl, Bt, 9

Paget of Northampton, Lord, 154
Parnes, Larry, 141
Peppard, Maurice, 304
Pierrepoint, Albert, 289
Potts, Paul, 162

Rankin, Sir Hugh, Bt, 72
Raymond, "Teasie Weasie", 284
Rose, Lt-Col Hugh, 253

Ross, Laurie, 5
Rush, Len, 302
Russell, Earl, 47

Shilling, Beatrice "Tilly", 204
Southesk, Earl of, 274
Sparrow, Gerald, 86
St Albans, Duke of, 90
St Davids, Viscount, 232
St Germans, Earl of, 58
Stevenson, Sir Melford, 50
Strickland, Mabel, 103
Stokes, Doris, 28
Swat, the Wali of, 44

Tennant, Stephen, 17
Tickell, "Kim" de la Taste, 187

Ventry, Lord, 20
Verney, Sir John, BT, 306
Vivian, Lord, 237

Watkins-Pitchford, Denys, 189
Wemyss, Lady Victoria, 324
Wharncliffe, Earl of, 29
Wilde, Gerald, 1
Williamson, "Father Joe", 61

Young, Canon Edwyn, 14